PROACTIVE DISCIPLINE FOR REACTIVE STUDENTS

A Guide for Practicing Effective
Classroom Behavior Management

PROACTIVE DISCIPLINE *for* REACTIVE STUDENTS

A Guide for Practicing Effective Classroom Behavior Management

Dr. Fred Johnson
and
Educational Resource Services

Dedication

This book is dedicated to the many teachers with whom I have worked during my career. They have struggled to manage classroom behavior while providing quality instruction and they have been an inspiration to many. In addition, this book is dedicated to the many teachers who have become frustrated in their efforts to manage classroom behavior. They have struggled in the face of enormous odds. Most of these teachers were only trained to teach, not to manage classroom behavior. But once they enter the classroom they realize that students have changed, family dynamics have changed, societal and cultural values have changed. While all of these teachers took course work in philosophy and history of education, they realize what they really need to know is how to better manage the disruptive behavior in their classroom so that teaching and learning can take place. It is my sincere hope that this book will serve to bring teachers the knowledge and skills to face the challenges of today's educational climate.

Acknowledgments

There are many people who have contributed to the development of this book. I think of the many teachers that I have known over the last twenty years. Their willingness to share their struggles has allowed me to refine my theories about effective classroom behavior management.

Gratitude must also be giving to the families who have discussed with me their frustrations with the school process. Their interest and cooperation has allowed me to develop and implement intervention strategies, make revisions, and re-implement the strategies that have led to much of the formation of this book.

I must also acknowledge my former graduate professors at the University of Louisville, Central Michigan University, and the University of Detroit. At each institution I have been encouraged to use my doctoral studies to develop a theoretical foundation for child behavior management that is not only supported by a theory, but also by practical and applicable interventions.

I also want to thank Bill Butler, my friend, colleague, and editor. Bill has been willing to work with me to make this project become a reality. I am thankful for his interest and expertise in creating a document that can serve as a framework for enhancing student-teacher relationships and improving the overall education process. I am grateful to those on Bill's staff who read and re-read the original manuscript and made suggestions to create a workable, user-friendly document.

However, I am most grateful to my family. My children, Hillary and Stephen, through their own academic and social struggles, have helped me to become a better educator and to understand the educational process, not only professionally, but also personally. In addition, this project would not have been possible without the patience and understanding of my wife, Barb. She has endured many days of my absence while I traveled throughout the United States and Canada to teach these concepts to teachers. The importance of her support cannot be overstated.

Table of Contents

Introduction

There are many reasons why teachers often struggle with issues related to behavior management. In many cases the emphasis has been on gaining specific teaching skills, and teachers have not been taught how to deal with disruptive classroom behavior. Increasingly, students with special needs are being placed in inclusion classrooms. Therefore, general education teachers often end up teaching atypical students. These teachers often continue to employ typical discipline strategies to atypical behaviors. As a result, teachers may provide a consequence to a disruptive behavior problem and never employ an intervention strategy. The consequence is only designed to change the behavior momentarily, while an intervention should bring about a more lasting change.

Teaching in today's current academic climate is one of the most difficult tasks one can undertake. Any experienced teacher will acknowledge that being a teacher has drastically changed over the last twenty-five years. In the past, teachers and the teaching profession were held in high esteem. In fact, in the past being a teacher was viewed much like being a minister. The profession was viewed as a calling. However, society has changed. The teaching profession is no longer viewed in such a positive light. Students have changed. Years ago, even if the student did not respect the person, they showed respect to "teacher." However, now students are willing to talk back, curse, become physical and even harm a teacher. Parents have changed, too. In the past, parents supported their child's school teacher; they were partners in the educational process. Now many parents complain, argue with, attack, and even file lawsuits against teachers. And, of course, the level of government involvement has changed. In the past, the school board and local administrators made most of the decisions. Now, however, IDEA '97 and '04 and No Child Left Behind (NCLB) often dictate to schools what they will teach and how they will respond to behavior. These layers of government involvement often served to create confusion while increasing the workload for the school teacher.

Another factor that has added to confusion in the teaching profession is what has not changed significantly; that is the way higher education continues to prepare teachers to teach. Fifty years ago, in order to become certified to teach, prospective teachers had to take coursework in philosophy of education, history of education, methods of education, systems of education, and curriculum. Today, these same classes are continuing to be taught. This is not to suggest that philosophy and history of education is not important, but to emphasize that few schools in the United States and Canada require general teachers to become proficient in classroom behavior management. In fact, one can go through almost any university or college and become certified to teach and never take a class in behavior management. This lack of change has occurred in spite of the fact that students, families and society have drastically changed and behavior is now the greatest issue confronting teachers.

There is ample research to support the fact that classroom behavior impacts on assessment scores, academic achievement, and teacher frustration and burnout. In the meantime, universities and colleges continue to place emphasis on the theory, history, and philosophy of education. Please don't misunderstand; the theory, history, and philosophy of education are important. However, if the classroom is disruptive and chaotic, teaching and learning cannot take place. The theory, history and philosophy of education are not going to help when students are creating a disruptive classroom environment. In addition, with the movement in education toward inclusion classrooms, all teachers are increasingly involved in working with students that are considered to be "difficult." Many of these teachers are in desperate need of the knowledge and skills to better manage classroom behavior.

The material collected for this book consists of intervention strategies that have been used during the past twenty-five years to help teachers better understand that discipline is not doing something to students; but rather, it is everything that goes on in the classroom. The idea for this book arose out of the constant concerns raised by teachers in seminars that "traditional" disciplining techniques, such as sending students to the principal, sending a note home, placing students in time out, taking away a privilege, putting a name on the board, writing sentences, and all the others things that are done, simply do not work. To verify this point all one has to do is review their local school's detention or suspension records. Most often one will find that 90% of the referrals to detention or suspensions are the same thirty or forty students. Albert Einstein stated that the definition of insanity is "doing the same thing over and over and expecting a change." It may be insane for teachers to continue using discipline strategies that do not result in changed behavior.

This book will provide you with a systematic and methodical approach to incorporating effective discipline strategies that not only work, but also will teach self-discipline. Obviously, the starting point for any such attempt must be with the teacher. If teachers do not fully understand their role, any efforts at discipline will not work. It is my contention that teachers must reclaim their importance to society. Education touches every fiber of a uniform society. Currently in the United States there is an emerging work force that is not prepared to respond to new trends in manufacturing, technology, and service trades. Research has linked the lack of education to the disaccumulation of wealth, criminality, and general decline of socio-economic status. Without teachers, our society simply cannot function. Yet, it seems that teachers have allowed their role to be diminished. Teachers cannot wait for society to suddenly begin valuing their role as teacher. Teachers must reclaim their importance to society. As difficult as it may be to admit, this will never be accomplished by unionization or making demands for more money. This reclamation is more intrinsic. These factors must be explored in detail.

Likewise, before one can effectively deal with students, he must understand student behavior. The premise of this book is that all behavior has meaning. Initially, this book provides an extensive description of those variables that result in typical and atypical behaviors. The atypical behavior patterns are usually more challenging. When typical strategies are implemented for atypical behaviors, the results are usually less than effective. These atypical students exhibit specific personality and behavioral indicators that can be used to help teachers understand and respond to behavior patterns. The information that will be presented will help teachers form a hypothesis for identifying the intervention strategies that will need to be implemented for typical and atypical behavior.

Obviously all relationships are based on specific levels of effective communications. For example, while couples may think that the conflict in their relationship is because of money, the kids, religion, or sex, most often it has to do with the way they listen to and talk with each other. Therefore, effective discipline has something to do with the way teachers and students communicate. What is often not understood is that communication is not just talking to students, it is also listening to students. In fact, research has suggested that the most effective type of communication is non-verbal. When teachers model effective communication with students, they are teaching students a skill that will help them function in a greater society. Without effective communications, effective classroom discipline will never be established or maintained.

It may be difficult to imagine, but there are many cases when teachers unintentionally contribute to the disruptive behaviors in their classroom. Therefore, in order to establish a system where effective and proactive discipline can take place, teachers must examine how they respond to students. Are the responses more of a reaction to negative behavior or a pro-action to the positive behavior? Are the responses consistent? Consistency is not contained in just one classroom, but it involves the entire school. For example, if a teacher reprimands a student for a behavior in his seventh grade math class and the teacher in the science class allows such behavior, the student may become confused and frustrated.

Two other issues that are worth exploring have to do with the structure of the classroom and the way in which the curriculum is taught. These two factors will have a significant impact on determining if the classroom supports positive discipline. Since effective discipline is not described as doing something to a student, but rather it involves everything that goes on in the classroom, it is important to examine the curriculum, the student, the teacher, and, of course, the specific interventions currently being used. However, there are no silver bullets. There is no one right discipline approach. What works today may not work tomorrow, and certainly what works for one student will not work for the next. Effective discipline is individualized and is constantly changing. That is why teachers must understand the difference between consequences and interventions. Perhaps we should define effective discipline as whatever works!

The focus of this book is on proactive discipline strategies that teach self-discipline. Much of the more chronic challenging behavior results when students do not have sufficient skills to practice self-regulation. Essentially, once they get going they do not know how to stop themselves. Therefore, when working with atypical students, emphasis must be placed on interventions that help them to self-control their behavior. Lastly, teachers must move beyond traditional discipline approaches and incorporate strategies to build responsible students. The aim is to develop students that can negotiate, make decisions by consensus, and set goals for themselves. This involves maintaining effective discipline while at the same time enhancing a student's sense of self-worth. In essence, effective discipline builds skills that will last a lifetime.

This book should be used as a guide for establishing and implementing effective discipline strategies. However, the real test comes after reading this book. The goal is for teachers to become excited about teaching and believe that they are really changing the world, one student at a time!

"Choose a job that you love, and you will never have to work a day in your life." (Confucius BC 551-479)

Chapter One

EFFECTIVE TEACHING FOR
PROACTIVE INSTRUCTION

Teachers make a serious mistake when they assume that student failure only occurs in the academic arena. Failure can also occur in social interaction, emotional adjustments, behavioral responses, or moral development. When a student fails behaviorally, effective proactive teachers are willing to develop and implement intervention strategies to correct the behavior just as if the student had failed academically. However, proactive discipline does not mean "*doing something*" to students. Proactive discipline involves everything that goes on in the classroom. Effective discipline is influenced by the teacher, by the curriculum, by the classroom structure, and by the student. This book is about those intentional, proactive, behavioral interventions that teachers can easily put into practice to bring about positive change.

The first question that must be asked and answered is, "What is proactive discipline?" Start by finishing this sentence: "Proactive discipline is ___." Try to identify what is involved in providing effective discipline strategies. Effective discipline has many components: it teaches, it is positive, it results in changed behavior, it provides guidance, it provides a choice, it teaches responsibility and independence, it is proactive, and it is strategic (Olivet, 2004). You may want to add your own components. Now ask yourself, "Do the discipline strategies I currently use include these variables?"

Think for a moment about the specific discipline strategies you or your colleagues routinely use. Some of the more common discipline strategies are:

1) Redirection
2) Taking away a privilege
3) Using the traffic light
4) Sending to the office
5) Losing recess
6) Parent conference
7) Time-out
8) Talking to student
9) Name on the board
10) In-school suspension
11) Writing sentences
12) Sending a note home

Look at this list for a moment and try to determine what all of these discipline strategies have in common. That's right – all of these strategies are reactions to negative behaviors. While these approaches may work some of the time for manipulative student behavior, they probably will not work for the more serious challenging behavior patterns. Typical manipulative behavior occurs when students display a mischievous personality that results in disruptive behavior; when they are in a specific age or regressed stage of development; when they are attempting to get attention or gain control; or when their negative behavior is being reinforced. In contrast, the more serious behavior patterns occur when students have a lack of self-regulation (Reid, Trout, and Schartz, 2005). A lack of self-regulation often results when students have a specific processing deficit (Gomez and Baird, 2005). While educators enjoy using various labels to discuss student needs, in reality these behaviors result from a processing deficit (Fielding, 1999). Labels such as learning disability, cognitive impairment, Attention Deficit Hyperactivity, autism, behavioral disorder, or emotional handicap are often used to describe these processing deficits (Reid, Trout, and Schartz, 2005). When students have processing deficits they will often process information much slower than their peers. It is the deficit that prevents the student from benefiting from discipline strategies that depend on learning through cause and effect.

Therefore, specific discipline strategies are necessary for different students, depending on what might be causing the disruptive behavior. While effective discipline does involve utilizing specific intervention strategies, proactive discipline includes a more comprehensive approach to classroom management. Proactive classroom discipline includes interacting with students on a positive level, having an understanding of student behavior, being able to relate, and able to utilize interventions that respond to the function of the behavior, rather than the behavior.

Introducing Proactive Change

The meaning of human existence has been debated by philosophers, theologians, and educators for generations. But the question remains basically the same: Is man inherently good or evil? Carl Rogers, the noted psychologist and founder of Client Centered Psychotherapy, stated that "Man is neither good nor evil, but is in a state of becoming." But becoming what? Rogers suggested that "becoming" means that human existence is fluid and ever-changing. Rogers was indicating that humans have the capacity for both good and evil, depending on the "state" of their existences (Rogers, 1961).

This initial chapter is written as a means of dealing with these issues of "becoming", and specifically, the importance of becoming an effective, proactive teacher. Perhaps the real issue for teachers is, *"What does it mean to be an effective proactive teacher?"* When a teacher is "effective" and "proactive," everything they do will have a specific outcome. For example, effective proactive teachers will not give students busy work, just for the sake of keeping them busy. In the effective proactive teacher's classroom *every* task has a purpose. Therefore, if the school principal walks into the classroom, the effective teacher is able to state specifically the objective of the task and the expected outcomes. Every task and every action will be purposeful and designed to help students succeed. Rick Warren, a minister from California, has written a very popular book, *The Purpose-Driven Life*, which encourages people to find "purpose to their existence." This current book is calling on teachers to become "purpose-driven" teachers, or "effective proactive teachers."

When teachers are effective and proactive, they will seek meaning to that which they do. Therefore, every activity will be designed to accomplish a specific "purpose." This approach does not allow teachers to waste time engaging students in non-essential tasks. *Everything* will have meaning! When the teacher asks a student to take the attendance role or lunch count to the office, there is a reason why this action is taken. Therefore, every task, day in and day out, will lead toward accomplishing the goal of helping students reach their full potential (Topping and Ferguson, 2005).

Teachers must also honestly ask themselves, "Does teaching give *me* meaning?" In some cases, the job of teaching may have become just that, a job! How does one reconcile this dilemma? One of the ways to ensure that teaching remains meaningful is to continually believe that teaching students is making a difference in the world. In essence, teachers are making the world a better place, one student at a time. If one truly believes they are making a difference in the lives of students, they cannot help but be excited and passionate about teaching!

Obviously teachers do make a difference in children's lives every day! However, it is amazing to realize just how many teachers approach their profession as if it were just another job. When most teachers graduate from college and obtain that first teaching assignment, they are full of excitement, hope, anticipation, and ideals. They truly believe they can make a difference in a student's life! However, after several years of teaching, many teachers face burnout (Butt, Lance, Fielding, Gunter, Rayner, and Thomas, 2005). They dread going to work. When teachers are burned out they often get to school at the last minute, and then leave as soon as the final bell has rung. These teachers rarely take on new assignments or participate in after-school activities. For these teachers, teaching has become a "job" of drudgery. Although these teachers assume that no one notices their lackluster effort, everyone sees their behavior. Administrators notice, colleagues notice, parents notice and, yes, even students will notice when teachers are going through the motions and doing just enough to get by (Brock and Grady, 2002).

Renewing the Excitement for Teaching

How does a teacher regain that initial excitement and zeal? Perhaps the best place to start is to look at what happened. What did happen? How does a teacher move from being excited about teaching to dreading to go to work, or worse, simply waiting for retirement? Circumstances occur over time to cause teachers to get zapped of their energy. It does not take a veteran teacher to realize that the teaching profession has changed. Students have changed, family systems have changed, society has changed, the demands have changed, and even the role government plays in education has changed. As teachers become increasingly disillusioned, they may even begin to wonder if they really can make a difference.

Years ago society held the teaching profession in high esteem. In fact, it was not so long ago that school teachers were viewed much like a minister, assuming that both had a calling. So, when did the perception of the teaching profession change? A quick review of some historical statements seems to suggest that a negative view is not so recent. Oscar Wilde (1854-1900), the famous Irish scholar of the 19th century, is credited with saying, *"If you cannot do anything else, you can at least teach,"* and *"Everyone who is incapable of learning has taken to teaching"* (Dover Publishing, 1959). These statements suggest that perhaps there has been a negative view of the teaching profession far longer than we realize. With all due respect to Mr. Wilde, his quote seems to be backwards. It should be, *"If you can teach, you can do anything else!"* If one can put up with the salary of a teacher, one can certainly deal with the salary of an accountant. If one can put up with difficult students and parents, surely one can put up with difficult customers. If one can handle the top/down decision-making by the central office, or the federal and state government, they certainly can handle the decisions made by a company CEO and board of directors. If one can manage all the paperwork involved in IDEA and NCLB, one can certainly manage the amount of paperwork found in almost any other profession. Mr. Wilde may have been a scholar, but he certainly had his statement wrong.

With the constant changing role of the school teacher in today's educational climate, it has become difficult to determine what it takes to be an effective proactive teacher. One of the ways to determine what makes a teacher effective is to remember a teacher from your elementary, middle, or high school experience that you consider to have been effective. This teacher probably had an impact on your life. In fact, this may be the very teacher that caused you to want to be a teacher. Who was this teacher and what was it that they did that you remember? Even though the memory of this teacher may be from many years ago, you can probably still remember their name. So, what was it that so impressed you? Was it that the teacher was a great science teacher, a great reading teacher, or perhaps a great elementary teacher? While being proficient at one's instructional subject is important, what you probably remember is how this teacher treated you. If you were asked to state what you remember about this teacher you would probably say that they were kind, patient, provided encouragement, expected a lot, believed in you, or some other kind of positive experience.

When asked this question rarely do teachers mention how well the teacher could teach. While students often do not remember what they are taught, they always remember how they are treated. When teachers treat students with kindness, respect, and dignity, they are forming a positive relationship. Therefore, having a relationship with students is the first ingredient to becoming an effective proactive teacher. However, in our current politically-charged educational environment, having a relationship with students is often viewed negatively. The importance of having a relationship with students will need to be explored in greater detail.

Establishing a Relationship with Students

Recently, there has been a rash of news reports about teachers engaging in inappropriate sexual behavior with students. It is confusing when these news reports refer to these behaviors as a "relationship", without differentiating whether they are positive or negative. Such reported behaviors are, indeed, inappropriate and negative. In fact, these behaviors should not even be referred to as a "relationship". When we think of a relationship, we think of caring concern and interest. Such behaviors have nothing to do with having a relationship with students. In fact, these reported sexual encounters are more about manipulation, control, immaturity, and a regressed emotional state. These behaviors are the opposite of having a meaningful relationship with students (Orange, 2000).

With this premise in mind, we must consider what it means to have an effective and positive relationship with students. Having a relationship simply means that students know that their teacher cares about their success! A few minutes ago you were asked to think of a teacher from your past who influenced you. That teacher probably took time for you; encouraged you; challenged you, or believed in you. They were engaging in a relationship. Even though this individual may have taught you ten, twenty, or thirty years ago, as a result of this relationship, you can even still remember their name. When teachers care enough to take time, encourage, or even challenge, they are demonstrating a deep level of care and commitment to their students' success. Therefore, a relationship means to care about students enough to be invested in their lives (Urban, 1999). Obviously, this has nothing to do with manipulation, control, immaturity, or a regressed state.

Another important characteristic of becoming an effective and proactive teacher is to understand that teaching includes not only academic, social, and emotional instruction, but moral instruction as well. In the current climate of political correctness, thinking about teaching students moral instruction is often frowned upon (Honig, 2005). However, in reality, moral values are taught whether we want to or not. Without getting into a debate about issues of political correctness, separation of church and state, or even conflicts related to Kolberg's theory of moral development, it is sufficient to say that values are "caught" not "taught." In fact, one cannot help but teach values and provide moral instruction.

The Character Counts program has stated that values are those things we do when we think no one is looking. Character Counts incorporates the "Six Pillars" of decision-making based on a belief system. The "Six Pillars" includes concepts of trust, respect, responsibility, fairness, caring, and citizenship (Harms and Fritz, 2001). The opposite of values is behaviors that one could do, and probably get away with, if they wanted. But most teachers do not engage in such behaviors because they "believe" they are wrong. Therefore, values and moral instruction have something to do with a belief system, and making decisions based on those beliefs. For example, when a teacher chooses not to steal from class funds, he or she is making the decision based on a value. Teachers could probably find a way to steal from the class funds and get away with it, but because of their belief system, they choose not to engage in such behavior. The DARE program is a good example of a program that is based on a value system and moral decision-making. DARE teaches students that the use of drugs and alcohol can be harmful, and DARE encourages students to make decisions based on that belief system (Kochis, 1995). There is an entire body of research based on value education found at the National Resource Centre for Value Education. However, for our purposes it is sufficient to know that values are taught when students observe teachers responding with kindness, being fair, or showing concern for their success.

What does it mean to have a relationship with a student? While some teachers have acted inappropriately toward students, this does not mean that they are effective, proactive, or have a relationship. While these teachers are the ones who are noticed and make the headlines, they are the exception. Teachers who engage in these negative behaviors have entered the teaching profession with a sense of immaturity, or perhaps some event has caused them to become regressed. It is this immaturity and emotional regression that allows them to become inappropriately involved with students

(Timmerman, 2003). These teachers have made decisions based on a faulty belief system. Sadly, our news media seems to focus on these inappropriate behaviors, while ignoring the thousands of teachers who develop positive relationships with students each year.

Having a positive relationship with students means that they know they are cared about and are important to their teacher. A relationship occurs when teachers take a personal interest in students' success. This interest in a student's success is not only academic, social, and emotional success, but in those factors that build moral character that will serve the student for a lifetime (Keith, 1991). It takes courage to be a teacher to care about students academically, emotionally, socially, and morally. It is possible to build and maintain students' academic, social, emotional, and moral development without compromising effective discipline. In fact, when teachers express this depth of concern for students, effective discipline becomes a natural by-product. Most students will misbehave in certain classrooms. However, when students know that their teacher respects and cares about them, they are less likely to misbehave.

My Story

As a student, I had a very difficult time adjusting to the academic and social climate of public education. I grew up in a poverty-ridden environment. I had nine brothers and sisters and two parents living in a three-room house in North Alabama. My parents had minimal education and could not read or write. I was the typical difficult student – poor grades, many unexcused absences from school, and behavioral problems. I received frequent suspensions from school because of behavior problems, and when I was at school, I spent most of my time in detention.

I recall returning to school on a Monday from a suspension and Mr. Denton, the school principal, told me that as part of my punishment, I was to work for a week doing chores around the school. (I later found out that one of the school janitors was off from work and they needed someone to help out.) I worked diligently that week cleaning restrooms, mopping the lunchroom floor, and emptying trash from classrooms. On Thursday of that week Mr. Denton saw me in the hallway and told me to go empty the large trash can in the outer office. As many adolescents might do, I took the trash outside and was placing one piece of paper at a time into the dumpster. However, after a few minutes, I noticed that I was getting purple ink all over my hands. I was not sure where the ink was coming from, so I started digging through the trash. I retrieved several pieces of purple paper and as I looked at them, much to my surprise, I discovered they were mimeograph sheets, used to make copies of tests. Evidently it was the practice of the school secretary to run off tests and discard the mimeograph originals.

While some people may have thought I was dumb, no one ever accused me of being stupid. Being one who was always looking for ways to make money, I put the sheets of mimeograph paper in my pocket, thinking I would try to sell these mimeograph tests to some friends. After school I found several of my friends and swore them to secrecy. I told them that I had the questions and answers to several tests that were being given the next day. Of course, they were immediately interested and wanted me to give them the papers. While we were friends, this was business; I told them it would cost them a dollar each to see the paper. They eagerly paid the money and I turned over the purple pages. The next day, which was Friday, Mr. Denton called me into his office and said that I had done a good job working in the office and on Monday I could return to class. Not wanting to ruin my newfound business, I told him that I enjoyed working in the office and wanted to continue. But he said I was missing too much schoolwork and that I needed to get back to class. After several minutes of begging and pleading, Mr. Denton agreed that I could continue working part-time. I told him that I had noticed that there seemed to be more trash on Thursday afternoon. After some more discussion, he agreed I could work in the office each Thursday afternoon. After all, since most tests were given on Friday, I assumed that most were copied on Thursday. This was a perfect setup!

After about a month of attending class and working in the office on Thursday, my grades and behavior were much improved. I was making about $20 each week selling answers to tests. I had quite an enterprise going! Then one day Mr. Denton caught me in the hallway and told me to come into his office. I remember being afraid that he had found out about my little enterprise. However, instead of being in trouble, he praised me. He complimented me on how well I was doing and asked me to tell him how he had helped me so much. Evidently, my teachers had reported that my grades and my behavior had improved dramatically. Mr. Denton said that he had some other students that he wanted to help and he wanted to know what he had done to help me make such a turnaround. I was a little stunned. After regaining my composure, I told Mr. Denton that I was not sure, but

I knew that working in the office had really helped me take more responsibility. Mr. Denton then said that I had evidently learned my lesson and that I should return to class on a full-time basis. I resisted and told him again how much I enjoyed working in the office. Finally he agreed to allow me to continue working on Thursday afternoons.

I continued in my pursuit of happiness and profit for about another month. Then one day something happened that I could never have anticipated. Three students in my 9th grade biology class got caught cheating. These students did not subscribe to my service! They were trying to cheat off of each other. I could not believe what followed. Mrs. Williamson, the 9th grade biology teacher, stood up in front of the entire class and said to these three students, "If you can cheat in my class and it not bother you, then I feel sorry for you because you have already become corrupt!" I could not believe what she was saying. Corrupt for cheating? She was making such statements to these three poor students, while I sat there with my little enterprise intact. Her statement struck me to the core. I kept hearing her words over and over, "If you can cheat and it not bother you, then I feel sorry for you because you have already become corrupt."

I was so bothered by her words that evening I decided to go to Mrs. Williamson's house to tell her everything that I had been doing. I knew that if she was disappointed with those three students, she would really be mad at me. But I was compelled to talk to her. That Wednesday evening I went to her house and knocked on the door. She allowed me to come in and I told her everything that I had been doing. I was ready for her to lower the boom, but instead of condemning me, yelling at me or rejecting me, she did something that was unimaginable. She put me in her car and took me to her minister. I can tell you, without a doubt, that night changed my life! Of course, I got into serious trouble and my grades declined. But from that day forward I was a changed person. This teacher not only cared about me academically, socially and emotionally, she also cared about me morally! I knew that this teacher really cared about me. From that day forward and even now, Rose Mary Williamson and I have a relationship!

Ingredients of an Effective Proactive Teacher

It has already been established that effective proactive teachers care about their students' success. So what does it take to become an effective proactive teacher?

1. Responsibility

Effective proactive teachers are those who take responsibility for establishing a classroom environment where learning can take place. Of course, all teachers could use more resources, more money and more assistance. But it is the teacher who is ultimately responsible for what goes on in the classroom. Effective proactive teachers know how much they can impact the behavior in their classroom.

2. Equality

Effective proactive teachers understand that they must live by the same rules and expectations that are established in their classroom. They realize there is a difference between rules and expectations. Expectations belong to the teacher, while rules belong to the students and the teacher. This means that effective proactive teachers trust students enough to involve them in the process of establishing the rules by which the class will live (Brady, Forton, Porter, and Wood, 2003). A common problem associated with rules and expectations is that rules are usually stated explicitly, while expectations are often stated implicitly. Research by Johnson and Edmunds (2006) suggests that greater success will be achieved when both rules and expectations are explicitly stated. Therefore, effective proactive teachers involve students in the formation of classroom rules and expectations. These agreed upon rules and expectations are applied to everyone, including the teacher. There are only two reasons for establishing rules in a classroom. These two reasons are based on what teachers are required to do: teach and keep students safe. In education, teachers and students have a *Bill of Rights*. A teacher's Bill of Rights includes, "I have a right to teach;"while a student's Bill of Rights includes, "I have a right to learn and to be safe." Safety is not only physical, but emotional as well. If anything is interfering with a teacher's right to teach, a student's right to learn, or a student's physical or emotional safety, then it must be dealt with.

3. Role Modeling

Effective proactive teachers realize that it is through one's actions, not their words, that cooperation within the classroom is established (Rusnak, 1997). It was previously stated that students tend to remember how they are treated, not what they are taught. This is not to say that competent academic instruction is not necessary. In fact, it is vital! But twenty years from now students will remember how they were treated by their teacher, not necessarily what they were taught. I recall a teacher telling me a story about his retirement party. He said a former student flew from Chicago to New York just to tell him how much he had helped him. The teacher was embarrassed when he could not remember having the student in his class. Sadly, most teachers often do not get to see the results of the seeds they plant or realize the impact they have on students. I recall conducting a seminar in Illinois for about 150 teachers and asking if they could recall a teacher that had influenced them. A thirty-something-year-old teacher all the way in the back of the room raised her hand and said she wanted to share about a teacher that had made the greatest influence in her life. She said that it was in the third grade and she was a little chubby girl that felt awkward. She had few friends and was often lonely. However, her teacher took a special interest in her, frequently praising her in front of her classmates and really made her feel special. Half joking, I asked her if she remembered the teacher's name. She responded immediately, *"Oh yes, it was Ms. Devoe."* About that time a sixtyish-looking woman about ten rows back stood up and turned around. Lo and behold, there stood Ms. Devoe. The two teachers ran from their seats and embraced. Ms. Devoe was lucky; she had heard first-hand what she had meant to that former student. Most teachers never have this opportunity.

4. Mutual Trust and Respect

Belvel and Jordan (2003) stated that effective proactive teachers are those who establish a high level of mutual trust and respect among students and themselves. These teachers not only establish trust and respect, they also acknowledge the importance of a high standard of performance. In acknowledging a need for high standards of performance, these teachers provide students with the tools necessary to succeed. To accomplish this, teachers must treat each student in a firm but fair manner. Firmness means that teachers provide structure and consistency to their students. But, what is fairness? Some wrongly assume that fairness means to treat all students the same or to have the same expectations for all students. The opposite is true. Fairness means to treat each student based upon his or her individual needs (Wendorf and Alexander, 2005). Some teachers struggle with the concept of fairness. They say that it is not fair to give one student special treatment. Also, students and parents may complain that the teacher is showing favoritism. When this happens, ask yourself: "Would it be fair to ask all students who wear glasses to remove them because it is not fair for only a few to wear corrective lenses?" Of course not! Fairness means to treat each student based on his or her individual needs (Campbell, 2003). Effective proactive teachers recognize that students have differences. Students have individual strengths and weaknesses. For example, you may have a rule in your fourth grade class that students will remain seated and continue working until they finish their math assignment. However, if you have a hyperactive boy in your fourth grade class, it would not be "fair" to expect him to remain seated working on a math assignment for an extended period of time.

5. Teaching for Success

Effective proactive teachers provide students with the tools needed to succeed. While it is important to have high expectations, unless you provide the tools to succeed, such expectations are unrealistic. Students must be taught in such a manner that will facilitate their success. Riedling (2002) suggests that effective proactive teachers will recognize that students have different learning styles. Some students are auditory learners, others visual learners, while still others may learn best from hands-on experiences. Effective proactive teachers will match their teaching style and curriculum to meet each student's individual learning style. When this is not done, some students miss out on valuable information. Without individualized instructions, some students will not receive the tools necessary to succeed. However, when tools to succeed are provided most students, even those with exceptional learning styles, will be able to attain academic skills at a high level of performance (Howard, 1999).

6. Continual Improvement

An effective proactive teacher is one who has an attitude of continual improvement (Smilkstein, 2003). Continual improvement for students is one of those expectations that is usually assumed, but not explicitly stated. It is expected that students will make continual improvement, and at the end of the academic year will have mastered the skills necessary to move to the next grade level. Effective proactive teachers will state explicitly: "Students, we are all here to learn. That's right, you and me. We will learn from each other." This statement suggests that learning is not just for the students, but rather is a joint partnership between the teacher and the students. This involves a continual learning process.

7. Acceptance

Effective proactive teachers recognize that learning new material always invites mistakes. However, mistakes should not suggest failure. Failure only means that students have not yet mastered the tasks. Students must try and fail, try and fail, try and fail, and then try and master. If students keep trying, they will eventually master the tasks. However, often when students try and fail they are ridiculed, demeaned, laughed at, or even punished. When this happens they will try and fail, and then give up. It is the giving up that results in students' failure. However, failure is not limited only to academics; students can also experience social, emotional, behavioral, and even moral failure.

Some failures are accepted, while others are not. When a note is sent home about a student's inappropriate behavior, parents often reprimand, ground, or even punish the child. However, on Sunday morning when that same child wants to learn to ride a two-wheel bike, the parent will push the child down the driveway, and as they get to the lawn, they let go of the bike. The child rides the bike for about five feet without assistance and falls to the ground. The parent rushes over to the child, picks him up and declares, *"You did great, let's try it again!"* However, in reality, the child just failed in his effort to ride the bike. Some failures are accepted, while others are not. When students are demeaned, laughed at, or even punished for their failures, it will lead to more serious academic, emotional, social, and behavioral problems. Effective proactive teachers recognize that there is no such thing as failure. Failure only means that the student has not yet mastered the task. These teachers are willing to accept students for where they are, then to take them to where they are capable.

8. Creative Teaching

Learning involves creative teaching (Lucas, 2003). Effective proactive teachers will utilize a variety of techniques and teaching styles to make the instructional material meaningful and applicable for students. These teachers know that when this is not done, students become bored or may not understand how the material relates directly to them. It appears that the lack of meaningful instruction is one of the primary reasons that students fail to achieve.

With all the emphasis being placed on grades and state assessment scores, it is not unusual for a teacher to become overly focused on the end product, rather than giving attention to the learning process. However, when too much emphasis is placed on the product, some students will become so frustrated that they will have difficulty with the process. For example, in a second grade math class the instructional objective is to learn various shapes. The teacher introduces the topic by asking the students to draw a snowman. However, a student draws a snowman using oval shapes. The teacher corrects the student and tells her to start over. The student may become frustrated, fearing that the picture will not meet the teacher's expectations, and decides to just not finish the picture. This is not to suggest that students should be allowed to do a project any way they wish. The level of acceptance will depend on the teaching objective. However, when a student's creative efforts are accepted, the student is empowered to achieve even more.

9. Commitment

It may be obvious at this point, but effective proactive teachers are those who are committed to their students, their school, and to the community in which they teach. This means that effective proactive teachers do not engage in gossip or spreading of rumors. These teachers will simply not allow themselves to become involved in these situations. When someone starts the "he said, she said, you said, I said" discussions, they excuse themselves. They know that they cannot solve a problem by complaining to someone else. They must deal with the problem directly. It is well known that if a teacher is willing to say negative things about one colleague, more than likely they will say negative things about others. Nothing will ruin one's reputation and relationships faster than constantly complaining, gossiping, or joining in cliquish behaviors.

10. Positive Relationships

Effective proactive teachers will seek to establish a positive relationship with their students (Sumsion, 2000). This issue was dealt with earlier in this chapter, but warrants greater discussion at this point. Please keep in mind that having a relationship with students does not mean becoming their best friend. Being a best friend to a student may be appropriate years later when they have become adults, but not as a student. Being a student's best friend suggests a peer relationship. Students do not need a peer relationship with their teacher; however, they do need a positive proactive relationship. In order to have a positive relationship with students teachers must be emotionally stable (Baldwin et. al., 1990). This may sound like a simple requirement, but one may be surprised at how many teachers are emotionally immature and/or unstable. Those teachers which were spoken of earlier, who engaged in inappropriate sexual behavior with their students, certainly are neither emotionally mature nor stable.

11. Emotionally Stable

What does it mean to be an emotionally stable teacher? When a teacher is emotionally stable, they do not get upset over minor irritations. They do not react to childish behaviors. They can differentiate between attention-getting behaviors and those that require more serious interventions. They know when to respond and when to ignore a behavior. I recall a 7th grade science teacher becoming upset because a student had placed a condom on his desk. Instead of ignoring the behavior, he held up the condom and stated, *"I wonder whose little bitty condom this belongs to."* He told me that he wanted to embarrass the student so they would not do it again. I assured him that those words would come back to haunt him. In fact, it is hard to embarrass a middle school student! Emotionally stable teachers are able to turn such behaviors into episodes of positive growth. Effective proactive teachers will know when to respond and when to ignore behaviors. This teacher's goal was to gain power by playing the "shame blame game." It suggests emotional immaturity and it just won't work.

12. Seek to Understand

Effective proactive teachers will seek to understand, before seeking to be understood. They will use their communication skills to better understand student needs. These teachers will find ways to get to know their students, their background, their hopes and dreams. Through their communication skills they will model for students how to become effective communicators. These teachers will communicate their faith in a student's ability to achieve and will find ways to bring that potential to the surface. Bringing out potential may be accomplished by demanding more than the student feels they can give, or it may be through encouragement and guidance. The effective proactive teacher will seek to understand, before they seek to be understood.

SUMMARY

Effective proactive teachers are those who understand the paradox of teaching. In most of life circumstances people spend time accumulating, in order to be sustained. For example, people save money for their retirement in order to be sustained in later years. However, if they do not save adequately, there could be problems later in life. People put gas in their car and as it is used up they replenish it. However, if they fail to take care and keep some gas in the tank, it could spell trouble. When it comes to being an effective proactive teacher, the process is far different. Teachers take in knowledge and then give that knowledge away. In doing so, they are fulfilled. This is the paradox of teaching. The more teachers give away, the more joy of teaching they will have.

Chapter Two

WHAT YOU SEE MAY NOT BE WHAT YOU GET: UNDERSTANDING DISRUPTIVE CLASSROOM BEHAVIOR

It is important for effective proactive teachers to understand the various factors that may influence classroom behavior. Without understanding what may be influencing student behavior it is impossible to develop and implement discipline strategies that are effective or proactive. In the previous chapter there was a brief discussion of the definition of effective discipline. Effective discipline is actually everything that takes place in the classroom. Since the influences on classroom behavior are so expansive, perhaps a good starting point is to review the influence teachers have on the behavior in their classroom.

It has already been stipulated that being a teacher is one of the most challenging jobs an individual will ever undertake. There are numerous factors that have resulted in teaching becoming such a difficult profession. It is difficult to explain logically why one would want to be a teacher. Certainly, it is not for the money. According to the USA Today newspaper teaching is among one of the lowest paying professions. It cannot be for the hours a teacher works. Effective proactive teachers are usually at school by 7:30 a.m. and often work late into the evening grading papers or writing planning lessons. Hopefully no one is ever so misinformed that they enter the teaching profession thinking it is going to be an easy job. There is nothing easy about being a teacher. There is ample evidence of the complications and conflicts associated with being a teacher.

It is difficult to explain logically why someone becomes a teacher. The only possible explanation is the belief that a teacher can make a difference in a child's life. When a teacher obtains that first job, they are so excited and really believe they can make a difference. However, after several years of teaching, teachers often began to experience burnout. They may question the validity of what they do. In order to reconcile this issue, teachers will need to reconsider their perception of their role. It may be helpful to hold onto the concept of "making a difference" by thinking of teachers as ministers. While some people may assume that ministry only takes place in a cathedral, mosque, temple, or church, the reality is that ministry takes place in classrooms every day. Ministry takes place when teachers treat students with respect and dignity and take time to care about them. Ministry essentially occurs when one's action makes the world a better place (National Science Teachers Association, 2004). That is what teachers do every day; they are making the world a better place, one child at a time.

So what is it that makes teaching so difficult? There are several factors that have contributed to this dilemma. Ample research supports the fact that students are just more difficult than they were thirty years ago (Soodak, L. C. and Podell, D. M., 1994). Family and community systems have broken down, creating more dysfunction, unemployment, poverty, poor housing, and various social ills. The residual effects of these problems often find their way into the classroom (Cook, J., 1996). Numerous federal and state mandates have certainly increased the demands on teachers and have made teaching more difficult (Stecher, B. and Hamilton, L., 2002). Almost all activities that are non-instructional have been eliminated. For example, over 70% of recess time has been eliminated over the past fifteen years. Thirty years ago recess was an important part of the total educational process. During recess students learn how to get along, how to share, and how to avoid conflicts and build relationships. Instead of recess, emphasis is now placed on the academic instructions and various state assessment scores. In the meantime, the United States has the highest rate of childhood obesity than any other country. Children receive little exercise at school, then often go home to an empty house and eat potato chips and play Nintendo while they wait for their parents to come home from work.

Since the federal government and state boards of education are basking in the fact that state assessment scores are increasing, one would assume that this would suggest that academic skills are increasing. However, the most recent data suggests that academic skills and standardized test scores such as the ACT and SAT are continuing to decline. The inference is that teachers may be teaching to the state assessment test, at the expense of teaching certain academic skills. In addition, there seems to be little correlation with increased assessment scores and actual learning. While state assessment tests are designed to verify that teachers are teaching what they are supposed to be teaching, however, since the inception of education reform in 1992, these tests have extremely poor validity and reliability (Johnson, F., 1996). If schools do not make a certain level of progress each year, they are considered "failing" schools. However, those who make such decisions do not seem to take into account various socioeconomic factors and the possibility that a school may already be proficient. If a school attains a state assessment score of 98%, it is still expected to make progress the following year, or it can be identified as a failing school. In contrast, schools with severe social and economic problems cannot be expected to make such progress, but they are still identified as failing. In the meantime, while providing this additional instruction, teachers are being asked to complete more paperwork and follow more mandates.

Another issue that has impacted the current education climate is that colleges often fail to provide realistic course work to prepare prospective teachers for the demands of the current classroom. Many colleges and universities continue to place emphasis on courses in foundations, theory, philosophy, and the history of education, while ignoring course work in classroom management (Johnson, S., Birkeland, S., Peske, H., 2005). Teachers report that classroom behavior management is the single biggest problem they face, yet very few schools require prospective teachers to take course work in this area. Course work in behavior management is often available as an elective, but in most cases prospective teachers do not realize they need behavior management training until it is too late (Harlan, J. and Rowland, S., 2002). This issue is further complicated by colleges developing a "fast track" teacher certification program for second-career professionals. This has been done in an effort to head off a potential teacher shortage. However, in many cases these individuals have entered teaching out of a background in business, sales, accounting and engineering and do not have adequate training to deal effectively with classroom behavior management.

The Challenging Student

Experienced teachers are aware that some days are more difficult than others. They will also tell you that some students are just more challenging than others. When attempting to understand what makes a student more challenging, it is important to remember the premise of this book; *that all behavior has meaning.* If all behavior has meaning, then all behavior can be explained and understood. If teachers can understand the meaning of behavior, then they are in a better position to use proactive discipline strategies that will be effective in changing behavior. For example, early work by Turecki (1985) indicated that there is a specific personality and behavioral profile of these challenging students. If teachers can identify students that are potentially challenging, they may be in a position to offer interventions that are proactive and will prevent the student from becoming a challenge. The following is a list of the identified areas of difficulty.

Personality Indicators

1. **Defiant:** Defiant students tend to do whatever they want and will basically ignore the teacher. These students often do the opposite of what they are told.

2. **Resistant:** Resistant students are those who refuse to listen or follow directions. They tend to dawdle, drag behind, and find excuses for their behavior.

3. **Stubborn:** Stubborn students are those who always have to have their way. These students will fight the teacher on almost everything and refuse to take "NO" for an answer.

4. **Shy:** Shy students are very timid and will not participate in class. These students will hide their faces when they are asked to perform a task. Shy students have difficulty with social interaction and teachers often spend a great deal of time trying to get them involved.

5. **Particular:** Particular students are those who are picky and want things a certain way. They are hard to please and will complain that the room is too cold or hot, the assignment is too hard or too easy, or their food is too hot or too cold. These students tend to move from one extreme to the other.

6. **Interrupting:** Students who interrupt will often break into conversations. It does not matter who the teacher is talking with—a student, a parent, the principal, or even the superintendent. These students appear

to have an overt need for excessive attention.

7. **Angry:** Angry students will yell at their teacher or peers. They may become verbally or physically aggressive. They often call others names or say will say, "I don't have to" to the teacher. These students just seem to be angry all the time.

These are just a few of the personality traits exhibited by these challenging students. Students that exhibit some, or all, of these characteristics are more than just manipulative; they are indeed a challenge! Typical discipline techniques of re-direction, time-out, taking away a privilege, putting the name on the board, calling home, or talking to the student will not be sufficient to change the behavior patterns of the challenging student. In order to correct the behavior of these students, a specific proactive and strategic intervention must be implemented (Jolivette, K., Barton-Arwood, S., and Scott, T., 2000).

To more fully understand these challenging personality and behavior patterns, it is important to review what may be causing the behaviors. This is typically referred to as the "function" of the behavior. There can be any number of factors that may influence a student's behavior. The student may have some type of physical problem, such as an ear infection or allergies and simply may not feel well. The student may have experienced various family dysfunctional issues that are being manifested in the classroom. If the student misbehaves in one classroom, but not in another, this indicates the behavior has something to do with events in the classroom. Challenging behavior may also be a manifestation of some type of neurological processing deficit (Davey, B. J. and Lignugaris-Kraft, B., 2005).

When students have neurological deficits they will process information at a much slower speed than their peers. Very often this delay in processing will cause a student to become frustrated, which is often expressed behaviorally. Even students with behavioral or emotional disorders are having difficulty processing social and behavioral responses. These deficits not only interfere with processing speed, but also cause students to have difficulty practicing self-regulation or self-control (Volkert, V. M., Lerman, D., and Vorndran, C., 2005). All of these factors must be given consideration when attempting to understand and respond to challenging behaviors. Turecki (1985) went a step further in his research and not only identified some of the personality traits and various processing deficits of these challenging students, but also identified some predictive behaviors that these students exhibit.

Predictive Behaviors

1. **High Activity:** High activity levels refer to students who are exhibiting hyperactive behaviors. Hyperactivity is a neurological disorder that is manifested behaviorally. This disorder interferes with students remaining seated for prolonged periods of time. When younger students have hyperactivity they squirm and fidget, while older students are restless. These students may want to sharpen their pencil, go to the restroom, or call home.

2. **Distraction:** Distracted students are those who have difficulty sustaining attention. This behavioral component may be manifested as having difficulty completing school assignments, staying on task, and will notice everything going on around them. While they may appear to be unfocused, in reality, they are over-focused. They cannot filter anything out.

3. **Poor Adaptability:** Poorly adapted students have difficulty handling transition. Change of classroom or even moving from one subject to another can become a challenge.

4. **Withdrawal:** Students who exhibit withdrawal are those who are poorly socialized. These students often are timid and shy and do not enjoy participating in social situations.

5. **Irregularity:** Irregular students are unpredictable. They become upset for no apparent reason. These students are difficult to read, and it is difficult to identify what has upset the student.

6. **Low Sensory Threshold:** Students who exhibit problems with low sensory threshold are easily over-stimulated. Minor irritations will upset the student.

7. **Negative Mood:** Students who exhibit a negative mood are often angry and sullen. In some cases their negative mood may be related to an unhappy home life or bad experiences at school.

8. **Illness:** Students who are sickly often have specific behavior problems. These students may have frequent ear infections, upper respiratory infections, or may have allergies. As a result, these students are often irritable and experience considerable peer conflict.

Impact of Difficult Behavior

No one is immune to these behaviors of the challenging student. In fact, these behaviors have an impact on every aspect of the student's life, and the lives of those associated with them. The student, peers, teachers, and family members are all affected.

The Student:

When inappropriate behavior remains unabated it can result in physical, emotional, social, and behavioral problems. Students with challenging behaviors tend to experience low self-esteem and feelings of inadequacy. If this process continues, it can have a cyclical effect. As students develop a poor self-concept and a poor self-image, they begin to act out these feelings and experience greater rejection by their peers and receive more reprimands and corrections from teachers. These rejections and reprimands result in the student's beginning to believe what they are hearing. The reprimands indicate that the student is bad, while the correction suggests that he just does not measure up to the expectations of others. Rejection by peers sends the message that the individual is not accepted. As students continue to encounter these responses, they begin to act in ways that will match their feelings. So if students are not good enough, do not measure up, and are not acceptable, they begin to take on these characteristics (Hyde, J. S., Else-Quest, N. M., Goldsmith, H. H., Biesanz, J. C., 2004).

It is not unusual for students to experience a self-fulfilled prophesy. When students have low self-esteem they will often give up without really trying. These students say things like, "I don't know how," or "I can't." As students become increasingly frustrated, rather than facing their feelings of inadequacy, they will blame others for their own mistakes. Eventually these students are ostracized by their peer groups, and they fail to receive the acceptance and approval they so desperately seek. It is not unusual for these students to develop a sense of low self-esteem coupled with feelings of inadequacy, loneliness and isolation (Curwin, R. L., 1993). Such experiences are a perfect formula for failure academically, emotionally, socially and behaviorally.

Students who exhibit challenging behaviors are not the only ones affected by this failure cycle. Peer relationships, school performance and family relations all suffer. Barkley (2003) reported that these students experience more conflicts with peers than students who do not exhibit such challenging behaviors. Teachers of the challenging students report higher levels of frustration than teachers of typical students. They report that a part of their frustration results from seeing these students rejected by their peers. Challenging students will also experience greater failure in the classroom and appear to have more difficulty sustaining attention, remaining seated, and handling transitions. As a result, these students have difficulty relating to peers or forming positive relationships with adults.

The Peers:

Peer conflicts can also become a major stumbling block for these challenging students. Students will often give an unvarnished opinion of how they perceive situations or others. If they perceive that a peer is acting inappropriately, they will often say so. However, when these students with specific challenging traits sense that they are being perceived negatively, they will often become defensive and lash out at their peers. These students use their coping mechanism to deal with this conflict. The basic meaning is they will reject others before others have a chance to reject them. It is their way of not having to experience rejection and such responses often result in even greater peer rejection and isolation (McElwain, N., Olson, S., Volling, B., 2002).

This situation is made even more complicated when the challenging behavior is the result of having a processing deficit. A processing deficit will impair a student's ability to comprehend and respond to various social cues or determine the appropriate social response. It is not unusual for these students to get into trouble and not even understand why. A processing deficit can interfere with a student's ability to follow directions or understand what they are supposed to be doing (Nelson, J. and Benner, G., 2003). For example, a student with an auditory processing deficit may not understand the directions and will lean over to a peer to ask what page he is on. The teacher sees this behavior and yells for the student to turn around. The student was simply trying to compensate for having an auditory deficit and gets into trouble. The next time the student may choose to just not participate rather than take the chance of getting in trouble. Another coping mechanism for these challenging students is to blame others for their own mistakes. Of course, these inappropriate responses lead to greater peer rejection and conflict. Coping mechanisms play an important role in the challenging student's efforts to maintain the status quo. For example, if the challenging student has an emotional/behavioral deficit, he is often highly anxious, insecure, or withdrawn. The anxious student is easily over-stimulated and often will react without thinking about the consequences; whereas the withdrawn student may be under-stimulated and fail to react. When these students experience conflict they may react by either cursing or hitting, or they might simply shut down and withdraw. Either of these responses will set the stage for challenging behavior in the classroom (Vitale, J., Newman, J., Goodnight, J., Dodge, K., and Pettit, G., 2005).

While most students are willing to give their unvarnished opinions, their opinions can also be very cruel. It is not unusual for these students who present challenging behaviors to be teased and called names by their peers. Such names as "shorty," "shrimp," "fatty," "four-eyes," etc., are just a few of the names these students must endure. As these students continue to experience peer rejection, they find themselves with fewer friends. Peer rejection has been identified as one of the primary indicators of adult maladjusted behavior (Sunwolf, L., 2004). As students continue to encounter these negative experiences, they tend to gravitate toward other students who have had similar experiences. This is the early stage of students becoming part of a negative peer group (Bolger, K. and Patterson, C., 2001). Students who display these personality traits and predictive behaviors have been identified as being associated with school dropouts, delinquency, drug use and promiscuous sexual behavior.

School Involvement:

Functioning within a classroom can be very frustrating for students with challenging behaviors. Classroom demands require students to function under specific structural demands and time constraints. Students are required to remain seated, complete tasks within time limits, and complete the work in a neat and orderly fashion. These are the very tasks that will prove problematic for many students with processing deficits and/or challenging behavior patterns. Students with processing deficits are often disorganized or slow to get their school work completed. These students frequently fail to write down their homework assignment, or will misplace it on the way home. If the student manages to get home with the assignment and complete the work, they will often lose it before they return to class the next day. These behaviors often lead to embarrassing moments and interruptions in the classroom. It is not unusual for these experiences to result in negative reactions from teachers and peers (Cooper, L. et.al., 1992).

These students with challenging behaviors and processing deficits often get labeled troublemakers or are seen as the class clowns. In an effort to assist these students, teachers may move them to the front of the classroom or refer them to the school counselor, all of which carries with it a certain stigma and causes further ostracization. As these behaviors continue, eventually the student gains the reputation of being a challenge and a troublemaker. Many of these students are smarter than is often realized and they quickly realize that their peers don't like them and their teacher wishes they were not in their classroom. When they sense rejection by others, they are quick to respond with behaviors that suggest that they don't care. This attitude is often a coping mechanism that is being employed to avoid rejection and conflict (Gould, M., Velting, D., Kleinman, M., Lucas, C., Thomas, J., and Chung, M., 2004). As a consequence, teachers may begin to ignore the students, verbally reprimand them, or send them out of the room. Such responses reinforce these students' self image that they are not good enough and not really wanted in the classroom. These students often drop out of classroom participation long before they actually drop out of school. Effective teachers must be aware of these warning signs and respond proactively.

Since most teachers have not been trained to deal with classroom behavior problems, they are often conditioned to use the discipline techniques to which they have become accustomed. However, these typical strategies do not work for these atypical behavior patterns (Irwin, L. and Nucci, C., 2004). It is normal for teachers to become frustrated when these techniques do not work for these challenging behaviors. As teachers become increasingly frustrated, they tend to become more negative toward students. As a response they may begin to demand less from the student just to avoid a conflict (Barkley, 2000). As the process continues, the teacher may begin giving up trying, decreasing expectations, or even ignoring inappropriate behaviors. All this is done with the hope that the inappropriate behavior will just go away. Unfortunately, these behaviors will not just go away!

Family Relationships:
Another area where these challenging students often have conflict is in their family relations (Sigfusdottir, I., Farkas, G., and Silver, E., 2004). Communication and sharing are two of the most important ingredients of healthy family relationships. However, communicating and sharing are two

of the greatest problems found among students who present processing deficits and challenging behaviors. When a child constantly interrupts or interferes with family activities, family members begin to experience exasperation and frustration, all of which result in family conflicts.

As a result of numerous family conflicts, children with these challenging behaviors are often seen as the problem within the family. It is a mistake to assume that a child's behavior belongs only to the child; it must be shared by everyone involved (Spotts, E., Neiderhiser, J., Hetherington, E., and Reiss, D., 2001). When children are seen as the problem, it sends a powerful message that sets in motion more problem behavior. Keep in mind that children become what they are told. This is the self fulfilled prophesy in motion (Rosenthal, R., 1987). If students perceive that they are a problem, they will work to become just that. When a child receives the message that he or she is not good enough, not smart enough or is a problem, it will cause them to act accordingly. Obviously such responses will lead to greater conflict and negative feelings within the family system. It is not unusual for these behaviors to show up in the classroom.

Barkley (1998) has suggested that teachers and parents alike go through a hierarchy of responses when dealing with their challenging students. Initially teachers will use those discipline strategies that they have been taught. These are the strategies that often work for students seeking attention or trying to gain power. However, when these strategies do not work, they move to a more stern approach. When the student rebels and begins to act out even more, they may remove the student from the classroom. Removing a student would not be a bad strategy if the student did not have to return. However, after a brief visit to the hallway or the principal's office, the student is back in the classroom. As the student's challenging behaviors continue to escalate, the teacher may begin to question the validity of their efforts, or blame themselves for the problems. Over time, as the student's behavior continues, somewhere along the way the teacher may begin to give up trying to correct the student. At this point, in an effort to avoid conflicts, it is not unusual for teachers to give in to the student, lower their expectations, or even begin completing tasks for the student. While assisting students and decreasing demands may be an appropriate academic accommodation, to do so in an effort to avoid conflict is never a proactive discipline strategy. Such responses from the teacher will reinforce the student's goal of power, control, or inadequacy. This process can become an endless cycle of classroom conflict and is counterproductive to proactive discipline.

SUMMARY

During this chapter we have explored some of the reasons why the role of the teacher has become more difficult. Obviously one of the reasons why teaching has become more difficult is because students have changed. There are specific personality and behavioral indicators that will help teachers differentiate between typical manipulative behavior and the more atypical behavior patterns. However, it is not just the teacher that is affected by these challenging behaviors. These conflicts impact on the student, peers, school functioning, and the family system. However, with help, the teacher can identify the personality and behavioral indicators and anticipate and intervene before the challenging behavior occurs.

Chapter Three

COMPARING APPLES AND ORANGES:
DIFFERENTIATING TYPICAL AND ATYPICAL BEHAVIORS

Thankfully, not all challenging behaviors are permanent. There are a variety of factors that can influence a student's behavior in the classroom to appear to be atypical. For example, a student may have a genetic predisposition toward misbehavior, may be in a regressed stage of development, may be reinforced by the teacher's response, or may simply be attempting to get a need met. These behaviors stand in contrast to atypical behavior patterns. Atypical behavior usually lasts much longer than typical behavior, is more intense, and is often related to the student's inability to process information.

It is not unusual for a teacher to have a current student and remember having one of the student's parents in their classroom years ago. The teacher may comment that the current student "acts just like his daddy did when he was a student." Such a response suggests a genetic link to the behavior. However, a student's behavior may result from a regressed stage of development. Students go through accelerated and regressed stages of development. A regressed stage of develop will typically last between three to six months. When students are in a regressed stage of development they will temporarily lose many of their physical, language, social, emotional and even behavioral traits. In essence, the student will act more regressed than their age might indicate. Teachers should keep in mind that the regressed stage is only a temporary setback. The student will eventually move beyond the stage. Of course the problem is that all students do not go through these stages at the same time. Therefore, at any give time, in a classroom of twenty-four students, six may be in a regressed stage. However, as three of the six students begin to make progress, another five may move into a regressed stage. If the student's inappropriate behavior is being reinforced by the teacher, the student will learn how to gain attention and power. Reacting to a student's negative behavior often only reinforces the behavior. Or in some situations students may be displaying negative behavior in an attempt to get a need met (Litrownik, A.J., Lau, A., English, D.J., Briggs, E., Newton, R.R., Romney, S., and Dubowitz, H., 2005).

It is not unusual, when these students' typical behaviors escalate and begin to interfere with academic achievement, that teachers may contact their pre-referral team (See NCLB, 2005), requesting an immediate appointment. These requests often take place after several attempts at intervention have failed. When meeting with the pre-referral team, teachers usually have collected sufficient data that accurately represents the student's behavior, but may not address the actual function of the behavior (Gresham, F. M., 1989). It will be important at a minimum to identify the possible antecedent and consequence of the behavior. This can be accomplished by conducting a series of observations and reviewing class records. This data can be recorded on an Education Performance Report Form (Johnson and Edmunds, 2006). When the behavior has been present for a few days or weeks, one may discover that there has been an abrupt change in the student's home life, or the student is going through a stage or phase or development that has resulted in the more challenging behavior.

All challenging behavior does not necessarily mean that the student has a severe behavioral problem. In fact, much of the behavior that teachers routinely struggle with is often typical behavior being influenced by the four components that were previously pointed out (Arnold, E., Goldston, D., Walsh, A., Reboussin, B., Daniel, S., Hickman, E., and Wood, F. B.,2005). However, it can be difficult to determine exactly what is causing the student's behavior. The goal of the Student Service Team is to help determine what might be causing the student's behavior and to suggest strategies to help address the presented concerns. This pre-assessment team may suggest that a psycho-educational evaluation be conducted, additional observations or some type of behavior modification program be implemented. A good rule of thumb is that if the behaviors are typical, they will continue only for a short period of time. These behaviors usually exist when the student is attempting to get attention or power, is in a regressed stage of development, or is trying to get a need meet (Johnson, F. 1996).

Typical Challenging Behaviors

Typically challenging behaviors can be very disruptive to a classroom. Although these behaviors do not call for long-term intervention, short-term strategies are necessary. As previously noted, there are four reasons why these children exhibit these typical inappropriate behavior patterns: genetic predisposition, the age or stage of development, reinforcement, and attempting to get a need meet.

Genetics:

Researchers have debated for years about the importance of inherent versus learned behavior. Most researchers agree that genetics plays a significant role in disruptive classroom behavior (DiLalla, L. F., 2002). Humans are born with a certain predisposition or temperament style. It is this temperament (personality) style that can influence how a student responds to various stimuli. For example, some students may overreact to a certain event, while others may not react at all to the same event. Teachers talk to the parents about their child's inappropriate behavior, only to be met with a response like, "He is just like his father." Such a response suggests a linkage between genetics and behavior. While researchers will continue to debate the importance genetics plays, it is sufficient to realize that genetics can be one of the contributing factors to misbehavior (Iervolino, A., Hines, M., Golombok, S., Rust, J., and Plomin, R., 2005).

Age and Stage of Development:

A student's physical, emotional, social, and behavioral development is all inter-related. Therefore, when students enter into a regressed stage of development, their physical, social, emotional, and behavioral skills will revert (Emick, J., and Welsh, M., 2005). During these regressed stages, a child may appear to be clumsy, become less coordinated, drop things, and trip over himself (physical). The student will often whine and complain and is more irritable (emotional). He tends to have increased arguments and be more withdrawn (social). It is during these regressed stages that a student will express greater frustration and tend to experience more peer conflicts.

The student will have difficulty completing tasks that were previously mastered and as a result become more insecure and frustrated (academic). For example, a second grade student may enter a regressed stage and suddenly engage in such behaviors as baby talk, thumb sucking, or temper tantrums. Research by Anstine, J. and Skidmore, M. (2005) suggests that students tend to go through various stages at predictable and approximate intervals. The younger the child the more quickly they move in and out of a stage. In addition, for some students the difference in behavior when in or out of a stage can be dramatic, while for others the change is more subtle. Older children will take longer to move through a stage and the changes are less dramatic (Johnson, F.L., 1996).

In order to make appropriate decisions about how to best respond to a student's behavior, it is important to understand specific behaviors that are present at each regressed stage of development. If teachers can understand and recognize these stages they will be in a better position to anticipate and plan for responding to the corresponding behaviors.

Age	Behaviors
12 months	At 12 months children are able to move about freely and tend to explore everything. They climb on chairs pulled out from the table, go up and down stairs and open drawers.
15 months	This period is represented by a growth spurt. The child is more active and will shift from happiness to sadness without provocation.
18 months	At this stage, the child's developmental skills will regress. Suddenly, the child becomes less social and will exhibit considerable emotional insecurity.
2 years	At this stage, the child's developmental skills make a rebound. Motor and language skills increase and they become more socially aware.
2 years, 6 months	This is one of those very difficult stages of development. Physical, language, social, and emotional and behavioral skills all regress. During this stage, children are often insecure and there may be many power struggles.
3 years	This is a time of adjustment for children. Three-

	year-old children are conforming and concerned about being accepted.
3 years, 6 months	This is another difficult stage. While at age 2.5 years the child's behavior was externalized, now it becomes internalized. Many children will become insecure and anxious.
4 years	At this stage, developmental skills rebound and the child appears to be well-adjusted and happy. It is during this stage of development that boys begin to exhibit oppositional-type behavior.
4 years, 6 months	It is at this stage that children begin to establish a system of rational thinking. They strive for more independence and use logic to argue. Children are highly imaginative and eager to learn.
5 years	This is another period of transition and a time for harmonious relationships. The student is often content and cooperative.
6 years	During this stage of development, students are now outgoing and ready to learn. They are able to process and conceptualize information and benefit from the learning experience.
7 years	At this stage, children may become shy, withdrawn and introspective. These children are moving from a stage of concrete reasoning to conceptual processing. While previously the child simply accepted what adults said, now he begins to use logic and reasoning skills to make decisions.
8 years	During this stage, students move into a period where they use trial and error for learning and problem-solving. These students are experimental and need to have

	permission to try new things and fail without ridicule.
9 years	At this stage of development, students tend to revert in their social skills. Girls tend to struggle more than boys with issues of self identity. (Please see Chapter Ten for more information related to self esteem.)
10 years	This stage is marked by greater cooperation and a need for approval and a sense of belonging. During the period of regression, these students seek approval, acceptance, and appear very needy.
11 years	At age eleven, physical development is vastly different for boys and girls. Girls will experience accelerated growth, while boys do not. Changes are also apparent socially. Boys continue to experience same-sex identity, while girls begin to become aware sexually.
12 years	This stage represents a physical growth spurt for boys. They often become more sexually aware, but they do not have sufficient social and emotional skills to regulate their impulses. It is during this stage of development that boys will say and do things that are socially inappropriate.
13 years	At age thirteen, girls have more difficulty reading social cues. Since they are so overly sexualized, they will often misread social meaning. For example, they may interpret a teacher's kind words or friendly gesture as sexual.
14 years	At this stage, boys and girls have the ability to relate platonically and intimately. They can have strong friendships with same sex and opposite sex peers, as well as a boyfriend/girlfriend relationship.
15 years	Students at age fifteen tend to become very competitive. This competitive spirit is not just with athletics, but with all aspects of life. These students

	may use sarcasm to put each other down.
16 years	At this stage, students move into a time when they are very conceptual and introspective. Their cognitive skills are almost complete and they will use logic and reasoning to argue.
17 years	At seventeen, students' cognitive skills are now complete. They are able to conceptualize and process information and use synergy to draw on concepts. Students at this age begin to seek meaning to existence as they make life decisions.

Social Learning:

Social learning occurs from those events in a student's life that influence behavior. While these behaviors are typical, they can be very worrisome. In Chapter Two it was suggested that students tend to not necessarily remember what teachers teach them, but rather how teachers treat them. For example, if the classroom experience is consistent, respectful, and provides encouragement, it will help students develop into healthy, functioning adults (Jeanpierre, B. J., 2004). However, if the classroom experience is inconsistent or does not match the student's learning style, this will be one of the contributions to the student's emotional struggles as an adult (Honigsfeld, A. and Schiering, M., 2004). It is for this reason that teachers must not only have an understanding of their students' behavior, but must also learn to respond in ways that will help the student move toward becoming a positive, healthy, functioning adult who can practice self-control. What are some of these events that can shape a child's personality and influence their behavior? It is easy to think of the big events, e.g. divorce, death, abuse. However, it may be the small events that result in the greatest difficulty. When teachers give attention on demand, are inconsistent, argue with students, call names, embarrass students in front of peers, tease or punish, these are all ways that behaviors can be reinforced. These are all events that may have a significant impact on a child's personality and behavior (Rubin, B. and Noguera, P., 2004).

Social learning can also involve the things that a child observes at home and then brings into the classroom. Some have argued that family relationships are becoming increasingly dysfunctional and are impacting on classroom functioning (Carich, M. and Stone, M., 1998). It is not unusual for children to hear their parents arguing, see the police come to their house at 2:30 a.m. to pick up the father on a bench warrant, or any number of events that may create anxiety for the child. The anxious child has been awake all night and then comes to school the next morning wired and tired. These students appear to not be interested when, in fact, they are only distracted by all that is going on in their private lives. They are tired and wired, and more likely to display challenging behavior.

Goal Seeking:

In some situations, students' misbehavior may exist as a means to simply get their needs met. These needs and/or goals can often be misguided. Obviously some students have greater needs than others. The objective of the teacher is not to deal with the student therapeutically - that is the role of the psychologist or therapist. Most often a needy child will become a needy adult. However, in the meantime the teacher must respond to the student's needs in order to minimize behavioral problems in the classroom. In many cases these behaviors are occurring secondary to a faulty belief system. These needs and/or goals are: attention, power or control, revenge and a display of inadequacy. While these needs are fairly typical, when taken to extreme they can become challenging (Kam, C. M., Greenberg, M. T., and Kusche, C. A. , 2004).

Attention:

Everyone wants and needs attention. However, when students demand excessive attention they are sending a message that they are only important when they are being noticed. Of course, students have different levels of need. For most students simply telling them at the end of the day or the end of the class period that they have done a good job is sufficient. However, some students may need to receive this attention and praise several times each hour (Kearney, C., and Albano, A. M., 2004). When students seek excessive attention they don't care who the teacher is talking with—the superintendent, principal, a parent, or another student—they will interrupt conversations or do something to get others to notice them. They will often interrupt, clown around, make noises, or pretend to be sick in an effort to gain attention. This need for excessive attention may be an indication of insecurity or feelings of inadequacy. The faulty belief system is *"I am only important when I am being noticed"* (Dubelle, S. T. and Hoffman, C. M., 1987).

Power and Control:

When students fail to receive adequate attention, they move into the next stage of seeking power. The faulty belief system is *"I am only important if I am proving that I can control others,"* or *"If I am proving no one can control me."* These situations often exist when students have too much power and control or, conversely, when they feel powerless. Students have too much power and control when they are able to control their family or classroom. Research by Knobloch, L. K. and Solomon, D. H. (2002) has pointed out that most children feel powerless when events occur in their lives over which they have no control, e.g. divorce, death, etc. They want to stop the events, but they do not have the power to do so. There are many ways that children either have too much power or not enough power, and they attempt to work out their frustration in the classroom. Behaviors that exist secondary to a student's overt need for power and control include: refusing to cooperate, acting bossy, behaving in ways to get sent to the office, and any other way that controls the classroom or where they can avoid a situation.

Effective teachers understand the importance of students' having their needs meet. For example, when students do not receive positive attention, they will seek negative attention. In fact, researchers (Boreham, N. and Morgan, C., 2004) have suggested that the need for attention and power are the cause for most of the disruptive behaviors by typical students. Therefore, if a teacher can adequately meet students' needs for attention and power, most classroom behavior problems of typical students should disappear. One of the best ways to provide positive attention include: greeting each student by name each morning and commenting on something specific about the student. For example: *"Good morning Stephen. Wow, is that a new shirt you have on?"* It is not really important what the comment is as long as it is personal or unique to the student. In addition, attention can be provided when teachers simply look at the student when speaking to him or her. Teachers can also provide attention by thanking students for their hard work during the day; *"Johnny, I noticed you really worked hard today. I really appreciate it."* Also, by allowing students to speak without interrupting gives them a sense of power. Lastly, one of the easiest ways to empower a student is to provide choices whenever possible. The teacher may say; *"Okay students, we finished early and you have about ten minutes. You can start on your homework or just spend time talking, as long as you do it quietly."*

Each of these efforts is a means of providing students with attention and power. When students are given attention and power, they will not have to seek it. In contrast, when students do not receive adequate attention and empowerment, they will move to the next stage of seeking needs or revenge.

Revenge:

When students misbehave because of feelings of revenge, they are essentially saying, *"I want to hurt you the way I feel I have been hurt."* These students feel that life is not fair, and now they want to get back or get even. The very idea of getting back or even suggests that students do not feel equal (Orth, U., Montada, L., and Maercker, A., 2006). When students fail to receive adequate attention and empowerment, they will begin to feel less than; worse than; lower than; not as good as; and they want to get even. Their goal is to simply feel even or equal with others. Even if the teacher sees the student as equal but they have not received adequate attention and power, they will often respond with, *"That's not fair."* Such events as failing a test, not being selected for the basketball team, or having a note sent home about their behavior will cause the child to feel that life is not fair. How does the student finally get even? When students are able to make others around them feel miserable, they have gotten even! Such behavior is a means of pulling others down to their level. It is not a pretty sight, but when everyone is miserable, at least they are even. The real definition of revenge is *"to make you feel the way I feel"* or *"I want to hurt you the same way I have been hurt."* (Johnson, F.J., 1996). Students who seek revenge are looking for acceptance, approval, attention, and power. In fact, research by Foster, L. G.; (1994) suggests that this absence of receiving attention and having power is at the very root of why students gravitate toward negative peers. The student may curse the teacher in order to receive attention, or shoplift to receive power. Of course they get into trouble, but they also receive this much-needed approval, acceptance, attention and power. Research has suggested in severe cases the lack of attention and power, and the inability to feel equal is at the root of gang affiliation. It is here that they can find attention, power, acceptance and approval (Chory-Assad, R. and Paulsel, M., 2002). These students may be experiencing low self-esteem that is being manifested as challenging behavior. When students have reached the revenge stage of attempting to get their needs meet, this is a very difficult perception to correct. Intervention must be proactive, and patience will be required. However, if students are not able to receive adequate attention, empowerment, and their efforts at revenge fail to make them feel acceptance, they will move into the last stage of need; they will display their inadequacy.

Display of Inadequacy:

When students misbehave because of feelings of inadequacy it suggests that they feel their mistakes are not acceptable (Cross, T. L., 2005). These students may feel that adults have unreasonable expectations, or whatever they do is never good enough. In addition, displaying inadequacies suggests that students want their teacher to think of them as incompetent. This is a sure sign that a student has failed and then was reprimanded, laughed at, or punished. Something bad, in addition to the failing, occurred (Byo, J. L., 2002). Now the student is afraid of making a mistake. The basic message to the teacher is: *"I am inadequate and I will prove it to you."* When students seek attention they are trying to be noticed, when they seek power they want control, when they seek revenge they want to "get even." What is the student trying to get when they display inadequacy? The thought process is, if the teacher thinks the student is inadequate, the teacher will have minimal expectations and then the student will not have to try and fail. Students display their inadequacy when they forget to do a homework assignment, when they refuse to participate, or when they engage in an inappropriate behavior. The mistake that is often made is to accept students' view of their inadequacy. This occurs when teachers lower their expectations or allow students to not complete their assignment because it is just easier. The message to the student is, *"You are right; you are inadequate and so pitiful that you cannot even complete your homework assignment."* This type of response reinforces the student's feelings of inadequacy and will result in even more misbehavior. The objective will be to not lower the expectations, but rather give the student the tools to succeed.

Reinforcement:

It is also important for teachers to understand just how much reinforcement can influence classroom behavior. Although teachers are only one of many factors that influence student behavior, they are one of the most important. However, other influences include the curriculum, the physical structure of the classroom, classroom organization and relationships to other students (Harrison, J.S., 1996).

In some cases teachers may not mean to, but unintentionally reinforce negative behavior. This unintentional reinforcement operates much like operant conditioning (McComas, J. J., Goddard, C., and Hoch, H., 2002). Of course, positive and negative reinforcement is one of the major concerns raised by teachers today. There are basically two models of reinforcing students. The first is referred to as the ABC model, while the other is the SRR model. Both of these theories are based on Thorndike's theory of motivation (Finkbeiner, C., and Koplin, C., 2002).

The ABC model refers to the Antecedent, Behavior, Consequence paradigm. The antecedent refers to that which happens just before the behavior occurs, while the consequence is that which happens just after the behavior (Codding, R. S., Feinberg, A. B., Dunn, E. K., and Pace, G. M., 2005). The theory is that if one can identify and control the antecedent and consequence, he can control the behavior. For example, in the classroom a teacher may announce that everyone is going to read a paragraph out loud. About that time a student becomes disruptive and is then sent to the office. While this may look like a simple process, upon closer examination the teacher may discover a specific process that is driving the student's behavior. The antecedent and consequence will give a clue to how to manage the behavior. Through observation, the teacher may discover that the student became disruptive when it was announced that everyone was going to read aloud. The teacher might speculate that since the student is a poor reader and is often embarrassed when trying to read, the student would rather be sent to the office than face possible embarrassment. When the student misbehaved, the teacher responded by sending the student out of the class, and thereby reinforced the student's behavior. The antecedent occurred when the teacher announced that the students were going to read aloud. The consequence was when the teacher sent the student out of the room. The goal of the student was to avoid reading so when he was sent out of the room his behavior was reinforced. As previously mentioned, the theory is that behavior can be managed if the antecedent or consequence is controlled. In this scenario, which can be controlled, the antecedent or consequence? Since the student's behavior is interfering with learning, it would not be reasonable to allow the student to remain in the room. However, can the antecedent be controlled? Yes. In this situation the teacher may talk to the student the day before the classroom assignment, and let him know which paragraph he will be asked to read aloud. Ask the student to practice the paragraph the night before. Then inform the student that just before it is his time to read, the teacher will stand close to him. This is his signal that he will be the next student to be called on. By controlling the antecedent, much of the acting out behavior can be controlled.

When behavior, negative or positive, is reinforced, the reinforcement causes the behavior to continue. Another way to understand this process is to review the SRR process. The "S" is for the stimulus, the "R" is for the response to the stimulus, and the last "R" is for the reinforcement of the response. The stimulus will involve one or more of the senses: touching, seeing, smelling, tasting, or hearing. Based on the stimulation, the student responds in some fashion. Then, based on the response, the student is reinforced. Reinforcement of behavior can cause a behavior to continue or discontinue (Scott, T. M., Liaupsin, C. J., Nelson, C. M., and Jolivette, K., 2005). The following is an example of this process:

A child comes into the kitchen where his mother is baking cookies. The mother takes the cookies out of the oven and sets them on top of the stove to cool. The child sees and smells the cookies (Stimulation). The child responds by walking over to the stove, reaches up and takes a cookie (Response). As the child takes a cookie, he touches the hot stove and burns his hand (Reinforcement). The reinforcement teaches the child not to reach to the stove again. The child was negatively reinforced. In contrast, if the child takes a cookie and does not burn his hand, the cookie tastes wonderful, the mother states, "I am glad you are having a cookie, have another." The child is positively reinforced and will probably repeat the behavior.

These two formulas can help teachers determine why students are behaving a certain way and help to formulate a hypothesis as to why the inappropriate behavior is continuing. It is entirely possible that the teacher may be doing something to reinforce the negative classroom behavior. Teachers reinforce negative behaviors when they:

1. Give attention on demand
2. Are inconsistent
3. Speak harshly to students
4. Belittle students in front of others
5. Are inflexible or controlling
6. Fail to provide adequate direction

      7. Compare students

      8. Show favoritism

However, since teachers can do things to reinforce negative behavior, they can also do things to reinforce positive behavior. This process suggests that teachers have considerable power when it comes to managing classroom behavior. The most important thing that teachers can do to promote positive classroom behavior is to offer proactive discipline strategies. However, students that engage in inappropriate behavior secondary to genetic predisposition, age or stage develop, reinforcement or attempting to get a need met are typically referred to as manipulative. This means that they are trying to get something. If they do not get what they want they will either stop trying, or will try a different avenue to get what they want. Students are usually trying to get attention, power, control, avoidance, or even something tangible (Johnson, F.L., 1996).

There are other students, atypical students, who do not respond out of a need to get something and their behavior is usually not short-lived. The behavior of these students is referred to as challenging. In later chapters when we deal with proactive discipline, we will discover that what works for these typical manipulative students will not work for these more difficult or challenging students.

Atypical Challenging Behaviors:

Students who exhibit these continuous challenging behaviors often do not have sufficient self-control to regulate their behavior. As a result, they are often in trouble with someone. These students are often frustrated and will act out secondary to their emotions. Without sufficient self-regulatory skills it is difficult for these students to stop when they begin to engage in inappropriate behaviors (Johnson, F.L., and Edmunds, A.L., 2006).

There are several reasons why these students have difficulty with self-regulation. One of the most common reasons why students display continuous challenging behavior is that they have difficulty processing information. This means that they will process information at a slower rate than most of their peers. It can be frustrating when everyone else gets finished with their work first or when everyone else seems to know the answers to the questions. As a result these students often are in a state of frustration, anxiousness, or tension.

Difficulty processing information is associated with the presence of a neurological deficit (Schunk, D. H., 2005). The word neurological refers to the brain and the word deficit means to have an injury or damage. Therefore, these students who have difficulty processing have some type of brain dysfunction or damage (Mayfield, J., and Homack, S., 2005).

This information was briefly discussed in Chapter 1, but now deserves a more complete view. There are three primary ways that information is processed—visual, auditory, and kinesics. The task of processing information involves encoding the information, decoding the information, and then interpreting and responding to the information. While this process normally takes only a millisecond to complete, for students with a processing deficit it can become a difficult task. Information is often processed simultaneously. This means that students can process all three tasks at the same time. They can listen, look and take notes at the same time. However, when a processing deficit is present processing information becomes an act of concentration. They process information sequentially. When one must concentrate on the task, they will complete the task at a much slower rate. For example, if a student has an auditory processing deficit and the teacher asks the class a question, most students begin immediately processing the answer. However, the student with a processing deficit must first process the question. By the time the student comes to the answer, the teacher has already moved on to another question.

Many terms are used to refer to a processing deficit. When students are referred to as having a learning disability, attention deficit hyperactivity disorder, cognitive impairment, autism, or even emotional disorder, in reality the problem is the way they process information. These students have a neurological deficit. However, saying that someone has a neurological deficit is too nonspecific and most teachers and parents do not like thinking that a student could have a brain deficit or damage (Weiler, M. D., Bernstein, J. H. B. D. and Waber, D. P., 2005).

There are many ways that diagnosticians relate this information in nonspecific and often less than helpful terms. For example, a teacher working in a birth-to-five program frequently receives reports from a neurologist referring to a child as having a Pervasive Developmental Disorder-Not Otherwise Specified (PDD-NOS) or Atypical Autism. Both of these terms are nonspecific. The diagnosis of PDD-NOS is basically saying the child shows multiple signs of developmental delays but we don't know why. The term "atypical autism" is rather confusing. We know that atypical is the opposite of typical. So, the child's autism is not "typical." Basically, the child's autism does not look like typical autism. These two diagnoses are very nonspecific and often not helpful for treatment purposes. They suggest that the child has some type of disorder but the physician is not sure what it is. Therefore, in an effort to make these neurological deficits more meaningful, differential diagnosis has been assigned to help better understand how the deficits are manifested. There are several "labels" that educators use to more specifically identify the neurological deficit: -

A. Attention Deficit Hyperactivity Disorder:

Attention Deficit Hyperactivity Disorder is a neurological disorder that is often poorly understood. Although the disorder is neurological in nature, it is manifested behaviorally. ADHD is manifested primarily in three domains of behavior-poor attention, impulsive behavior, and hyperactivity (Mullins, C., Bellgrove, M. A., Gill, M., and Robertson, I. H., 2005).

1. Attention difficulty is often thought of as not paying attention or as unfocused when, in fact, it is the opposite. It is not that the student cannot pay attention, it is that he is paying attention to everything. An attention deficit is really a filtering problem (Power, T. J., Costigan, T. E., Eiraldi, R. B., and Leff, S. S., 2004). For example, most people can listen to music and read at the same time. However, the ADHD student cannot filter any of the stimuli out. The student is listening to the teacher, but he is also wondering why the police car is in the parking lot; he is thinking about what he is going to do when he gets home; he is listening to the students behind him whisper, and he is thinking they are probably talking about him. He cannot filter out any of the stimuli so everything gets his attention (Eisenberg, Nancy et. al., 2004).

2. Impulsive behavior is seen when students appear to act without thinking about the consequences of their behavior. A teacher may call an impulsive student out into the hall and discuss his inappropriate behavior. The student can state in clear terms the appropriate way to deal with the conflict in the classroom. In fact, the student agrees to respond appropriately in the future. However, five minutes later the student exhibits the same inappropriate behavior. The student is able to retrieve the knowledge of how to behave in a calm setting, but under stress and the immediacy of the moment is unable to do so. The student is unable to learn from discipline strategies involving cause and effect.

3. Hyperactivity is a behavior that is often misunderstood. This behavior is manifested differently, depending on the age of the student. Young hyperactive students, ages three to eleven years, will squirm in their seats, play with items on a table, kick their feet or fidget. However, hyperactivity in older students is seen more as a sense of restlessness. These older students are up every five minutes to sharpen their pencil, they need to go to the restroom, they have a headache and want to go to the office, or they need to call their mother. These students are restless. However, the real definition of hyperactivity is "as if a motor is running" (Wood, J. G., and Benton, S. L., 2005). This involves involuntary muscle movement. The next time you are in a staff meeting look around the room and see if anyone's leg is moving. Most likely they do not even realize it, but their leg is just tapping away. This is that "motor" running inside them.

Questions usually arise concerning possible over-diagnosing of ADHD. While the disorder may not be over-diagnosed, there is certainly evidence to suggest that it is often misdiagnosed. The usual mode of treatment for ADHD children is to prescribe a stimulant medication. Certain medical conditions are mistaken for ADHD. For example, a depressed child will often appear distracted; a highly anxious child will appear impulsive, while children with Tourettes Syndrome will appear to be hyperactive. This misdiagnosis often results in the way in which the student is diagnosed. For example, a teacher complains to a parent that a student is creating a behavior problem in the classroom and provides the parent with a pamphlet on ADHD. The parent in turn goes to the family doctor to discuss the problem. The doctor takes the parent's statement and offers a prescription for a stimulant. However, if the student is not ADHD but rather depressed, anxious, or has Tourettes Syndrome, taking a stimulant will do what it is designed to do—that is, stimulate. Therefore, if a student is misdiagnosed and is given a stimulant, it will exacerbate underlying pathologies. The child taking a stimulant may become withdrawn, weepy, and just stare out the window. Or, if the child is anxious instead of impulsive, after taking a stimulant the parent may complain the child became aggressive and irritable. The child may have been diagnosed and the underlying pathologies have been stimulated.

Teachers of students with processing deficits often become frustrated when their usual discipline strategies are not effective. One of the residual effects of a processing deficit is poor self-regulation (Schunk, D.H., 2005). This condition can be made worse when a teacher minimizes the impact the disorder has on behavior. Parents may also have difficulty believing their child is unable to control his or her behavior. A statement such as, *"that teacher is not strict enough"* is a signal of denial or a lack of acceptance. Students with processing deficits will need a multimodal approach to treatment. Interventions may involve family therapy, school accommodations, and changes in their community involvement. For example, interventions may include a modified school schedule, change in curriculum, small group instruction or social skills training. In some situations, these students may benefit from a behavioral modification program or medication (Cole, K., Mills, P., Jenkins, J., and Dale, P., 2005).

B. Learning Disabilities:

A learning disability is another neurological deficit which can influence student behavior (de Bildt, A., Sytema, S., Kraijer, D., Sparrow, S., and Minderaa, R., 2005). It is a mistake to think that learning-disabled students are not very bright. It is true that in some cases, learning-disabled students may have a limited cognitive ability. However, many learning-disabled students are very bright but have a specific deficit in a certain area of processing. It is not unusual for a student that is learning-disabled to become frustrated in the classroom. They often have difficulty processing visual, auditory or kinetic information. Imagine what it is like to be a bright student but not understand directions from the teacher, or to have difficulty writing down the homework assignment from the chalkboard. These students often have concomitant language deficits that can prevent them from expressing how they feel. Therefore, when they are frustrated they will act out their frustration (Frost, J., and Emery, M., 1996).

One of the primary difficulties associated with a learning disability is having difficulty following sequences or multiple steps for task completion (Harris, C. et. al., 1995). These students often have difficulty following simple two- and three-step sequences for problem solving. Teachers may become equally frustrated when students fail to follow directions. The teacher may tell the class to turn to page 119 in their math books and complete the first 10 problems in section one. If the student did not understand the sequence, steps or directions he may lean over to the student sitting beside him and ask, "What did she say?" The teacher thinks the student is just goofing off and yells for the student to turn around. The student will get into trouble and all they were doing was trying to compensate for having an auditory processing deficit. These students may also fail to comprehend multiple tasks involved, and fail to complete the problem. When any of these events occur the student may become frustrated and then attempt to retaliate. Therefore, an important part of proactive discipline is to understand how a processing deficit might impact on daily classroom functioning. Instructions will need to be clear, concise and frequently repeated. Also, it may be important to guard against asking a learning-disabled student to complete multiple-step tasks.

As was mentioned in Chapter One, effective teachers are those who provide students with directions. However, some teachers may become frustrated when they have to show a student more than once how to complete a task. It is ironic that a coach does not hesitate to instruct students over and over how to hit a baseball. However, in the classroom that same teacher may feel that a student should not have to have academic instructions repeated. When working with students with processing deficits, it is imperative to be patient and always be willing to repeat instructions (Doyle, M. L., 1990).

Some teachers may not be aware of how a processing deficit may impact on classroom behavior. For example, if a student has an auditory processing deficit, the teacher cannot expect the student to understand or follow directions. Therefore, accommodations will need to be provided. The teacher will need to repeat instructions or check with the student for clarification. On some occasions the material will need to be re-taught. However, even with assistance, these students are often more challenging and may display greater behavior problems than will the previously mentioned manipulative students (Toro, P. A. et. al.,1990).

C. Teacher Skills:

It is important for teachers to provide classroom instructions that will match their student's learning style. The lack of adequate instruction will enhance the possibility of misbehavior. Effective teachers will recognize individual differences that exist among students and rather than seeing them as a challenge, they will see these differences as an opportunity. As a result, effective teachers celebrate diversity and use various teaching styles and methodologies in the classroom to match the needs of each student. Therefore, effective teachers recognize that classroom instruction must be designed to maximize students' strengths in order to meet individual needs and different learning styles of students.

Just as students have differing learning styles, they also exhibit different types of behavior patterns. Some behaviors are viewed as typical or normal behaviors while others are more atypical or challenging. While typical behaviors may be influenced by a genetic predisposition, social learning, the age of the student or the needs of the student, the more challenging behaviors are influenced by issues related to a lack of self-regulation. An inability to self-regulate is often at the root cause of atypical students' getting into trouble in the classroom. Effective teachers must realize that just as specific academic instruction must match students' learning style, specific discipline interventions must be provided to match students' behavioral needs. These teachers recognize that proactive discipline is not doing something to a student, but rather involves everything that goes on in the classroom.

SUMMARY

During this chapter we have explored the differences between typical and atypical behavior patterns and some of the ways that teachers tend to reinforce these behaviors. Research has suggested that approximately 65% of students express typical behaviors while 35% are more atypical. The vast majority of students process and integrate information, assimilate, and basically benefit from the learning experience. Do these students ever misbehave? Of course they do. But they also learn from cause and effect and other typical discipline strategies. However, approximately 35% of students seem to have more serious issues. These students may have a cognitive, academic, emotional, social or behavioral impairment. These numbers are in stark contrast to the national average of only about 13.4% of students receiving special educational services. As was noted, these atypical characteristics are often assigned labels, e.g. attention deficit hyperactivity disorder, learning disability, autism, emotionally handicapped, etc. Regardless of the impairment or label, teachers are left to contend with these students in the classroom. However, when teachers provide typical discipline strategies for these atypical behaviors, little benefit will be realized. Therefore, it is important for teachers to understand the difference between typical and atypical behavior patterns and the factors that may influence such behavior.

Chapter Four

"HEY, CAN WE TALK?"
COMMUNICATION IN THE CLASSROOM

When people hear the word "communicate," often the first thing they think of is talking. While talking is important, it is only one part of the total communication process. In fact, talking may be one of the least important parts. Researchers (Do, S. L. and Schallert, D., 2004) have estimated that one will remember only about 18% of what is actually said to him. For this reason alone, we can rightly conclude that if talking is our only means of communication, it is fairly ineffective. The other important part of the communication process is listening and non-verbal communication. Julius Fast (1971) first explored the concept of body language. However, effective teachers are those who are able to utilize a variety of communication skills in their classroom in order to enhance learning and teach effective discipline. In fact, researchers have suggested that students recall efforts at teacher communication in the following categories:

Verbal—what teachers say 7%
Vocal—how teachers say it 38%
Visual—how teachers look, act, etc. 55%

What makes a teacher an effective communicator? It probably has something to do with his or her ability to talk, listen, and act (Kramer-Dahl, A., 2004). In contrast, an ineffective communicator is one who has limited talking and listening skills, and whose actions often send the message of disapproval. Most people like to be listened to. Have you ever been in a situation where the other person dominated the conversation? How does it feel when one person dominates the conversation? Even more importantly, how do people act when caught in such a situation? The following experience will demonstrate this point more clearly.

I recall being at a social function and caught in a conversation with an individual who talked on and on and on. I ate all the hors d'oeuvres on my plate as quickly as possible and excused myself. However, my real objective was just to get away from the person who was dominating the conversation. Much to my dismay, as I turned around from the table where the food was located, there was this individual standing, ready to resume the conversation. I immediately pretended to see someone I knew and went in the opposite direction. I felt that this individual thought that what he had to say was more important than what I had to say. In effect, this person was communicating to me that what I had to say was not important. Most people look for excuses to avoid people who talk excessively.

When teachers lecture excessively, students will either tune them out or find other ways to avoid the conversation. Students will avoid them by trying to get out of the room, sleeping in class, drawing, or finding other ways to entertain themselves. This occurs because students are just like adults; they want people to listen to them (Murphy, B., 2004). Being a good listener is one of the important qualities of an effective teacher. When teachers listen to students, it communicates that what they are saying is important. However, the opposite is also true. When teachers do most of the talking, the message is communicated that what students have to say is not important.

There are many benefits to listening to students. When students are listened to they feel valued and important to their teacher (Baw, S. S., 2002). In addition, when teachers listen to students, teachers learn valuable information that they may otherwise not know. Lastly, when students are allowed to talk about what is important to them, it acts as a ventilation process to "get it off their chest." In essence, by allowing students to talk about their feelings, frustration and anxiety is reduced.

Expressing feelings and thoughts is an important part of the communication process. When talking with students it is important to be honest and make sure they fully understand your thoughts and feelings. One of the goals of an effective communicator is to determine when it is appropriate to talk and when it is appropriate to listen.

Talking as a Form of Communicating

An important part of a teacher's day is consumed with talking. In order to effectively talk with students, teachers must have excellent communication skills. If the issue is helping a student solve a problem, the teacher must first determine if the presenting problem is one in which they actually need to become involved. Teachers need to only get involved when asked to or when it is necessary. When teachers intrude into problems unnecessarily, students learn to be dependent and irresponsible. After all, if the teacher is going to solve the problem, why should students take responsibility? And, if the solution offered by the teacher does not work, the students can blame the teacher. When students have problems, let them know of your concern and express confidence in their ability to make appropriate decisions. When this is done students are learning to be more self-reliant, and helping them develop confidence and responsibility to solve their own problems (Sutton, R. E., 2005).

When attempting to determine if it is appropriate to become involved, ask yourself, *"Who owns the problem?"* Keeping students safe is one of the major responsibilities of teachers. When students are engaging in behaviors that could result in injury, teachers may decide to get involved. The other reason to become involved is when the conflict interferes with the teacher's right to teach, or student's right to learn (Dufresne, J., 2005). To decide the appropriate course of action teachers will need to answer the following questions:

1) Does the behavior interfere with my rights and responsibilities to teach?
2) Does the problem involve the safety of the student or someone else?
3) Does the problem interfere with learning?

If the answer to these three questions is no, then the problem belongs to the student. If the answer is "yes," then teachers will need to become involved (Seay, H., Fee, V., Holloway, S., and Giesen, J., 2003).

If the decision is to get involved, teachers must decide how to respond. Should you talk with the students about the importance of respecting each other or getting along, or should you allow them to work out problems on their own? If students are physically fighting, the situation obviously involves a safety issue and a teacher is required to become involved. Others situations which require teacher involvement include when students place themselves or others at risk; when students are destroying school property; or when behavior is interfering with a teacher's right to teach or a student's right to learn.

When teachers encounter a problem involving students, two important questions must be answered:

1) What is the goal of the misbehavior?
2) Who owns the problem?

Once these two questions are fully understood, teachers can make a better decision about whether to get involved and, if so, to what extent. In most cases teachers will need to allow students to solve their own problems (Lee, Y., Baylor, A., and Nelson, D., 2005). However, if the decision is to get involved, the teacher will not only need to understand the goal of the behavior and who owns the problem but also, how to talk to students. Obviously, when teachers talk to students barriers often exist. These barriers, if not corrected, can interfere with the overall success of problem solving.

Communication Barriers:

When preparing to talk with a student, be aware that it is not unusual for teachers to create barriers to the communication. One of the inherent problems in conversing is that it is easy for conversations to take on a business-like tone (Church, E. B., 2005). This often results in fact-finding, with the teacher asking endless questions. When students are asked question after question, they begin to feel like they are being attacked. This type of conversation is usually devoid of emotion and most often does not allow teachers to get to know their students on a personal level. When conversations are limited to asking questions, teachers miss an opportunity to get to know their students better.

Students are often very hesitant to share their feelings and emotions. If this appears to be the case, it will be important to determine what is causing the hesitancy. In many situations when students have been open and honest, it has come back to haunt them. When students are honest, teachers may become angry, judgmental, or even reject the student. If this happens students are quick to realize that it is not acceptable to say what they really feel.

Another problem encountered when trying to communicate with students is that teachers are often not very good at expressing themselves.

Many adults, including teachers, have grown up in families where feelings and thoughts were not valued and should be kept to oneself. As a result, some teachers may feel uncomfortable talking or listening about issues involving conflict and, as a result, fail to model positive communication skills in such situations (Black, L., 2004).

The importance of effective communication cannot be over-stated. In fact, communication is often at the core of most problems that occur in relationships. When teachers consider their involvement with students as a relationship, then one may rightly conclude that the way they and their students communicate will enhance or interfere with that relationship. A variety of reasons can exist to keep students from talking to their teacher about problems. Teachers at times unconsciously fail to pay attention to the student. When this occurs students feel that what they have to say is not really important.

I recall as a child attempting to show my father a picture that I had drawn. I was very proud of the picture. I said, "Daddy, look at this picture I drew!" He responded, "Yes, that's very nice." However, years later I still remember that he never looked away from the newspaper that he was reading to actually look at the picture. Even though his words indicated approval, his behavior indicated a lack of interest. The message came through loud and clear that he was not interested in my picture or in me.

When teachers fail to give adequate attention to students it sends a powerful message, suggesting a lack of interest.

In some situations teachers may take a student's words too literally and overreact to what was said. If what the student is saying is negative, one must be careful not to criticize the student for having such feelings. While it may be appropriate to disagree with students, it is never appropriate to criticize or put them down for having such feelings (Prusak, K. A., Vincent, S. D., and Pangrazi, R. P., 2005). When teachers respond negatively to students for sharing their honest feelings, it gives students the message that honesty and openness is not permitted.

There are always feelings behind the words. Effective teachers are those who seek to understand what students are feeling and understand how those feelings may be resulting in a negative statement or behavior. For example, a third-grade student may say to his teacher, *"I hate you; you are the meanest teacher in the world."* Teachers are often tempted to say, *"Johnny, we do not talk like that in our classroom,"* or respond, *"But, I love you."* Both responses fail to get at the feelings behind the words. One must examine what are the feelings behind the words. Ask yourself what is the opposite of love? At first we may think the opposite of love is hate, but it is not. In fact, love and hate appear to result from the same emotion. One must be emotionally involved to love, but also emotionally involved to hate. Love is not the opposite of hate, indifference is! When students are indifferent, they are usually lethargic, passive or non-participatory. These students are not interested in learning, regardless of how intriguing the curriculum may be. They are indifferent! Therefore, when a student responds with a statement such as, *"I hate you,"* it is important to be thinking, *"Something important must have happened."* This statement suggests that the student is still emotionally connected.

In some cases teachers may jump to conclusions, not allowing the student to finish his statement. This type of response is inappropriate and occurs because of poor concentration or when teachers think they know what the student is going to say. Interrupting a student will communicate a lack of interest (Brady, S., Peters, D., Gamel-McCormick, M., and Venuto, N., 2004). Obviously, the way one responds to students when they are talking will influence whether they continue to be open and honest or withdraw. Review the previous discussion in Chapter Three concerning the use of reinforcement and how important reinforcement is used to influence the continuation or discontinuation of a behavior.

(Hutchinson, L. M., and Beadle, M. E., 1992) has identified the following negative communication styles. Try to determine if your way of communicating matches any of these inappropriate styles.

Inappropriate Communication Styles:

1. **The Boss:** This individual tends to order students to get rid of their emotions. They say such things as, "Don't you dare talk to me that way," and "Look at me when I am talking to you." This style of communication will tell students they do not have permission to express their feelings.

2. **The Philosopher:** This communication style occurs when teachers tell students what they should or should not feel. These teachers say things like, "You shouldn't let him upset you."

3. **The Teacher:** This individual has all the right answers and tends to lecture, give advice, and in general act superior to students. They say things

like, "I could have told you that."

4. **The Judge:** This individual evaluates and pronounces judgment on students' feelings. The Judge says things like, "Well, what did you expect?"

5. **The Joker:** This individual has the same motives as the Boss, Philosopher, Teacher, and the Judge—that is, to be correct. However, the Joker also uses ridicule or sarcasm in a joking manner to put the student down. The teacher may say things like, "Why don't you use your head?"

6. **The Counselor:** This individual tends to try to gloss over the feelings and tells the student what they need to do. It is like giving the student a cup of hot soup or cookies, thinking this will make the hurt go away.

There are many reasons why people take on these roles. Most people simply do not know what else to do. They want to get their student on the right track, but unfortunately such responses often send students down the wrong track. These responses do nothing to encourage open communication and responsible decision-making. More than anything else when students attempt to communicate their feelings, they want to be heard (Buerk, D., 2000).

When students are listened to, they feel accepted for what they are saying. Acceptance does not mean that the teacher agrees with what the student is saying. It simply indicates that the student has a right to have such feelings. I recall one day when my daughter came storming into the house and yelled, *"I've had it with school, I hate it, I'm quitting and I'm never going back."* She was only eight years old at the time and I knew that she would have to return to school the next day. If I had attempted to discuss the logical benefits of finishing school or the legal aspects surrounding going to school, she would have felt that I did not understand her feelings of anger. Such a response would have communicated that I did not understand her feelings and she may have withdrawn or rebelled.

When teachers attempt to use logic and reasoning with students that are acting illogically, such responses will only escalate problems. It is important to first respond to the feelings and then the content. How, then, should teachers respond? First, in the situation with my daughter, I had to first let her know that I understood her feelings. Therefore, I responded, *"Sounds like you had a really miserable day at school."* This type of response attempts to identify the feelings that are behind the words and it gave my daughter an opportunity to tell me what had happened to get her so upset.

Had I demanded that she go to her room until she settled down or told her that she would be going to school the next day, or offered her some milk and cookies and dismissed her feelings, she would have withdrawn and probably been hesitant in the future to share her feelings.

It is through the ventilation (blowing off steam) or cathartic process that allows the upset student to calm down enough to look for ways to solve their problems. With my daughter, even if I had given a good suggestion, jumping in too soon would have caused her to reject any ideas that I might have. When students are upset they do not want to hear about solutions; they simply want someone to listen to them. Listening is the single most important factor that teachers can do to encourage students to talk (Margolis, H., 2005). Remember the old saying: *If I cannot tell you how I feel, I will show you.* This statement suggests that by allowing students to talk about their feelings, there will be a reduction in the acting-out behavior.

Hearing and Listening:

There is an important difference between hearing and listening. Hearing is an automatic reaction to a sound (Toro, J., Sinnett, S., Soto-Faraco, S., and 2005). Therefore, hearing is involuntary and it happens naturally without effort on the part of the person who is hearing. For example, it is easy to talk with someone and hear the television playing at the same time. While we may not be listening to the noise, it is still being heard. Listening, on the other hand, is deliberate and involves making a conscious effort to hear or pay attention to what is being said (Dewatripont, M., and Tirole, J., 2005). A teacher must want to listen to a student to communicate the message that what is being said is not only being heard but is understood. Listening communicates a level of interest and sends the message that what is being said is important.

Problems with Listening:

There are several common problems associated with listening. It is not unusual for teachers to hear, but fail to comprehend what their students are actually saying. This often results when one only hears the content, and fails to understand the feelings or emotions that are behind the words. Another common problem that teachers often have is being too analytical or logical about what the student is saying (Greenspan, S. I., 2005). When teachers respond this way they tend to play the forty questions game. They probe and question students about factual information, rather than looking for feelings behind the words. As was previously discussed, there are always feelings behind words. The first objective is to determine the feelings, then attempt to understand the content. When teachers focus only on the content, students may begin to feel that their teacher really does not understand what has been said. When teachers hear only the content, and fail to listen for feelings, there is a tendency to react with negativism or criticism. Reacting teaches students that it is not a good idea to share feelings, especially if they are negative.

Reflective Listening:
When communicating with students one of the best ways to encourage them to talk is to use a reflective listening statement. Reflective listening is a technique that means what it says; it allows the speaker to reflect back the feelings that are behind the words. Making a reflecting statement is very simple. An example of a reflective statement to a negative comment is: *"You seem angry."* This simple statement tells the student that you not only understood the words but the feelings as well. Reflective listening involves not only hearing the words that are spoken but also making a guess about the feelings behind the words. Such a response sends a message to students that they are cared about and invites them to share their feelings. In essence, this statement provides a mirror for students to see themselves more clearly. Students may initially reject a reflective statement because they do not understand their own feelings (Boyd, J., and Boyd, S., 2005).

Open Response:
Reflective listening is best demonstrated with an open response. Open responses demonstrate that not only are students heard, but also understood. The understanding involves hearing both the content and the feelings. An open statement does not blame or give advice, or try to solve the student's problem (Ryfe, D. M., 2006). An open statement only means that the student has a right to feel a certain way and state those feelings. This is in keeping with the statement, *"If I can't tell you how I feel, I will show you."*

Closed Response:
In contrast to an open response, a closed response blocks communication by showing students little or no understanding of their

feelings. A closed response denies students the right to say what they think and feel. In essence it blames, gives advice, and does not recognize students' feelings. Please recognize that teachers often make these "closed" statements without even realizing it. For example, when a teacher innocently says; "You should not let him upset you," they have just given advice, blamed the student, and told them not to feel. A common experience is when a student complains that the other students will not let him play with them during recess. The teacher may respond; *"Just go play with some of the other kids."* This statement is a closed response because it blames the student for the problem. It offers a solution to the problem, and it does not identify the student's feelings. In contrast, an open response would be, *"It sounds like you feel it is unfair that the other students will not let you play."* An open statement provides students the opportunity to talk about what they feel is unfair. When making an open response, teachers not only attempt to identify the feelings but also why students may be feeling a certain way. Also, when making an open statement it is important to check to see if the student agrees or disagrees with the reflective statement. This can be accomplished by simply asking, "Is that right?" By checking with the student, the statement becomes more of a question, rather than telling students what they feel (Gordon, T., 1975).

There are several advantages to using a reflective listening statement with students. A reflective listening statement allows students to see things from a more rational perspective. This is especially important for students who exhibit challenging behavior patterns and then hold irrational perceptions or blame others for their own mistakes. Some may question the value of allowing students to express their feelings. However, when students are allowed to express their deepest emotions, this ventilation process helps one see more clearly the realities of a situation.

Often when teachers ask their students about their behavior, students typically respond with "I don't know." When initially using a reflective statement, it is not unusual to receive such responses. Remember, it takes time to break old habits. Teachers must remember that their students have been communicating a certain way for several years, and it will take time to change this pattern. Also, because using a reflective or open statement is a new approach, students may be hesitant initially to share their feelings. Initially, it is not unusual for students to fail to understand or be confused by this new way of communicating. This approach will take time. Be patient and do not give up trying to improve communications in the classroom.

Encouraging Effective Communications:

Teaching effective communication to students is one of the many things that teachers do that will leave a lasting impression. There are several things that teachers can do to encourage the student to communicate more effectively (Black, L., 2004).

1. **Make a guess:** When you see a smile or frown or an angry expression, comment on it. You may say, *"Gosh, you seem happy about something,"* or *"It looks like you are really feeling down today,"* or *"It seems like you are upset."* However, be aware that if you point out only negative feelings, students may deny them. If this happens, accept the student's response and try again later. Also, be aware that you may guess at a feeling and the student will begin spilling their guts. Be prepared for how students may respond.

2. **Be a model:** Do not expect students to do all the sharing. Teachers must be willing to share their feelings about things that happen. Take a few minutes to tell students how you feel about some of the current events. However, when initially establishing more effective patterns of communication, it is not the time to talk about areas of conflict. Instead, talk about your job, friends or whatever. Your modeling will demonstrate that it is acceptable to share feelings.

3. **Ask for comments**Students like to be asked about their day, things that interest them, or their opinion about certain issues. Teachers often get an "I don't know" response. These are ways of saying, "I'd rather not talk." If this should happen, don't force the issue; respect students' decisions and continue to indicate interest at other times.

4. **Increase your communications:** Everything that happens in the classroom will increase or decrease the level of communication with your students. If students fail to listen, talk or do not cooperate, it may be because you are sending a "you message" instead of an "I message."

You Messages:

Another critical mistake that many teachers make is giving student a "you message." This type of statement tends to put students down and blames others for their feelings. A "you message" is similar to a closed message in that it will criticize students for their feelings. "You messages" often cause students to become angry, hurt, or feel misunderstood. Such a statement can also cause students to be embarrassed or even feel worthless (Bippus, A. M., and Young, S. L., 2005). When teachers make statements like, "Why don't you use your head," the student may hear the message that he lacks personal value. It is these little throw-away lines that a teacher will forget in a few minutes, but the message may remain with a student for the rest of the day. If students already have a negative self-concept, they probably expect criticism, and when they receive a "you message," it reinforces their negative feelings. A "you message" also teaches irresponsibility to students. When a teacher says to their students, *"You are really making me mad today,"* they are suggesting that the students are responsible for the teacher's feelings. No one is responsible for another person's feelings. To claim such is to suggest irresponsibility.

I-Messages:

Teachers must strive to use "I messages." An "I message" is the alternative to a "you message" (Osgood, J., 2005). These messages allow teachers to share their feelings and concerns with students and communicate a sense of trust in their ability. An "I message" communicates understanding of students' feelings and does not blame or criticize students. It only states what the teacher perceives in relationship to their feelings. An "I message" is a way of claiming responsibility for one's own feelings and is an excellent model for students. Also, an "I message" says that it is okay to have feelings. When teachers say, *"I feel angry,"* it serves as a model for students to talk about their own feelings. This modeling gives students permission to claim ownership and express their feelings. The fact that the teacher said "I feel angry" instead of "You make me angry" is an effective way to take responsibility for one's own feelings. Students must realize that they "choose" to get mad or upset, no one makes them. An "I message" conveys respect to the student and models for students that they must take responsibility for their feelings.

An "I message" is simply an attempt to identify the student's feelings. Therefore, when stating, *"I feel very frustrated when you refuse to complete your homework assignment,"* teachers are identifying what students are doing (their behavior) and how it is affecting you (the teacher). An "I message" statement will encourage students to modify their unacceptable behavior, while increasing their acceptable behaviors. In addition, "I messages" are much less likely to provoke resistance and rebellion (Smith, A. B., 2004).

There are several ways to make an "I message" that will help teachers better communicate with students. The following is one of the formulas that works effectively:

"When you. . ." (Student's behavior)
"I feel. . ." (My feelings)
"Because. . ." (Consequence)
"What do you think?" (Ask for feedback)
"Next time would you. . ." (Asks for agreement)

The *"when you"* part of this statement identifies the specific behavior that is being exhibited. The *"I feel"* component indicates that the teacher is accepting responsibility for his or her own feelings. The *"because"* part of the statement indicates when behavior and feelings come together, there is a consequence. Therefore, teachers may say to students, *"When you refuse to complete your school assignment, I feel worried, because you may not be ready to go to the next grade."* It is important that the message match what you really feel. Therefore, if you are really frustrated, you need to convey this, but not in a negative fashion. The next part of this statement is, *"What do you think about what I just said?"* This statement gives students permission to agree or disagree and it asks for feedback. The last part of this process is to ask for an agreement to change. *"Next time would you . . ?"*

Another important aspect of communication involves non-verbal communications. Research by (Frascarolo, F., Besse, V., and Favez, N., 2005) has suggested that sixty percent of all communication is non-verbal. Likewise, research by Best, W. (2005) has indicated that seventy-two percent of the time we can correctly predict what a person is feeling based on their non-verbal expression. A teacher can often tell if a student is upset simply by looking at the student's facial expression. When it comes to effective communication, teachers must become equally skilled at determining what students are experiencing through non-verbal behavior. Teachers must learn to pay attention to students' facial expressions, posture, voice tone, and a variety of non-verbal means. Teachers can also use their non-verbal expressions to communicate acceptance, care and concern. Such non-verbal expression as patting the student on the back, touching him or her on the arm and smiling are all ways to demonstrate non-verbal acceptance and approval.

Silence is also a form of non-verbal communication (Panteli, N. and Fineman, S., 2005). Silence may simply suggest that a student does not want to talk, or may suggest that the student has difficulty expressing their feelings.

This can be especially true when students have a speech or language deficit. However, silence may also mean that students do not trust the teacher enough to share such feelings. It is important when dealing with students that their silence is respected. If a teacher is concerned that something may be wrong, be honest and tell the student about your concerns. For example, the teacher may respond, *"Lately you seem angry almost every day,"* or *"I noticed that you seem worried, is something going on?"*

Non-verbal messages can also be useful when dealing with young students. Teachers working in a pre-school program must realize that when they are holding or touching students this is a form of non-verbal communication (Frascarolo, F., Besse, V., and Favez, N., 2005). Non-verbal communication can be an important part of the discipline process for young children. For example, if a student is standing in a chair, the teacher may need to physically pick the child up and move him to the floor. Likewise, positive messages can be sent by giving hugs, pats on the back, or even an approving look. Non-verbal responses can be used to demonstrate irritation about a certain behavior, or that you are very pleased with the student.

SUMMARY

One aspect of becoming an effective teacher is to incorporate positive communications into an overall classroom discipline program. Teachers must realize that a proactive discipline program will always teach lifelong living skills. Therefore, when teachers model positive communication skills and encourage their use in the classroom they are teaching students skills that they will use for a lifetime.

Effective communication involves talking, listening, and understanding non-verbal cues. When teachers talk with students it is important to use I-messages and open-ended questions. Effective teachers avoid using statements that blame or teach students to be irresponsible. Likewise, when listening, these teachers not only listen for the words that students are saying, but also the feelings behind the words. In essence, proactive teachers use their communication skills to enhance their relationship with their students and to reduce behavioral conflicts.

Chapter Five

UNINTENTIONAL REINFORCEMENT: REDUCING TEACHER CONTRIBUTIONS TO MISBEHAVIOR

In order to establish a well-disciplined classroom, teachers must be willing to go the extra mile to ensure smooth functioning. There are several ways teachers may contribute to the disruption in their classrooms. Since communication is so important in any relationship, this is a good place for teachers to begin the evaluation process. As was previously discussed, proactive discipline is not doing something to students, but rather it is the intentional actions taken by teachers that are designed to bring about a change in the learning environment. Therefore it is necessary to evaluate every aspect of the classroom in order to determine what, if anything, may be contributing to the misbehavior. This evaluation process will include the physical structure of the classroom, the curriculum, the teaching style, and how one responds to students. This chapter is not designed to blame teachers for classroom disruption, but rather to explore ways in which teachers may inadvertently contribute to disruptive classroom behavior.

Effective Problem Solving in the Classroom

One way that teachers may exacerbate disruptive behavior in their classrooms is through inappropriate communications. While this was dealt with in the previous chapter, it deserves mentioning again. Obviously, one important aspect of the teaching process is to lecture to students. However, if teachers respond in a vague or nondescript manner, student behavior will be influenced.

When talking with students about behavior problems, teachers will need to be specific when describing the behavior that is being disruptive. If, for example, a teacher states to a student, *"Your desk is messy,"* or *"Clean up your desk,"* both statements are nonspecific. The student's perception of a messy or clean desk may be vastly different from the teacher's perception. While this may seem like a small issue, nondescript statements can contribute to ongoing classroom disruptive behaviors. For some students a clean desk is like a prepositional phrase. If they can go through, under, over or around it, then to them this is clean. Therefore, when giving instructions to students, be descriptive and specific (Botting, N., and Adams, C., 2005).

It is equally important to be specific when talking to students about behavior problems. For example, if a teacher says to a student, *"You have a bad attitude,"* it is unclear what is actually meant. Does a "bad attitude" mean that the student is being disrespectful, refuses to complete an assignment or is talking back? The term *"bad"* suggests that something about the student's behavior is negative, but the "something" is not identified. Therefore, in order to ensure compliance, it is important to identify specifically what it is about the student's "bad attitude" that is problematic. After all, it is not the student's "bad attitude" that is the problem, but rather the behavior. If students know specifically what it is that they are doing that is problematic and if the information is communicated properly, there is a greater chance that students will respond positively. When talking to students about behavior problems there is a systematic way to ensure understanding. A good description includes a detailed breakdown of the behavior and specific information about the behavior. Information about the behavior should convey:

1. Who was involved?
2. Where the behavior occurred?
3. When the behavior occurred?
4. How often the behavior occurred?

When statements do not contain these four components, the statement is considered to be non-specific and vague (Elder, L., and Paul, R., 2004).

When talking with students about their behavior it may be helpful if the student is provided with examples. An example of a specific statement might be as follows: *"This morning when I asked you to return to your desk you just stared at me and said, "You are always telling me what to do."* This statement specifically describes who was involved, what the student was doing, when it occurred, and how the student responded. When talking with students about problem behaviors, it is important that the statements specifically describe the behaviors the student is exhibiting.

Vague emotional statements are inappropriate and usually result in greater misbehavior. For example, if a teacher says to a student; *"You are being bad"* or *"You are being good,"* each statement is vague, non-descript in nature, emotionally laden, and tends to set the stage for conflict. Equally important is to avoid using generalizations. Words such as *"always," "never"* and *"good"* are gross generalizations that are designed to shame and blame a student into obedience (Meier, D., 2004). For example, if a teacher says, *"You are always out of your seat,"* this is an obvious generalization that cannot possibly be true. No student is *"always"* out of his seat. He may be out of his seat a great deal of time, or even most of the time, but never "always" out of his seat. Teachers must make sure what is being said is not a generalized subjective allegation that is being stated as a fact. Using the example mentioned above, if a teacher says to a student, *"Your desk is always messy,"* the teacher has made a non-specific generalized statement. The student may take this as a personal put-down. Therefore, it is important to talk with students in specific descriptive terms about behaviors that are problematic.

In an effort to bridge the concept of appropriate communications and proactive discipline, teachers will need to take every opportunity to respond with comments suggesting positive regard for students. When teachers see students acting appropriately, respond in such a way as to compliment the student with attention, appreciation, and praise. It is easy to catch students acting inappropriately, but teachers rarely focus on a student's positive behavior. When my daughter was in the second grade, I recall her coming home one day with her spelling test. She had studied her spelling words and she knew them forward and backward. However, when she took her test, she missed two of the twenty words. As a concerned parent, I responded, *"I thought you knew how to spell those two words."* I had just missed the opportunity to communicate positive regard. Instead I chose to focus on the negative.

Far more success will result from providing attention to positive behaviors rather than focusing on the negative behaviors (Meisinger, E. B., Schwanenflugel, P. J., Bradley, B. A., and Stahl, S. A., 2004). However, just as statements of reprimand must be specific, so must statements of praise and appreciation be specific and descriptive. Statements such as, *"I appreciated your helping take up the homework sheets,"* or *"I really like it when you complete your math work,"* are specific statements that provide praise and encouragement. In the case of my daughter, it would have been far more appropriate had I indicated how proud I was of her for knowing 18 out of 20 words. While remembering to focus on positive behavior is a simple concept, it takes practice to consistently praise students for performing positive tasks. Providing students with positive reinforcement for specific behaviors will help them internalize their behavior and will offer greater compliance in the future. Had I focused more on the positive behaviors with my daughter, perhaps she would have worked more diligently on the next test to master all of the words!

There are several ways to increase behavioral compliance or noncompliance in the classroom. In order to increase compliance teachers must be consistent and willing to see a task through to its completion. Statements to students should be presented as a polite directive, not as a request or asking the student to do the task as a favor to the teacher. Teachers may increase the inappropriate behavior simply by saying, *"Will you please stop talking?"* This statement gives students a choice to stop or continue talking. Although this statement needs to be made as a directive, it should not be made in a negative tone. The directive must be made clear and indicate that the teacher is serious about the task. The same statement becomes a directive by saying, *"I want you to stop talking now!"* This type of statement does not give the student a choice and identifies specifically the *"what"* and *"when"* of the directive.

Students with processing deficits will often exhibit disruptive behaviors because of their frustration related to not being able to follow directions or to perform tasks involving multiple steps or sequences. When communicating with these students, it is even more important for statements to be simple—one or two steps, rather than information involving multiple steps or sequences (Scott, T. M., and Caron, D. B., 2005). Also, it is important to allow adequate time for the initial task to be completed before proceeding to the second directive. If the student fails to complete the first task before it is time to move to the second activity, let the student know that there will be an opportunity to return to the task at a later time. Also, if the student is given multiple-step tasks, he or she will often become confused about what to do and may act out that confusion and frustration.

Another thing that can increase classroom disruptions is when there are many distractions. Before beginning any kind of instructions, teachers will need to reduce the distractions. For example, if students are engaged in a fun or enjoyable activity, discontinue the activity before giving instructions for the next activity. If these highly stimulating or fun activities are not eliminated, it is doubtful that the teacher will have success in getting the students' attention or gaining their cooperation.

When giving a directive to students it is important to maintain eye contact. Yelling out instructions from across the room will only increase the chances of non-compliance. Looking at students when talking to them will help in gaining their undivided attention. When necessary, have students repeat the instructions in order to make sure they understand what they are supposed to do. Repeating instructions will also reinforce the memory of the instruction and increase compliance (Barton-Arwood, S.; Morrow, L.; Lane, K.; and Jolivette, K.; 2005).

It is also beneficial to assign a specific time limit for completing a task. The specific timing allows students to pace themselves. When instructions include time limits, compliance can be increased by setting the timer on the desk or making sure students can see a clock. By providing a timer or clock the constraints of the time limit becomes more concrete. However, students may become overwhelmed and anxious when they realize that time is running out to complete a task. If this happens, and students have been working diligently, assure them that they will have an opportunity to complete the task at a later time.

Including steps or sequences to task completion instructions can also increase compliance. This is especially true when the students are visual learners. When the steps or sequences are provided, student compliance becomes greater. By adding the steps or sequences students are able to complete the assignment in an orderly fashion. When this is coupled with concrete information related to time constraints, student success is further enhanced (Mixon, K., 2004).

Some students will work harder if they know they will be able to engage in a fun activity when they are finished. However, again, this may invoke anxiety for some students. Some may rush through the assigned task or turn in careless work, especially if they see other students finishing their assignment before them. This is another reason why it is so important for teachers to know their students and their potential.

Unintentional Reinforcement

Another factor that will influence compliance is the way in which classroom rules are communicated. Because of the limited attention and poor processing skills of many students, it is important that rules are structured, specific, concrete and positive (Thompson, R. H., and Iwata, B. A., 2005). Rules should always be concise and to the point. To make them concrete, they should also be written down and posted so they will serve as a constant reminder and visual cue of what is expected. To enhance compliance, rules will need to be framed in a positive way and limited to no more than five. For example, one rule may have to do with respect for self and others. This may include such things as no teasing, bullying, talking back to the teacher, wearing a shirt tucked in, etc. (Johnson, F. and Edmunds, A., 2006). Rules should also provide students with information about consequences for failure to follow the classroom rules. If rules are not specific and informative, there will be a greater level of non-compliance.

A teacher's presentation style can also influence student behavior. Many teachers continue to teach in a dictatorial manner (Rassuli, A., and Manzer, J. P., 2005). This style usually involves a teacher standing at the front of the room lecturing while students take notes, especially in secondary schools. This style of instruction allows little time for questions or discussion. When students are exposed to a dictatorial style of teaching, they tend to be withdrawn, become disinterested, and may well act out their frustrations.

Another common response by teachers is to try to solve problems for students. They think this is helpful when, in fact, it only causes more problems. In most cases students are quite capable of solving their own problems. Therefore, when teachers attempt to solve problems for students, it causes students to become dependent and irresponsible. It also sends the message that teachers do not trust students to come up with their own solutions. Allowing students to solve their own problems, when possible, will help them to become more responsible and learn valuable problem solving skills that will last a lifetime. In addition, by allowing students the opportunity to solve their own problems, their self-esteem is enhanced and it builds their social skills (Howes, C., Phillipsen, L. C., and Peisner-Feinberg, E., 2000).

Teachers will also contribute to a student's misbehavior when they take responsibility for the students' completing school assignments (Jeffrey, B.; 2002). This is not to suggest that students should not be given assistance when needed. However, when teachers allow students to display incompetence and then compensate for such incompetence by accepting inferior work, or assignments that are turned in late, the student learns to be irresponsible. Actions in the classroom are designed to help students function in a larger society. Students of all ages and learning styles must learn how to function in situations where there are expectations. Therefore, to accept an assignment that is inferior to what the student is capable of producing is setting the student up for future failure later in life. The school experience is designed to enhance responsibility and independence. At each increasing grade level greater expectations are placed on the student. For example, in the 2nd grade teachers may walk around the room and take up the completed homework assignment, while in the 4th grade teacher may ask the students to place their homework assignments on their desks. Then in the 7th grade the teacher expects the student to turn in their homework assignment without a reminder. These increasing demands are slowly helping students prepare to live and work in a society that is less forgiving than a classroom.

Having expectations and giving students responsibilities communicates that their efforts are important and that they are capable. Unfortunately, in many classrooms, when students fail to complete a task or perform at an expected level, teachers often simply lower their expectations and accept inferior work. When this is happens it communicates to students that they are inadequate and they can get away with being inferior. Unfortunately, in a greater society such accommodations are not provided. Any time a teacher lowers expectations, it is contributing to negative behavior (Malveaux, J.; 2004). When adequate instructions are provided and students' capabilities are known, expectations should not be lowered. However, in some cases teachers may have too high an expectation of their students. Teachers must know their students and understand at what level they are capable of achieving. However, capacity to function does not always correlate with grade placement. Just because a student is in the 4th grade, does not mean the student will be functioning at that grade level. While most students will function at that grade level, some students may function below their grade level. Therefore, it is important for teachers to know what grade level a student is capable of achieving, and then have instructions and expectations appropriate to the student's ability (Ainsworth, J. W., and Roscigno, V. J., 2005).

Teachers also contribute to their students' misbehavior by becoming angry or retaliating in inappropriate ways. When teachers do this they exacerbate classroom disruption and destroy students' self-esteem. In subsequent chapters we will discuss issues related to self-esteem. It is important to remember that students have the same feelings as adults; they are just contained in smaller bodies for a short period of time. Just as teachers should never allow their administrators to yell at them, point their finger at them, call them names, compare them, use sarcasm to make a point or embarrass them in front of their colleagues, teachers should never respond in these ways to students. However, on occasion teachers will attempt to use shame and blame, yell at them, or discipline students when they are angry, all in an effort to maintain control. When teachers do these things, they are contributing to the disruptive behavior in their classrooms.

It is interesting that most teachers are quick to say that they would never call a student a name, compare students, or in general put students down as a means of controlling their classroom. However, one may be surprised to find just how often teachers engage in these very behaviors. They make statements such as: *"Don't go thinking you are all grown up,"* or *"Look at me when I am talking to you,"* or *"Why don't you sit still like Mary over there? See how nicely she is sitting?"* or *"I had your sister in my classroom last year, and she was a nice girl. What happened to you?"* These are all statements that will drive students' self-esteem down and will leave them with feeling rebellious or feeling like giving up. Becoming rebellious or giving up are forms of misbehavior that will cause classrooms to be disruptive. Teachers often forget these responses by the end of the day, but students may well remember such statements for a lifetime.

Giving attention to students when they demand it will also cause greater classroom disruption. When students misbehave and receive attention for their behavior, they are reinforced to act that way again (Ruenzel, D., 2001). There is an old saying: *"Bad attention is better than no attention."* This saying suggests that when students do not receive adequate attention they will act out in ways to draw attention to themselves. This is another reason why it is important for teachers to understand each student's individual needs and provide adequate attention. Teachers must find ways to focus on what students are doing that is positive and provide attention to those behaviors, rather than focusing on what they are doing wrong and providing attention to the inappropriate behaviors (Harlin, R. P., 2000). However, teachers must recognize that some students need more attention than others. There may be a student in the 4th grade that comes from a stable functioning family and she does not need much attention. So, at the end of the day all I need to do is thank her for how hard she worked today. However, another student may be one that is floating around in foster care, is the victim of abuse, or have parents going through a divorce. This student will need much more attention. Therefore, every five minutes I go over to her desk and make a positive comment: *"Wow, I can't believe how much work you are getting done today,"* or *"Did you come up with that answer on your own?"*

Being inconsistent is another important factor that can influence negative classroom behavior. Inconsistency can be confusing for students (Sinkinson, A. J., 2004). When a certain behavior is accepted one day, then punished the next, students can become frustrated. However, inconsistency can also exist from one class to the next. For example, if a teacher in the 7th grade math class allows certain behavior, while the 7th grade teacher in the Social Science class does not, disruptive behaviors will often result. This is why it is so important for the school faculty to establish and consistently follow a school-wide discipline program.

Being overly rigid or unstructured will also contribute to student misbehavior. In fact, it is not unusual for some students to rebel against classroom control and rigidity, while others may become submissive and dependent (Beachum, F.; and Dentith, A. M.; 2004). Regardless of the student's response, such behaviors by teachers will contribute to classroom disruptive behavior. It is important that teachers find a happy medium between being consistent and structured, while not being overly controlling or rigid.

SUMMARY

The purpose of this chapter was to point out some of the ways teachers inadvertently add to the disruptive behavior of their classrooms. These actions are often done unintentionally and without the awareness of the teacher. Being a proactive teacher suggests that one is open to exploring any and all factors that may contribute to misbehavior in the classroom, including themselves. Such inadvertent behaviors are displayed not only by the novice teacher but also by seasoned teachers as well. In psychology there is a term, "functional dysfunctionalism." This suggests that teachers can become accustomed to responding in a certain way until they do not even realize that it may be contributing to the disruption in their classrooms. Proactive teachers must always be concerned about self-improvement and looking for indications that they may be a part what is causing disruptive classroom behavior. Proactive teachers know that there are always more ways to learn and ways to improve on their teaching skills. These teachers realize that it is through reviewing and struggling with issues related to effective classroom discipline that they become an even more capable teacher.

Chapter Six

ESTABLISHING A PROACTIVE CLASSROOM ENVIRONMENT: SETTING THE STAGE FOR EFFECTIVE DISCIPLINE

There is no part of teaching that is more difficult than consistently using effective discipline. Some teachers think the word "discipline" means to punish or at least do something to a student. However, discipline is a method by which students are taught appropriate behavior and it helps them to become more responsible and independent (Smith, A. B., 2004). Discipline involves preventive as well as corrective measures for helping students learn to make appropriate decisions for the rest of their lives. Discipline should also lead to self-discipline. Through effective discipline, students learn from the consequences of the decisions they make. However, some students do not seem to learn from cause and effect. These are students who must first learn how to self-regulate their behavior and gain the art of self-discipline (Skiba, R., Rausch, M. K., and Ritter, S., 2004).

Very often the conflict occurring in classrooms is not related to using the wrong discipline technique, but rather the power struggle between the teacher and student. In essence, teachers and students are trying to prove to each other who will be the most powerful (Watson, C., 2005). When power struggles occur, both the teacher and student become losers. When a student enters into a power struggle, teachers often feel threatened. They may take the approach to "clamp down" or assert their authority.

However, when teachers do this, students often rebel or simply withdraw and become very passive. Rebellion will occur when students feel controlled. In order for the response to be proactive, teachers will need to determine how to avoid creating a power struggle (Tan, K. H. K., 2005).

One of the most effective ways to teach students positive behaviors is by serving as a role model. When teachers demonstrate the behaviors they are seeking in students, students not only get to hear about them, they can see them in action. In simple terms, students learn better when teachers "practice what they preach." In contrast, teachers can also demonstrate inappropriate behavior. When teachers are inconsistent, over-react, show a lack of interest and/or respond disrespectfully, they are modeling inappropriate behaviors. Human nature teaches us that it is much easier to be a negative role model than it is to be positive. In order to be a positive role model, teachers must be diligent and constantly be on the lookout for opportunities to teach students such skills as problem solving, managing conflict, and acting respectfully. Actions always speak louder than words, and this is especially true in the classroom (Espelage, D. L., Bosworth, K., Simon, T. R., 2000).

When making decisions regarding discipline, teachers will need to try to determine what might be causing the student to misbehave. Ask, *"What is the student attempting to accomplish through his misbehavior?"* It was previously postulated that all behavior means something. Most often it is the *"something"* that is not known. When the something is not known, teachers will respond to the behavior, but not the function of the behavior. For example, in a seventh grade language arts class the teacher tells the students to get their books out because they are going to take turns reading aloud. About that time a young girl turns her back to the teacher and refuses to participate. At the same time a young boy turns his back and refuses to participate. While the behaviors are the same, the "function" of the behavior may be completely different. The young girl may have a slight reading deficit and is afraid that if she reads out loud everyone will laugh at her. However, the young boy is angry because I will not allow him to sit with his friends. The behaviors are the same, but the function of the behavior is vastly different. If the discipline strategy is directed only to the behavior it will miss the mark.

There are various reasons for misbehavior. The difference will depend on whether or not the behaviors being exhibited are typical or atypical.

Typical behaviors occur secondary to a genetic predisposition, a specific age or stage of development, reinforcement, and/or because the student is trying to get a need meet (Johnson, F.L., 1996). In contrast, the more challenging atypical behavior often occurs because the student has not developed sufficient self-regulatory skills (Johnson, F. and Edmunds, A., 2006). In essence these students do not know how to stop themselves, so they often take things too far.

Setting up a Classroom to Support Positive Intervention:

Before developing a plan for changing behavior, teachers must assess their own actions that may be contributing to the classroom disruption. It may be difficult to accept the fact that teachers contribute to classroom misbehavior; however, it does happen to the best of teachers. In the previous chapter some of the inadvertent contributions were briefly mentioned. For example, when students demand immediate attention, and it is given, their misbehavior is reinforced.

Being inconsistent is another problem that will contribute to misbehavior. Inconsistency is one of the variables that will ruin even the best behavioral interventions. Inconsistency may occur by the same teacher, or it may occur from class to class by several teachers. When students experience inconsistent responses by the same teacher or among several teachers, they will become confused about what is expected. Such confusions will contribute to the misbehavior that occurs in classrooms (Kim, H., Arnold, D. H., Fisher, P. H., and Zeljo, A., 2005).

A lack of structure or boundaries in a classroom will also cause students to become confused. Consider the following scenario in relationship to a lack of structure and/or boundaries. One day your principal comes to you and says, *"You can come to work whenever you want."* In fact, *"While you are at work you can do whatever you want. From now on you do not have to turn in lesson plans."* And, while you are at it, *"You can leave whenever you want."* However, *"If you mess up, you will be terminated immediately."* Initially such a proposal sounds great, but with the possible resulting consequences, the offer does not seem so appealing. What changed to make the offer unacceptable? It is the structure and boundaries that allow teachers and students to feel secure. Students will not learn from sporadic consequences, limited structure, or a lack of boundaries (Tracey, T., and Robbins, S. B., 2005). The lack of structure and boundaries will lead to insecurity and misbehavior in the classroom.

Treating students disrespectfully is another response that will contribute to misbehavior in the classroom. Screaming, yelling, belittling or name-calling students are obviously acts that do little or nothing to teach students appropriate behavior. In fact, such responses cause students to think and feel poorly about themselves and will result in greater non-compliance. When students feel put down, demeaned or made fun of, they tend to respond by becoming more aggressive. After all, students basically act the same way they feel. When students feel or think badly about themselves; they will respond accordingly (Edwards, C. H., 2000).

When teachers punish in anger, the potential for misbehavior is increased. Such responses are ineffective and they teach students the way to handle anger is through outbursts or revenge. In addition, when teachers respond impulsively in anger they are reacting, rather than acting toward a problem. In essence, they are reacting, rather than pro-acting. When one reacts, it is not unusual for the response to be emotional, and this is the opposite of being a proactive teacher. In contrast, to "act" means to respond with a specific *"intentional"* plan in mind to facilitate change (Parish, T. S., 2000).

Another way teachers may influence students' misbehavior is by being inflexible, rigid, controlling and demanding. Being flexible does not suggest that one is inconsistent. Flexibility indicates an understanding of the issues confronting the student. In essence, the teacher is empathetic. If the situation warrants, the effective teacher is flexible enough to provide an alternative response to the inappropriate behavior. For example, a teacher may be aware that a student was up all night studying for an exam. Therefore, the teacher may choose not to reprimand the student for putting his head down on the desk.

It is also important to have a clear understanding of why a specific intervention is needed before it is actually implemented. It is surprising how many teachers utilize punishment rather than an effective discipline approach. The proactive teacher will select a specific intervention strategy to match the student's needs and the objective that is to be achieved. If a strategy is not specifically designed to meet students' needs and to teach students more appropriate ways of behaving, the response will probably be ineffective and will result in greater disruption. For example, most teachers use some form of time-out in their classroom. This strategy may be referred to as quiet-time, the thinking chair, think-space, the hallway, back of the room, principal's office, another classroom, or in-school suspension, but it is still removing the student from the situation and is time-out. Time-out can be effective for some students, but should never be used for others. Time-out is a form of isolation and should never be used for children with low self-esteem, or students that have experienced some time of traumatic loss; e.g. parents are going through a divorce, being kicked around in foster care or displaced by a natural disaster. This is why it is so important for teachers to know and understand the needs of each student (Readdick, C. A., and Chapman, P. L., 2000).

In contrast, there are several positive things that teachers can do that will help students learn from proactive interventions. In order to maximize the benefit of any discipline strategy, a classroom must be set up to support positive behavioral intervention (Long, James D., Williams, Robert L., 2005).

1. **Always make sure students understand what is expected.** Having established rules and identified consequences gives students knowledge of what is expected and what will happen if they fail to follow predetermined rules. This knowledge will provide students with a sense of structure and serves as a constant reminder of the parameters in which they can operate. This is an important point because structure is equal to security, and security builds self-esteem. If students know what is expected, most often they will respond to the expectations.

2. **When developing rules and consequences, allow students to have input when appropriate.** This can be accomplished by talking with students about rules and why certain rules are important. There are only two reasons why classroom rules are needed. First, so learning can take place, and second, so everyone will be safe. It is best to identify several reasons why the rules are needed. With students in grades K-3 it will be important to provide examples, such as, *"If the parent is driving down the street and fails to see a stop sign and another car is approaching, what might happen?"* It is also important to discuss the importance of rules in relationship to learning. For example: *"Rules will allow everyone to learn and get ready to pass to the next grade."*

3. **Have positive expectations of students.** It is amazing what students will do when it is expected, and what they won't do when it is allowed. This involves the theory of self-fulfilled prophecy. If students are

expected to obey rules and to accept the consequences of violations, they often will respond positively. However, when teachers will accept sloppy or inferior work, students will respond accordingly. More specifically, if teachers hold negative expectations of a certain student, the student will pick up on these expectations and respond accordingly.

4. **Make sure students understand the consequence of a behavior before it occurs.** When writing down rules, be sure to list the resulting consequences for violating each rule. It will be helpful to post the rules and discuss them with students. This will serve as a constant reminder and a visual cue for students. It may be appropriate to allow students to have a list of the rules and the consequences at their desk or to send a copy home and have parents sign them. This approach helps remove the teacher from the role of continually reminding students of the rules and consequences.

5. **Always be willing to give students a reminder when their behavior seems to be getting out of hand.** Students have short attention spans and often do not realize when their behavior is becoming inappropriate. This approach also allows students to make a choice about discontinuing the behavior or dealing with the consequences. Providing a reminder is different from a threat. A threat is a demand, whereas a reminder provides students information about their options.

6. **When explaining inappropriate behavior, stay simple.** Remember, students do not have the same vocabulary or conceptual skills as adults. Therefore, do not use words or concepts that are vague, non-descript, or are too advanced for students to understand. When teachers talk to students they will often agree with anything, even if they do not understand what the teacher is saying. Their objective is to get the teacher off their back. If teachers use words that students do not understand, they are likely to misunderstand the rule and continue the misbehavior.

7. **Show empathy and remember that students have bad days.** When teachers feel bad physically, they have the option of taking a sick day. In fact, some school districts allow for "mental health" days. It is difficult for parents to take off from work to stay home with a sick child. Students often come to school when they should be home in bed. Teachers will need to be aware of students who have allergies, respiratory infections or other illnesses that may cause them to be more irritable and disruptive. In addition, students often come to school feeling sick emotionally. It is no secret that many families experience various types of dysfunction. It is not unusual for

parents to argue or engage in physical altercations in front of their children, for the police to show up at 2:30 a. m. with a bench warrant, a parent to get drunk and fall off the front porch, or any number of other dysfunctional behaviors to occur. In the meantime, children lie awake in bed worrying about their family or their own safety and security. These same children must attend school the next day. They come to school and they are wired and tired and ready for a fight. Teachers will need to take into consideration these issues. This is not to suggest that teachers should be inconsistent, but rather should be empathetic and understand that students have bad days.

8. **Try to use humor whenever possible when handling a problem.** In no way should teachers take students' negative behavior lightly, but rather they should use humor to ease the situation. Many students become irritated when teachers point out that their behavior is becoming disruptive. It is often helpful to work out a system with the student whereby the student can receive a signal that their behavior is becoming disruptive or unmanageable. This signal should only be known by the teacher and the student. For example, the teachers may tell the student when they take their glasses off and hold them in their right hand this is a signal to indicate that their behavior is becoming unmanageable. Then put the glasses back on when the student corrects their behavior. It really does not matter what the "secret" signal is, as long as the student understands its meaning. This approach has many benefits. It eliminates the need to constantly be calling the student's name and it will soften the conflict, while serving as a reminder to return to work.

9. **If possible, include the student in the problem solving process.** Sending students to time-out or sending them to the office is a consequence, not an intervention. An important part of proactive discipline is to teach students a replacement behavior. Consequences are done basically for the remaining students. An intervention is a strategic process whereby the student learns a more appropriate way of behaving.

10. **Talking to students is also an important part of proactive discipline.** If the behavior has become so unmanageable that a consequence is needed, it would not be appropriate to spend time talking with the student. Talking about the behavior should wait until after the consequence has been completed. In fact, many students will attempt to "talk" to the teacher before the consequence is implemented in an effort to talk the teacher out of taking action. When teachers talk to students before the consequence is completed, it will create greater conflict, because the student will most likely attempt to

control the situation. It is important to talk with the student after completing the consequence or as a part of the overall intervention process. Talking to students after the consequence allows the teacher and student to calm down so greater understanding of the ramifications can be achieved. Also, talking with the student after the consequence allows the teacher to conclude the consequence with positive reinforcement.

11. **Allow students to talk about their feelings.** Allowing students to discuss their feelings reduces anxiety and frustration and allows them to feel that what they have to say is important. This does not necessarily mean the teacher is in agreement with the students, but rather that their feelings are respected.

12. **It is important for teachers to give students choices, when possible.** Choices allow students to have power and input when decisions are being made. When students are given a reminder about their behavior, this in essence provides students with a choice to either stop the misbehavior or accept the consequences.

13. **Always be firm and fair with students.** The firmness part of this component is the consistency and structure that teachers must provide. Structure must be present in the classroom organization, the curriculum, and in the way teachers implement interventions. The classroom must be organized in such a way that it is comfortable and provides maximum opportunity to learn. A messy, disorganized room will contribute to classroom disruption. The curriculum must be presented in an organized fashion that makes sense to students. In addition, the curriculum must match students' learning style and be meaningful, practical, and exciting. The fairness part of this equation is not to treat all students the same, but rather to treat them based on their individual capabilities. The fairness part does not mean to treat all students the same, but rather to treat all students based on their individual needs. For example, a fourth grade teacher may have a rule that all students must sit quietly and finish their math assignments. However, if there is a young ADHD boy in the class, it would not be fair to expect him to remain seated for forty-five minutes working on math. Students must receive firmness and fairness.

What does it take to respond appropriately to student's misbehavior, while continuing to show respect and dignity? Teachers must first understand the goals for the behavior and the messages behind his behavior. In Chapter Three, the goals for misbehavior were discussed in great detail. Also, teachers will need to consider what it is about a student's behavior that they find disturbing. This will require teachers to analyze not only the student's behavior, but also the level of expectations they have for the student (Maag, John W., 2001). Lastly, it is important to consider what the student is attempting to communicate through the misbehavior. Keep in mind that a student does not have the same communication or conceptual skills as an adult. A student may not be able to process and communicate feelings of anger, sadness or even fear. If students are unable or not allowed to verbalize their feelings, they will act them out. Remember, when students are not allowed to tell you how they feel, they will always show you. It is this acting out or showing of negative feelings that most teachers refer to as misbehavior.

There are as many ways of dealing with students as there are teachers. When deciding a discipline approach, teachers should select one with which they feel comfortable. Obviously, most teachers seek a teaching and discipline approach that will have a positive outcome. Several factors exist whereby students' positive behaviors can be reinforced in order to reduce, or in some cases even eliminate, the negative behavior. Positive behavior supports don't just happen, teachers must create them. It is important for teachers to ensure that their classrooms are places where positive discipline can actually take place. The following is a list of things that will help ensure that the classroom is conducive to effective discipline (Belvel, P.S., and Jordan, M. M., 2003).

Ten Ways to Improve Classroom Functioning

1. **Be firm and fair: These two characteristics are not mutually exclusive.** The firmness part means to be consistent and direct, while the fairness part means to be understanding and empathetic.

2. **Don't become overly concerned about being perfect: In fact, there is no such thing as a perfect teacher.** When teachers make mistakes and acknowledge them, students learn that it is acceptable to make mistakes. Therefore, teachers need to relax, be professional and allow students to see that you, too, are human.

3. **Be consistent: Nothing is more important than being consistent.** The very best discipline strategies will be ineffective when teachers are inconsistent. When teachers are inconsistent, students become confused about what is acceptable and what is not. This confusion often leads to frustration which is often manifested in misbehavior. It is not only important for individual teachers to be consistent, proactive discipline is most effective when all teachers practice school-wide discipline strategies. Therefore, when

students move from class to class, there is consistency.

4. **Separate the student from the behavior.** This may sound like a simple task, but it is more difficult than it appears. It is easy to become frustrated with the student and say things that are degrading. However, if teachers can remember that all behavior occurs for a reason, then we have a better chance of separating the student (person) from the behavior (actions).

5. **Encourage independence through problem-solving.** When students are asked to make some decisions about their own behavior, they are being encouraged to become more independent. Interestingly, in many cases students will decide on a punitive action far more harsh than the teacher intended. Allowing students to participate in decisions regarding their behavior sends a powerful message that they have some control over what happens to them. This will encourage students to be more responsible and independent.

6. **Do not pity or feel sorry for students.** Even though many students come from some very difficult situations, feeling sorry for or pitying students will create more problems. When students are pitied, it is actually a put-down. The message is that the students are so poor, pitiful, and inadequate that they cannot possibly handle the consequence of their behavior. Remember, when students are given a reminder and their misbehavior continues, they are choosing to suffer the consequence of their behavior. When teachers feel sorry for or pity students, there is a greater opportunity to be inconsistent. Pity actually decreases students' self-esteem, increases their misbehavior, and teaches student to be "helpless."

7. **Do not be concerned about the "right" discipline technique: In fact, just as there is no perfect teacher, there is no "right" discipline technique.** What works for one student may not work for another; what works one day may not work the next day. This is why it is important for teachers to develop several intervention strategies. If only one type of discipline technique is used, there is a good chance that the efforts will become ineffective. The right proactive discipline technique is whatever works today.

8. **Recognize who owns the problem.** Another way of asking this is, "Whose problem is it?" In previous chapters we have discussed this concept. If the problem belongs to the students and they are not about to hurt themselves, hurt someone else, or destroy property, then they need to be encouraged to solve their own problems. In some cases, the problem may

belong to the teacher. The teaching style may not match the students' learning style. The curriculum could be boring and not stimulating. The classroom could be poorly organized. Or, the teacher could be having a personality conflict with students. In reality some teachers are poorly equipped to work with and relate to young students. These teachers may need to consider working with adults or perhaps computers. This is not said to be cruel, but teaching is such an important profession that teachers must be honest about their strengths and weaknesses.

9. **If action is necessary, then act.** Unfortunately, when action is called for, many teachers continue to give reminders, negotiate or, in general, quarrel with students. Such responses give students the opportunity to manipulate their way out of the consequence. Simply inform the student that you will talk with them once the consequence has been completed.

10. **Encourage students to be responsible.** Students need to be held accountable for their behavior. When this occurs it encourages students to be responsible for solving their own problems. However, many teachers will jump in and tell students what they should or should not do. It is important that students be taught problem-solving skills and then be allowed to practice them. Depending on the way teachers respond to students, their behavior will be reinforced positively and negatively. E.L. Thorndike in his Law of Effect (1932) demonstrated how behavior is learned. B.F. Skinner's (1957) Operant Conditioning theory and experiments showed how behavior can be reinforced positively or negatively. Therefore, reinforcement can impact appropriate and inappropriate behaviors. In essence, consequences for behavior can be positive or negative. A positive consequence will increase the likelihood that a behavior will reoccur, whereas a negative consequence will result in the likelihood that the behavior will diminish or discontinue. For example, when a student performs a task and is given a treat, there is a greater chance that the student will continue to perform the behavior that has resulted in the reward. Likewise, when behavior is followed by a negative consequence or the absence of a reward, the opposite is true. If the misbehavior is not reinforced, the likelihood that it will reoccur decreases. This is why some psychologists have suggested ignoring certain behaviors as an effective discipline strategy (Perlman, M., and Ross, H. S., 2005). However, in order to determine how to respond, teachers must understand what the behavior is attempting to achieve. For example, if a teacher decides to ignore a behavior, there is an assumption that the student is attempting

to gain attention. In other words, positive reinforcement (rewards) maintains or increases the behavior it follows, while the absence of reinforcement or negative reinforcement decreases behavior.

There are a variety of positive ways to respond to students to bring about meaningful change in behavior. As has been pointed out, the most powerful way to change behavior is through positive reinforcement. In other words, catch a student displaying appropriate behavior and reward or reinforce that behavior. However, most consequences are given in response to negative behaviors (Call, N. A.,Wacker, D. P., Ringdahl, J. E., and Boelter, Eric W., 2005). Since positive reinforcement or rewards are things that people want or like, when using reinforcement, be sure that the reward is something important to the student. If the reward or positive reinforcement is more important to them than what they are receiving from the negative behavior, it will serve to decrease or eliminate the negative behavior, while increasing the positive behavior. There are many different types of rewards or positive reinforcements (Simons, J., Dewitte, S., Lens, W., 2004).

Social Rewards:

A social reward is one of the most powerful rewards for students (Hendley, V., 2000). Social rewards include giving hugs, smiles, praise and attention. These are the easiest and least expensive rewards to give and they are always available and are a natural part of the interaction between teacher and student. Social rewards can also be negative. Negative forms of social rewards include yelling, arguing, sarcasm, criticizing, comparing, name-calling and angry looks. These responses can also reinforce negative behaviors and as a result increase or maintain problem behavior.

Exchange Rewards:

Students also respond to exchange rewards. This type of reward includes money, tokens, points, stars, or anything else that the students can use to "buy" things that are important to them (Dobbs, J.; Arnold, D.; and Doctoroff, G., 2004). These types of rewards will be discussed in greater detail in Chapter Seven. Very often a behavior modification system will use exchange rewards in order to motivate students to amend their behavior. An exchange reward system is usually continuous and will require data collection to keep a record of the student's progress. However, this type of system is flexible and can be used with students of all ages.

Activity Rewards:

Activity rewards can also be used to reinforce positive behavior. These are activities and behaviors that the student enjoys doing. Activities can be used to reward behavior by structuring them so they occur when the positive behavior is exhibited (Reynolds, B., and Schiffbauer, R., 2005). These types of rewards are usually very effective for changing certain inappropriate behaviors. For example, allowing a student to have ten additional minutes on the computer if they complete their class assignment within a certain amount of time is an activity reward. Selecting an activity reward that the student likes or enjoys is necessary for this approach to be successful. If the reward is for the student to read a favorite book when he finishes his math assignment, and he dislikes reading, he would not be positively reinforced. However, if the student enjoys reading this may be a positive reward. It is important to know what rewards motivate students.

Timing Rewards:

Timing rewards are rewards that are given every time a positive behavior occurs or when the behavior occurs at intermittent intervals. This type of reward is very effective for students in lower elementary grades (Lindberg, J. A.,and Swick, A. M.,2002). Timing rewards require teachers to provide the reinforcement immediately following the behavior. Rewards are usually more effective when they are applied immediately following the desired behaviors. If the teacher attempts to reward a student several hours after a positive behavior occurs the reward becomes less effective. For example, if the class is on a field trip and the teacher says, "Just wait until we get back to school!" When this happens, the reward or consequence loses its effectiveness. Remember, students, especially younger students do not conceptualize time very well. Therefore, when a reward is delayed, the student may not even understand why they are being rewarded. If this is the case, providing a reward or consequence later may result in more confusion, anger, and disruptive behavior. Therefore, in order to increase effectiveness, give the rewards immediately when the positive behavior occurs.

Verbal Rewards (Praise):

The use of praise can be a very powerful reward when used at appropriate times and for specific, positive behaviors. Since teachers are so important to students, the use of praise can be a strong motivator for changing behavior (Witzel, B. S., and Mercer, C. D., 2003). A reasonable approach is to give praise when students are behaving appropriately and try to ignore the inappropriate behaviors. Whenever using this technique, always describe to the student the behavior that is being praised. Using praise as a behavior change agent will be discussed in greater detail in Chapter Seven.

Attention:
Attention received from a teacher is another powerful reward that can be used to motivate students to discontinue inappropriate behaviors, while increasing positive behaviors (Hamre, B. K., and Pianta, R. C., 2005). From the very birth of a child, adults typically supply enormous amounts of positive attention to their children. Such initial acts of attention include holding the child, rocking, and even making baby-like noises. As the child grows older, the types of interaction change. In fact, it is not unusual to find both parents and teachers giving more attention to the negative than the positive behaviors. This is done in an effort to get students to stop their misbehavior. Since attention is a reward, when attention is given for inappropriate behavior, students are actually being rewarded.

Even negative attention for negative behavior is viewed as a reward. This kind of attention includes such responses as yelling, threatening, criticizing, frowning, complaining, lecturing, and looking at the student in a negative way. On the surface these negative forms of attention may not appear to be rewards. However, each of these responses sends the message that the teacher is reacting to students and giving them the desired attention and power. When students receive more attention for their negative behavior than for their positive behavior, they will continue the misbehavior in order to sustain the attention that they are receiving.

Some teachers may not understand why their students continue to misbehave, even when they are scolded or punished. Generally, if the misbehavior continues, in spite of efforts at discipline, it may be that the attention is rewarding the misbehavior (McComas, J., Goddard, C., Hoch, H., 2002). If this is the case, the discipline techniques being used to decrease the inappropriate behavior, are not as effective as is the attention that is sustaining the negative behavior.

Obviously, no one discipline technique is effective for all students at all times. In fact, no one discipline technique will work for all students all of the time. Therefore, it is important for educators to be skilled at using a variety of discipline strategies. Please note that if a student's misbehavior stays at the same level or increases following several attempts at intervention, then the strategy is not working. As Hernandez, T., and Seem, S. (2004) pointed out, in some cases focusing on the misbehavior, while ignoring the positive behaviors actually causes the student to become even more difficult.

Rewarding students with activities is another approach that can maintain or encourage problem behavior. Before children can talk they will often cry when they want something. Crying was their only means of communication when they were infants. However, even after children are able to talk, they remember that they can get their way by crying, whining, or throwing a temper tantrum. Even though children may know perfectly well how to ask for something, if they have been rewarded when acting in such inappropriate ways, they will revert back to these inappropriate behaviors because they worked in the past (Dobbs, Jennifer, Arnold, D., and Doctoroff, G., 2004).

When teachers acquiesce to students' inappropriate behavior and give them what they want, the inappropriate behavior often stops temporarily. However, such a response actually strengthens the inappropriate behavior and they are encouraged to continue misbehaving. An activity reward can be ruined when teachers reward students for stopping their misbehavior. This becomes no more than a bribe to get students to stop their misbehavior. This process is related to the stimulus-response-reinforcement paradigm that was discussed in Chapter Three. Teachers must keep in mind that when students want something and the teacher refuses, they will initially try harder to get their way. As the misbehavior escalates, and if the teacher eventually gives in, the behavior is reinforced and becomes much more difficult to change. The message the student receives is, "*I can still get what I want; I just have to try harder.*" It is not unusual to find this process occurring even in high school. A student who does not want to complete the class assignment acts out in class and the teacher sends them out of the room. In such cases, the misbehavior is reinforced and is certain to reoccur. It is this type of response that establishes a pattern of negative classroom behavior.

Another type of response by teachers that often results in rewarding misbehavior is allowing students to escape or avoid certain activities. Students learn this type of manipulation very early from their parents. The child may overhear his parent calling into work saying he is sick when he really just needs a day off, or the parent may make up an excuse to avoid going to a social function. Likewise, students may misbehave or make excuses in order to avoid or escape a task or an activity. This usually occurs when students realize that behaviors such as complaining, arguing, or becoming belligerent will get them out of doing an undesired task. When teachers give in to such behaviors it allows students to avoid the activity, thereby rewarding the problem behavior. Since this process is rewarding inappropriate behavior, the behavior is likely to reoccur (Gootman, M. E., 2001). When this process takes place, students learn a very powerful lesson about how to get out of situations they dislike. Such responses will have long-range implications. When students are allowed to avoid certain activities or tasks, the message is sent that using manipulation is a preferred way of behaving. This process, of course, will eventually have a significant impact upon how the student deals with various social, relational, and occupational situations.

SUMMARY

It is important to realize that effective classroom discipline is not "doing" something to students. Discipline involves every aspect of the classroom. Before considering specific discipline interventions, teachers must reconcile the possibility that they may be contributing to the disruptive behavior in their classroom. They must ask themselves if their classroom is organized in such a way that supports efforts at effective discipline. Is their curriculum interesting, practical, and applicable to students' everyday life? It is also equally important to review one's own discipline style. What are the strategies with which you are most comfortable? Ask yourself if in the past your responses increased or decreased student misbehavior. If you are not sure, keep a journal for one week, recording how you typically respond to student behavior, positive and negative. Such an approach will help you identify specific behavior patterns and responses that create problems.

There are many discipline strategies that can be employed that will result in changed behavior. In later chapters we will explore specific intervention programs. Using a reward system is one way to respond proactively to students. However, in some cases, teachers may end up rewarding students' negative behavior, thereby achieving the opposite of what was intended.

Chapter Seven

PUTTING THE PUZZLE TOGETHER: RESPONDING TO TYPICAL BEHAVIOR PATTERNS

Teachers often feel that neither rewarding nor punishing is an effective means of helping students correct their non-compliant behavior. The concern most often voiced is that students should be intrinsically motivated to change behavior or comply. These teachers are correct in that rewards or punishment have never worked very well as discipline strategies. A reward is something given by someone in a superior role to someone in an inferior role. Students that are motivated by rewards or punishment may have a tendency to become dependent, self-centered, fearful and insecure. On occasion, these students may even begin to rebel against the classroom structure and expectations (Covington, M. V., 2005).

Educators often use a reward program more as a system of bribes to get students to behave. When rewards are used as bribes, such efforts cannot be considered an effective discipline strategy. Bribes tend to have strings attached and can also set the stage for blackmail between the teacher and student. The basic message of a bribe is, *"If you do this, I'll do that."* However, strings are attached at both ends of a bribe and it is not unusual for students to end up basically saying, *"I'll do that, if you'll give me this."* Some researchers (Akin-Little, K. A., Eckert, T. L., Lovett, B. J., Little, S. G., 2004) feel that rewarding positive behavior also teaches students to expect something for everything they do. As a result of rewarding behavior, students often fail to develop the intrinsic values and motivation skills needed to complete a task for the sheer pleasure of cooperation or mutual respect.

As previously discussed, the goal of proactive discipline is to help students learn to function responsibly on their own. Learning and growing cannot flourish when students are constantly fearful of punishment or they are seeking a reward for every effort. In most cases appropriate behavior is not learned from punishment or rewards, but rather from an understanding of one's relationship within the order that is around them. There are many other positive classroom behavioral interventions that can be implemented that are far more effective than rewarding or punishing. These proactive discipline strategies will help all students, typical and atypical, learn more appropriate behaviors and teach them how to become a successful part of the classroom and school population (Johnson, F. and Edmunds, A., 2006).

The type of discipline strategies being proposed are referred to as proactive disciplines. In the past the term discipline has taken on a negative connotation. The word discipline actually means to offer guidance to students. Effective discipline implies that actions are being taken to guide students toward more acceptable behaviors. When teachers use proactive discipline strategies, their actions should be considered positive because they are guiding students toward more appropriate and acceptable behaviors.

Components of Proactive Discipline

Proactive discipline strategies include several components:

1. **The first component of positive discipline is that it will focus on the present and the future.** However, in many classroom situations efforts at discipline focuses on the present and past. When students are constantly reminded of their behaviors of the past, responses by the teacher become more of a game of shame and blame. When teachers tell students how bad their behavior has been in the past, it is essentially telling them that they expect the inappropriate behavior to continue. When teachers focus on students' past behaviors their efforts at discipline will become ineffective.

2. **Another important component of proactive classroom discipline is that it provides student with a choice.** One of the misguided goals of disruptive classroom behavior is to gain power or control. When students are given a choice they are empowered. Therefore, when students

are provided with a reminder about their behavior and possible resulting consequences, they are given a choice. For example, if a teacher says, *"If you do that again, you will have to stand out in the hallway,"* the student is being given a choice to amend his or her behavior or to suffer the consequences. Notice how the statement focuses on the present and the future.

3. **Enhancing or building a student's self-esteem is another building block of proactive discipline strategies.** When the discipline strategy focuses on the present and future and provides a choice, it will enhance the student's self-esteem. However, in many situations, rather than using proactive strategies, teachers react to the negative behaviors and impose punishment. Reactive actions that constitute punishment will destroy a student's self-esteem. When students are embarrassed, ridiculed, or demeaned in front of their peers, their self-esteem will become depleted. When this occurs, students essentially have two choices: they can fight back or acquiesce. The disruptive classroom behavior with which teachers often must contend may be the result of this fighting back, while the unmotivated, lethargic student has often acquiesced or given up. It is not unusual for these students to work hard to get their teachers to give up on them.

4. **A fourth important aspect of any proactive discipline strategy is that it will teach students new ways of behaving.** Since teaching is an important component of proactive discipline, if the disruptive behavior is continuing, one must conclude that students are not learning from the discipline strategy. Teachers make their discipline strategy a proactive learning experience when they teach students replacement behavior. While this may seem like common sense, it is surprising how many teachers never take time to teach their students a different way of handling a conflict. Without teaching, there can be no learning. If teachers expect a change to occur from their discipline strategy, then teaching replacement behavior must be included.

5. **The last component of a proactive discipline strategy is that the intervention must be logically related to the behavior.** This can be a little tricky because many discipline strategies used are not logically related to a student's misbehavior. What this really means is that a proactive discipline strategy must be designed so that it makes sense to the student. Sometimes the logical relationship is to get a student out of the classroom so they can calm down, and so teaching can continue. However, if the discipline strategy has no logical relationship to the behavior it is not proactive and will probably be ineffective.

In Chapter One, a great deal of time was spent discussing the "intentional" teacher. When considering proactive discipline strategies, the concept of intentionality becomes even more important. An effective teacher will take actions that are intentional. In fact, the very word "strategy" comes from the word "strategic" (Shulman, J. H., 2004). This suggests that actions taken are logically or intentionally planned. When teachers use proactive discipline strategies they are not reacting to a student's misbehavior. Proactive discipline involves an intentional plan of action that is designed to achieve a specific purpose. A haphazard reaction to misbehavior is not proactive!

Students who exhibit habitual challenging behavior will often respond best to an intervention program that helps to modify their behavior (Newman-Carlson, D., and Horne, A. M., 2004). A behavioral modification program is a systematic approach in which an effort is made to modify or change a student's behavior over an extended period of time. Since implementing a behavioral modification program takes a great deal of effort, it is best to first determine if other intervention programs will be effective in minimizing problematic behaviors. Other effective discipline approaches include ignoring the behavior, taking away a privilege, using a reward system, behavioral charting, some form of time out or setting up a token economy (Putnam, R. F., Handler, M. W., Rey, J., and McCarty, J., 2005).

Ignoring:
The desire to get attention is one of the primary reasons why students misbehave. When students have been receiving attention for their negative behavior, the logical alternative is to provide attention to the positive behaviors while ignoring the negative ones. When initiating this program teachers will need to rearrange the situation so that attention does not follow the student's inappropriate behavior. This means that the behavior will be ignored when the student is acting out. Ignoring means that teachers will not confront, argue, or even try to reason with the student when they misbehave. In fact, when the student is disruptive the teacher will not even look at the student (Perlman, M., and Ross, H.S., 2005). Although this approach may sound simple, ignoring a problem behavior can be very difficult to achieve.

When students have been accustomed to receiving attention for their negative behavior and teachers begin to ignore the behavior, it is not unusual for the misbehavior to initially escalate. When this pattern occurs, the student is simply trying harder to get the desired attention. At this point the student has not yet realized that he can receive just as much attention for positive behavior as he can from the negative behavior. Therefore, when first starting to ignore behavior, be prepared to follow through, regardless of how long it takes. If the behavior is ignored for a while, then attention is provided, inconsistency occurs and the inappropriate behavior will become even more severe. For example, a teacher may plan to ignore a student's misbehavior then, as the behavior becomes worse, the teacher gives in to the student and provides attention. The negative behavior is reinforced. The student receives the message that he can still get attention or gain power, so he just works harder.

When attempting to ignore inappropriate behavior, it is important to understand when it is appropriate to ignore the behavior and when it is necessary to respond. Unless a student is about to hurt himself or others, or destroy property, then most behaviors can be ignored (Willert, J., and Willert, R., 2000). When ignoring is done consistently, it is an excellent discipline method that can reduce or perhaps even eliminate disruptive classroom behavior. However, in order to be effective, teachers must ignore the behavior every time it occurs. If the behavior is ignored at infrequent intervals, the behavior will be strengthened and may become even more difficult to change. Once the decision has been made to ignore certain behaviors, the strategy must be used consistently.

Teachers must also decide how to ignore a student's disruptive behavior. The easiest way to ignore a behavior problem is to lose the situation, physically and mentally. This may mean turning away from the student, getting involved in another activity or simply continuing to do what you were doing without providing attention to the student. There are situations, however, where it is simply impossible or impractical to completely ignore a student. The behavior can still be ignored by turning away from the student, not talking to him, or not even glancing at him (Peskin, J., and Olson, D. R., 2001). Just by glancing at a student while they are being disruptive can provide enough attention to reinforce the misbehavior. When using ignoring as a proactive discipline strategy the teacher should not scold, give warnings, or even tell the student what you are going to do. If the teacher says to the student, *"I am not going to deal with you while you act this way,"* this response by itself is giving the student attention.

Before implementing ignoring as a behavior strategy, teachers will need to determine what might be expected from the student. By attempting to anticipate the student's response, teachers can plan their course of action before the behavior occurs. If the student has a long history of getting attention for inappropriate behavior, you can be almost certain that the behavior will become worse before it begins to subside (Lane, K. L., Pierson, M. R., Robertson, F. E. J., and Little, A., 2004). If the teacher is prepared for this increased negative behavior, then they will not be taken by surprise or give up so easily. When the student increases his misbehavior, he is surmising, *"My tantrums used to get me what I wanted and now they are not working. I may need to scream louder."* The student is only testing this new response. After all, the misbehavior has paid off in the past. As the ignoring strategy continues, at some point the student will realize that the behavior is no longer working and he will then be more open to talking about other ways to get his needs met.

How long does it take before one can determine if the ignoring strategy is working? This is something that is often omitted from the literature. The time it takes for ignoring a behavior to be effective is different for each student. If the student is stubborn or has practiced this technique for many years, it may take quite a while. However, if the student is young and more compliant, the positive results may be seen very quickly. Generally, it will take two to three weeks of consistently ignoring a behavior before it will subside (Perlman, M., and Ross, H. S., 2004). Ignoring disruptive behavior can be difficult to achieve because it takes only a glance at the student to send a message that he still has your attention.

When the teacher and student both agree that ignoring the inappropriate behavior will be used in the classroom, students learn that they must find more acceptable ways of getting what they want. It is equally important to teach students how they should behave in order to get the attention or rewards they desire. This may be accomplished through the use of praise and positive reinforcement when appropriate behavior occurs. It is amazing what students will do when they are told how to behave!

Talking to Students to Avoid Manipulation
Where do students learn these skills of increasing their misbehavior until the teacher gives in? Most likely it is learned from early social experiences. These social experiences are all around us and are a part of everyday experiences.

I recall my daughter, Hillary, at age three years learning the act of manipulation. In her case, the learning experience took place in a grocery store. Believe me you should have great respect for the marketing skills found in grocery stores. These people have come up with an ingenious plan to get customers to come into their store, buy all their groceries, and then as they are leaving, make one more purchase. I am convinced that checkout lanes have been strategically designed to accomplish this task. The checkout lanes are about four feet wide and the grocery carts are just wide enough to barely fit into the lane. Then inside the lane on either side, they have placed racks of all sorts of candy that goes from the floor to about five feet high. As the customer enters the checkout lane with a child, the child can easily reach over and get a treat. This marketing strategy has led to many parent/child power struggles and millions of dollars spent! On this particular day I was in a hurry to get to the cleaners before they closed to pick up some dry cleaning. But since the grocery store was on the way, I wanted to get a few grocery items for dinner. I had just picked up my daughter Hillary from day care. We hurriedly went into the grocery store to get some milk and bread. Since I had so few items I thought I would check out in the express lane that required five items or less and cash only. Two people were in front of me and Hillary was standing in the grocery cart. As we waited in line, Hillary reached over and grabbed a candy bar. I said to her, "Put it back." She said, "No!" I said, in a louder voice, "Put the candy back, now." She matched my voice tone and said, "No!" I decided to use a different approach. I explain logically to Hillary why she needed to put the candy back. I said, *"Honey, you need to put the candy back because we will be having dinner in about thirty minutes and the candy will spoil your appetite."* In spite of my best logical statement, she responded, "No!" At this point I was becoming frustrated and embarrassed. Several people in the store had stopped shopping and were watching this father scream at his daughter and the daughter was screaming back. In the meantime two or three people had gotten in line behind me so I was even more embarrassed by Hillary's behavior. I raised my voice again and said, "Give me the candy!" But, instead of putting the candy back, she started crying and held on tightly to the candy. The two people who were in front of me had checked out, and the woman at the cash register motioned for me to move forward. I said in my most determined voice, "Hillary, put the candy back before I count to three!" The reason I counted was to make my command more concrete. However, Hillary just started to cry louder.

I decided just to take the candy out of her hands. But Hillary held on tighter and leaned backward over the grocery cart to so I could not reach her. With all the commotion, people were now staring at us. The woman checking groceries called out that people were waiting and for me to move forward. Once more I attempted to remove the candy from my daughter's hands, and said in a loud voice, "Put the candy back!" But she would have nothing to do with my demands. As I leaned forward to take the candy, the man in line behind me bumped me with his cart and said, "Give her the damn candy, I'll pay for it!" With that comment, and the embarrassment I felt, I gave in and allowed Hillary to keep the candy. She learned an important lesson on that day: "If I try harder, even when my daddy says no, I can still get my way."

Similar events occur every day in classrooms, on field trips, during assemblies, in cafeterias, and on playgrounds. One of the ways to prevent an escalation of negative behavior is to talk to the student about how you plan to deal with inappropriate behaviors before the event occurs. When talking with the student about using a particular discipline strategy, make sure that it is at a time when the student is not having a problem (Black, L., 2004). When teachers attempt to talk with students about their inappropriate behavior and the student is upset, one can anticipate even greater conflict occurring and rejection of any plan for proactive discipline. When talking to students about trying a new discipline strategy, do it at a time when there is not a problem. In addition, the discussion should be kept simple and concise in order to assure that the student fully understands. It is usually a good idea to talk to students when it is convenient to the student and when other students are not around. What this means is to avoid talking with students during their fun times, such as recess, gym, or any time when they are doing something that they enjoy. Also, do not talk with a student about a behavior problem when their peers are nearby. The student may be embarrassed or may try to show off by acting defiant. It is usually a good idea to approach a student about a problem behavior as if you needed help. Tell the student, *"I really could use your help in solving this problem."* Be sure to ask for feedback by asking, *"What do you think?"* This allows the student to agree, disagree, or ask for clarification. If there is a general agreement between the teacher and student about how to handle a problem in the future, make the agreement concrete. Shake hands or sign a contract to make the agreement concrete. When these procedures are followed and proactive discipline strategies are used, most often there will be a decrease in the inappropriate behavior.

Removing A Privilege

Another effective technique that can be used to alter students' inappropriate behavior is to remove a privilege. However, as with any strategy, it is important that certain steps are followed. First, it is important that the privilege that is being removed is something that is important to the student. For example, if during recess a student misbehaves, they may be required to discontinue playing and sit out for five minutes. Some situations present opportunities to remove desired objects or activity rewards. In order to make removing a privilege a proactive discipline strategy, use these five steps that were previously discussed: 1) focus on the present and future; 2) provide a choice; 3) enhance self esteem; 4) teach the student an alternative behavior; and 5) make the action logically related (Brinker, S. R., Goldstein, S. E., and Tisak, M. S., 2003).

Removing a privilege is also an excellent technique to use when two or more students are having conflict. For example, if during a basketball game in the gym two students are arguing about how best to play, make them discontinue the activity until they can jointly decide how to play without arguing. This will encourage the students to work together to solve the problem. When encouraging students to resolve their own conflicts, it may be necessary to provide some supervision to ensure that one student is not taken advantage of. It may also be necessary to teach students how to problem-solve. When used correctly, removing a privilege can be a proactive discipline strategy that will teach students how to settle their own disagreements through negotiation rather than fighting (Pickering, J. S., 2003).

When using the removal of a privilege discipline strategy, be sure to follow a systematic approach to maximize effectiveness. The following is a step-by-step description of how to use removing a privilege as a proactive discipline strategy.

1. **Give students a reminder:** By giving a student a reminder, they are given a choice to either discontinue the inappropriate behavior or experience the consequences.

2. **Inform students of the possible consequences:** When giving students the reminder, make sure they know what will happen if the

misbehavior reoccurs. When students know what the consequence is, there is a greater chance for compliance.

3. **Make sure the lost privilege is important:** When removing a privilege or taking away an object, make sure that the privilege or object is important to the student. If a student does not see the privilege or object as important, they will continue misbehaving.

4. **Determine the goal:** It is important to ask, *"What is the student trying to communicate through his misbehavior?"* In essence, what is causing the behavior?

5. **Take action:** Once a reminder has been given and the misbehavior continues, take action immediately. Of course, a part of the proactive responses is to be consistent. To do otherwise is to render the strategy ineffective. Also, to respond immediately means that the teacher must know specifically what action to take.

6. **Reinstating the privilege:** Make sure students know what has to happen for the privilege to be reinstated or object returned.

7. **Talk to the student:** After the consequence has been completed, talk with the student about what happened that caused him to lose the privilege, object or activity. If he does not know, explain the inappropriate behavior.

8. **Accentuate the positive:** Express appreciation to the student for having the ability to handle the consequence and being willing to talk about the behavior. This allows a teacher to re-establish his or her relationship with the student and will serve as a transition from dealing with the negative behavior to responding to the student on a positive level.

9. **Provide a replacement behavior.** After praising the student for his effort to handle the consequence, talk about other possible ways of behaving. This could be introduced with, *"What other way could you have handled that problem?"*

10. **Reinstate the privilege and provide a reminder:** Ask the student if he is ready to resume his activity. Remind him why he lost the privilege and offer an alternative activity, such as, *"You may want to play over there with some other students; however, you can play wherever you wish. But if you have more problems you will have to come back and stand with me."* This provides the student with a choice and a reminder.

At this point you may be thinking that this process is too involved and will take away valuable time for the other students. When followed correctly, time away for other students should be not more than two minutes. By following a systematic approach, the discipline strategy is made proactive because it incorporates the previously discussed five components of proactive discipline. When approaching removing a privilege as outlined, there is a greater opportunity for success.

Penalty/Reward System

When it is not possible to ignore a behavior, talking has not worked, and there are no immediate privileges to remove, teachers may decide to apply penalties or other negative consequences to reduce behavior problems. A penalty/reward system is a popular discipline strategy because it is usually effective and because it is visible and flexible. The penalty/reward system can be designed to work well within time constraints or location issues. For example, penalties can be applied during a gym class, while students are in the cafeteria, on a field trip, at recess, or when attending an assembly (Gnezda, N. M., 2004).

When using a penalty/reward system, teachers must first identify the behaviors that are to be increased or decreased. It is usually best to work on only one behavior at a time. When a student exhibits appropriate behavior, a reward of some type is provided. However, when the student fails to exhibit the appropriate behavior, a reward or point is withheld. Typically a student must receive an agreed-upon number of points in order to purchase other privileges. This strategy is effective because when the student fails to behave appropriately, they can get back on track and continue earning points. The consequence for inappropriate behavior is to not receive the points. This program is different from a behavioral modification program because the penalty/reward program is ongoing. For example, a teacher may walk around the room giving tokens to students who are on task. The students can accumulate a certain number of tokens to buy free time on the computer (Desiderio, M. F., and Mullennix, C., 2005).

Using a Behavior Chart

Changing behavior patterns can often be accomplished and enhanced by using a behavior chart. There are many advantages to using a behavior chart. A behavior chart will serve as a visual cue to students and allow them to monitor their successes. Behavior charts can be a wonderful tool for teaching self-discipline skills. However, again, teachers must incorporate specific components to make this strategy proactive. Behavior charts have been used to reduce or eliminate almost any type of behavior, ranging from helping students to stay at their desks, to stop talking back, and to complete school assignments.

To be proactive, the behavior chart must be designed so that students can understand what they need to do to receive a specific reward. An example might be that a student is given a point for every fifteen minutes that he does not talk back. If the student receives an agreed-upon number of points during the day, he will be allowed to play on the computer when his class assignment is completed. When the student masters the required task, the level of difficulty can be increased. For example, rather than receiving a point every fifteen minutes for not talking back, the time interval is increased to twenty minutes (Anguiano, P., 2001).

One of the benefits of using a behavior chart in a classroom is that teachers are relieved of the responsibility of constantly reprimanding or reminding their students. A behavior chart program works best when an entire class participates in the program. This allows everyone to be working on the same task. In order to individualize the program, teachers may provide each student with his own behavior folder. Another way to accomplish individualization and enhance compliance is to allow students to design their own folder and decorate their chart. This level of involvement will allow the teacher and students to agree on what privileges will be received based upon the number of points accumulated. Posting a record of the earned points can also enhance compliance and motivate student to achieve. However, there are also some drawbacks to this program. Some students will attempt to manipulate or sabotage others so they will fail. Other students may become frustrated because most students are receiving more points than they are. However, by posting the chart in the classroom students can take responsibility for marking their own points and keeping up with what rewards or privileges are to be received. This intervention strategy also takes teachers out of the role of telling students about their failures or constantly nagging them to stay on task (Buehl, D., 2001).

When first starting the behavior chart, it is not unusual for some students to be resistant to the program. After the first day, it is a good idea to sit down with the students to talk about the chart and how they have responded to the program. This will also be a good time to review the charts for correctness and effectiveness. Remember, nothing is cast in stone, so if adjustments are needed, make the changes early. Making changes does not indicate failure. In fact, making early changes to the charts is positive because it allows all of the kinks to be worked out so that students can succeed.

Most students will initially like the idea of a behavior chart because of the rewards they will receive. Teachers often become excited about this initial success, but then are disillusioned when the chart is no longer effective. Most students become bored or frustrated with a behavior chart after a period of time. When this happens, students will attempt to find ways to avoid using the chart. They may *"forget"* to put down their points, or may argue about their behavior as related to receiving the points. This may be a sign that the tasks are too difficult or the rewards are not sufficient to sustain the students' interest. In order to guard against this happening, it is important to incorporate short-term, mid-term, and long-term rewards. For example, students can be rewarded at the end of each day, at the end of each week, and then at the end of each month. In this way, if a student has a bad day, he can get back on track and focus on the mid-term and long-term goals.

Time-Out

Time-out is one of those discipline strategies that many do not realize they routinely use. Most teachers say they do not use this strategy because it is just does not work. However, as teachers take a closer look, they may discover that they often do use some form of time-out almost every day. Time-out is essentially the removal of a student from an environment to another environment. Regardless of what it is called it is time-out! It should be noted that time-out is most often used for the remaining students. Also, teachers should not be fooled thinking that sending a student to the hall is going to have any lasting impact on the student's behavior. Psychologists and educators can debate the effectiveness of time-out, but what they cannot argue about is the fact that time-out continues to be used each day in almost every school (Gartrell, D., 2002).

Even though hundreds of books have been written about time-out, teachers continue to say that time-out is ineffective for changing behavior. Essentially time-out involves removing a student for a short period of time from the environment in which he is misbehaving. This isolation process seems to be effective because most students enjoy the attention they receive from being around other people (Essa, E. L.,2000). Any time a student is sent from the room because of his behavior, in essence a form of time-out

118

has been used. However, in order for time-out to be proactive, very specific strategies must be followed.

Time-out should only be used when ignoring the behavior has not worked, when there is no privilege to remove, when the student has not responded to the teacher talking to him, or when some type of charting system has failed. Placing a student in time-out sends the message that the student's behavior is such that he cannot be permitted to continue in the activity or be around people.

Why is time-out effective? Isolation has always been a powerful tool. Even in state prisons, where there are some pretty terrible people, when they act out they are placed in *"isolation."* Isolation is powerful because people are human beings, not human doings. To be a human being means that social contact is important. Isolation can be very painful. However, this is exactly what time-out does—it isolates a student. Consider the last time you were at home alone. There was nothing to do, no dish washer to empty, no floors to sweep, no clothes to wash; nothing to do but spend time alone. What did you do? You probably listened to music, watched television, read a book. These are all forms of stimulation. Being alone sounds like the perfect evening. However, what if you are told to sit at the table and do nothing but think. Suddenly, this does not sound so appealing. The next time a student refuses to sit quietly in time-out, remember how difficult it is to be alone and not create some type of stimulation.

Before using time-out, teachers need to know why they are using time-out. What is the purpose of using time-out and what does one hope to achieve by isolating a student? Some teachers may say that they want the student to *"think"* about what they have done, while others may say they just want the student out of the room so they can teach. Neither of these statements is an acceptable reason for putting a student in time-out. Proactive teachers know that there are only two reasons why time-out is ever used: a) to calm the student down, and b) as a consequence of the student's misbehavior (Elkind, D., 2001). However, regardless of why time-out is used, teachers must implement the strategy in such a way as to make it a proactive intervention.

When students are placed in time-out to help them calm down, it is not necessary for the teacher to prescribe the amount of time the student is to remain in time-out. Simply tell the student that he will need to stay in time-out until he calms down. This may take two minutes or five minutes.

The student stays until his anger has subsided and he is more rational. In contrast, when students are placed in time-out as a consequence of their misbehavior, teachers may choose to allow the student to remain in time-out for a specific period of time. After the prescribed period of time has passed, the student is allowed to leave time-out if he is ready to talk about his inappropriate behavior. For example, when a student has misbehaved, teachers may say, *"You can come out of time-out after five minutes if you are ready to talk about your behavior."* Therefore, the student can choose to sit in time-out for a brief period of time or stay for an extended period of time if he is not ready to talk about his behavior. At some point the student will need to talk about his inappropriate behavior (Wolfgang, C. H., 2001).

One of the problems with the time-out process is that students can be very oppositional and they may choose to stay in time-out for a longer period of time than is deemed appropriate. If this happens, teachers should go to the student after a brief period of time and tell him that you are concerned that he is staying in time-out and missing too much class work. If the student indicates that he wants to remain in time-out, it is important that he be monitored to ensure his safety, as well as to provide an assurance that he is cared about.

Many teachers are reluctant to use time-out because they feel that it is not effective and they are concerned about the emotional trauma it may cause the student. While time-out should not be used with all students, with appropriate strategies, it can be both effective and proactive. It is important to look at some of the ways in which effectiveness of this strategy can be enhanced (Elias, M. J., 2004). The following are the essential steps to be taken when using time-out as a proactive discipline strategy:

1. **Establish and Post Rules:**
Before any proactive discipline strategy can be implemented, students must know what is expected. Therefore, the teacher must first discuss with the students what the behavioral expectations for the classroom are. Second, in order to make these rules more meaningful, it is always a good idea to post the rules. This will serve as a visual reminder and make the rules more concrete.

2. **Resulting Consequences and Behavioral Expectations:**
Students not only need to know what the rules are, they need to know what will happen if a rule is violated. Also, this discussion should

inform students about what behaviors will result in being placed in time-out and what behaviors are expected while in time-out. When talking with students it is important to be specific. Vague descriptions of being good or bad are too subjective and will result in failure. It is best to describe specifically or give examples of behaviors that will not be tolerated. If students do not fully understand the behaviors that are expected in time-out, they will continue to misbehave, even in time-out.

3. **Behavior while in time-out:**

The purpose of time-out is for students to focus on their inappropriate behavior and to calm down. As previously indicated, most students do not enjoy being along and when isolated may become anxious. Also, the process of thinking about one's behavior works best without distractions. Therefore, students need to be told specifically what is expected while they are in time-out. This information should include both positive behaviors that are expected and the inappropriate behaviors that will not be allowed.

4. **Time-out Location:**

Time-out should take place in a location where students cannot see or hear other students or classroom activity that might be stimulating or distracting. When students are placed in a location where they can observe other students playing, they often will act in ways to get attention. During time-out do not allow students to play with toys or go to sleep. Time out is not a time for entertainment or sleep. However, if the objective is for the student to calm down, taking a rest may be appropriate.

Time-out works best when there is a designated location in the classroom where time-out always takes place. Using the same location each time for time-out will eliminate excessive discussion and decision-making when placing a student in time-out. In fact, when students know where the time-out location is located, they will often place themselves in time-out.

Time-out may include a specific a chair or table in the room, a different classroom, the hallway, the detention room, or the principal's office. If the student is in lower grades, has exceptionalities, or generally tends to be insecure, avoid using locations that might create fear. Students should never be put in a dark closet, bathroom, or any place that is degrading. While in time-out supervision should be provided at all times. Close supervision ensures students will remain in time-out, behave appropriately, and stay safe.

5. Length of time-out:

How long a student stays in time-out depends on the objectives and the student's age. If time-out is being used as a consequence, a certain period of time is prescribed. However, if the goal is for the student to calm down, the student can decide when to leave time-out. Young students do not conceptualize time very well, so a timer or clock will be necessary for them to know when they can leave time-out. A clock or timer will make the time sequence more concrete and result in greater compliance. Using a clock or timer during time-out will also give the student a greater sense of security that he will eventually get out of time-out.

6. Taking Action:

Once the decision has been made to place a student in time-out, this is not the time to talk, regardless of the student's various attempts. Talking is often an attempt to avoid having to go to time-out. If teachers have made sure students know the rules and have provided them with a reminder about their misbehavior and the student continues to misbehave, he or she is in effect choosing the consequence of time-out over discontinuing the inappropriate behavior. To allow a student at this point to talk his way out of time-out will be a signal that he can still get his way. When teachers give a second, third, or fourth reminder, they are being inconsistent. The student does not know if the teacher means business on the first, second, third, or fourth warning. When teachers are inconsistent and finally take action following the fourth or seventh warning, they are essentially placing the student in time-out for themselves. They have finally become sufficiently frustrated that they now take action. If the teacher was placing the student in time-out for the student he or she would have taken action after the first reminder. When teachers are inconsistent, the time-out strategy is rendered ineffective. Students often employ a variety of techniques to avoid going to time-out:

a) A frequent technique that students use to avoid going to time-out is to ask to go to the restroom. Most students are able to control their bladder for a short period of time. Therefore, unless the student has a urinary tract problem, do not allow a student to go to the restroom during their time in time-out.

b) Another common response from students who have been placed in time-out is to say things like, "I hate you," or "You are the meanest teacher in the world." Even though such a statement may hurt a teacher's feelings, this is nothing more than a manipulation to try and avoid going to time-out. When this happens, respond with a sense of reassurance that even though the student feels angry he must remain in time-out.

As previously indicated, talking with students while they are in time-out only increases the potential for failure. If the student attempts to manipulate or wants to talk while in time-out, simply ignore him. If, however, the student continues to call out or cry, you may indicate that if the behavior continues the timer will have to be re-set. In other situations, students will attempt to move the chair or tip it over. If this should happen, provide the student with a reminder that if the chair is tipped over again, you may have to re-start time-out. While in time-out students often complain of being tired, hungry or thirsty. These are all forms of manipulation and should be ignored. If attention is given to these manipulative efforts, the student's negative behavior will be reinforced. Students may occasionally refuse to go into time-out or attempt to leave time-out. When this occurs, the student is testing to see if the teacher is serious about using this strategy. Keep in mind that time-out is not an appropriate technique for all students. However, if necessary, you may have to accompany the student into the time-out area. If this is the case, it will be necessary to have the teacher assistants handle the classroom.

7. **A successful completion:**
Once time-out has been completed, it is important to provide immediate positive reinforcement. This can be accomplished by giving the student a hug or making a statement praising him for his ability to remain in time-out. After giving the student attention and praise, ask the student, *"What caused you to have to go to time-out."* If he says he does not know, explain the misbehavior and remind him of the class rules and the fact that a reminder was given. Be sure to ask him again if he understands.

8. **A replacement behavior:**
Before completing the time-out process the student will need to be told how to avoid time-out in the future. Based on the behavior that has resulted in time-out, provide the student with an alternative way of dealing with the conflict or problem behavior. For example, if the student was placed in time-out for shouting out during the lecture, ask the student what was going on that caused the response. He may say, *"John kept reaching over and pushing my arm while I was writing."* The teacher can respond, *"Oh, I did not know that is what was going on. If that happens again just tell John to stop,*

and if he does not, come and get me because I will stop him." This provides the student with an alternative or replacement behavior the next time something happens.

9. **Offer a choice and a reminder:**

At the completion of time-out, offer the student a choice. Let him know that there is another desk in the room he can sit in if he wishes. Also, provide a reminder. Say to the student, *"If you want you can go back to your desk, but if you yell out again, you will have to go back to time-out."*

Is time-out an effective discipline strategy? Does it incorporate the five components of proactive discipline? Is it focused on the present and future? Does time-out provide a choice? Does it enhance the student? Does it teach the student? Is it logically related? When the teacher initially provides a reminder, the teacher is focusing on the present and future *("If you do that again you will have to go to time-out.")* In addition, this gives the student a choice. When the teacher praises the student for handling time-out and when the student is talked to, the student's self-esteem is enhanced. When the teacher discusses with the student an alternative behavior, teaching is taking place. When the student is removed from the group for disrupting the class, the removal is logically related. Time-out can be an effective discipline strategy and it can be proactive if these steps are followed. However, if any of these steps are omitted, the time-out strategy will not be proactive and will probably fail.

Time-out is not for all students, however. The primary component of time-out is that it isolates students. There are certain students who do not need to be isolated. Students who are insecure, students of a recent divorce, students who have been kicked around in foster care, and students who have been abused are the types of students that teachers should never isolate. Isolation means to cut off one's relationship. The above-mentioned students are those whose relationships with teachers should never be cut off. There are many other discipline strategies available for these students (Johnson, F., 1996).

Regardless of what discipline strategy is being used, if there is a history of being inconsistent, students will probably try to do everything they can to disrupt your efforts and get you to change your mind. Inconsistency can exist with just one teacher, or can exist among several. If teachers respond inconsistently to a student's misbehavior, this will cause the student to be confused and unsure of what is really expected. Therefore, a discipline strategy will not be as effective if one teacher allows a particular disruptive behavior and another does not. Likewise, the student will become oppositional if on one occasion the student commits a misdeed and is punished and the next day the same teacher ignores the behavior. Imagine if you told a joke and everyone laughed, then the next day you told the same joke to another group and no one laughed. You would not be sure if you should tell the joke again or not. Inconsistency by one teacher or among several teachers can render a discipline strategy ineffective.

SUMMARY

Discipline has often been thought to be something that teachers do to students. However, proactive discipline is strategic action that is taken to bring about self-discipline. In order for the discipline to be proactive it must include five components: focus on the present and future, present a choice, enhance students' self-esteem, teach students alternative behaviors, and be logically related. While traditional methods of discipline have been frowned upon, when including these five components, the methods become effective and proactive.

Discipline strategies for typical misbehaving students may include ignoring the behavior, talking with students to avoid manipulation, a penalty/reward program, using a behavior chart, removing a privilege, or using time-out. Since most typical students misbehave in order to get a need meet, get attention, power or avoidance, when used properly even typical discipline strategies can be effective and proactive for meeting Best Practices of classroom management.

Chapter Eight

SOLVING THE RUBIK'S CUBE: PROACTIVE DISCIPLINE FOR ATYPICAL BEHAVIOR PATTERNS

Responding to students with chronic challenging behaviors can be frustrating for any teacher. As with the typical students, these atypical students are not misbehaving in order to get a need meet. Their behavior usually results from more serious issues. As was noted in Chapter Three, these students often exhibit disruptive behaviors because their inability to process information is frustrating them. When a processing deficit exists it prevents the student from understanding information that is presented in a visual, auditory, hands-on, or even language format. As a result, these students will often complete a task at a much slower rate or not understand what they are supposed to be doing. These students become frustrated and their frustration is manifested as misbehavior in the classroom.

It is not unusual for these students to experience conflicts with adults and peers. Therefore, efforts at proactive discipline must teach these students how to self-regulate or self-control their behavior. If these atypical students fail to learn the art of self-control, they may continue to experience conflict throughout their life. Consider a typical event. You are driving down a busy expressway, and someone cuts you off. What do you do? You may blow your horn at him, or you may even curse him under your breath. However, if the individual in the other car responds by making an obscene gesture, curses at you, and hits his brakes in an attempt to get beside you or even swerves toward you; then what do you do? You would probably slow down or maybe even take the next exit. Even though it is not your exit, you will take it in order to avoid a conflict. You would do anything to avoid the conflict because it has become far too dangerous. However, how would a student who does not have self-regulation respond? The same event occurs, but instead of avoiding the conflict, the student responds back to the inappropriate driver. The student flips the dangerous driver off with a bird. He rolls down his window and screams a profanity. The student may even motion for the dangerous driver to pull over. Both drivers pull over and an argument ensues. Someone may pull out a weapon. Someone gets hurt or killed and someone gets sent to prison. All this occurs because the student had not learned how to self-control. This is why the focus of discipline for these more atypical students must teach self-discipline or self-regulation. Believe me, typical discipline strategies such as time-out, taking away a privilege, name on the board, sending to the principal, or even talking to the student will simply not teach atypical students the skills they need to self-control.

When working with more chronically challenging behaviors, it is important to differentiate between a consequence and an intervention. Teachers will need to provide a consequence for the immediate behavior problem, but respond with an intervention to teach the student how to change his behavior. It is often this *teaching* component that is missing for the teacher's approach to effective discipline. Therefore, one of the primary components of proactive discipline for atypical students is to include an intervention program that works in small incremental steps to teach self-regulation (Reid, R., and Lienemann, T. O., 2006). There are several intervention strategies available that will focus on the present and future, provide a choice, enhance students' self-esteem, teach them an alternative behavior, be logically related to the behavior, and help students develop their self-regulatory skills.

Tokens/Points

Setting up a token economy or point program in the classroom, and perhaps the entire school, is one of the intervention strategies that meets the definition of a proactive discipline strategy. This approach is designed to stabilize the classroom so a behavior modification program can be established.

In addition, both the token economy and the behavior modification programs will help students develop the ability to self-control.

Using a token or point program in a classroom has many advantages. When used correctly, a token or point system can result in a more rapid behavior change than will occur with simply ignoring or praising a student. Also, a token or point system will not only result in changed behavior, but it will help students become more responsible, independent and will facilitate emotional growth. A token economy program can be used very effectively with students as young as three years of age and up. Not only can a token or point system be used to reduce oppositional or defiant behaviors, but it is also effective for eliminating worrisome behaviors such as thumb-sucking, poor hygiene, or generalized disruptions (Reitman, D., 2004).

One of the advantages of using tokens or points is that it can be implemented in a variety of settings. These tokens or points can be given almost any time. While time-out or removing a privilege may not be feasible in certain situations or locations, tokens or points can be given or taken away even while on a field trip, in the classroom, or during any other activity. In addition, tokens or points tend to have a more lasting effect on students in that they are constantly working toward receiving enough tokens or point to "buy" an activity, privilege, or some item (Spencer-Matthews, S.,2001).

Another advantage is that a token or point system is easily understood by students because it very concrete and it operates much like a monetary system in most societies. Therefore, while helping students better manage their behavior they are also learning multiple skills like math, self-monitoring, good decision-making, prioritizing, time management, delayed gratification, and socialization. Rather than using paper money or metal coins when working with younger students, teachers can use items such as poker chips or buttons that can be kept in a container. However, when working with middle and high school students, using a point system is more appropriate. These points can be recorded in a bank register, the ones that adults record their deposits and withdrawals. As in our larger economy, this system allows students to earn chips or points for performing certain tasks, or displaying compliance behavior. These chips or points are then exchanged for a variety of activities or rewards. Children under age three have difficulty conceptualizing, and the token economy program would not be effective (Christensen, L., Young, K., and Marchant, M., 2004).

Using a token or point system is not particularly new to most teachers. In fact, it is not unusual for teachers to supplement their praise and attention with promises of special privileges, activities, or tangible rewards for appropriate compliance. What has often not been included, however, is a record-keeping system to quantify the student's progress. Keeping a record of progress and a means of "earning" will keep the teacher and students informed of the progress that is being achieved. A token or point system also allows teachers to more quickly reinforce students' positive behavior, as opposed to focusing on the negative ones (Kehle, T. J., Bray, M. A., Theodore, L. A., Jenson, W. R., and Clark, E., 2000).

Using edible treats or stickers to reward instead of tokens is not as effective, especially if the student is older than age four. However, using a token or point system has many advantages to the classroom teacher. It allows teachers to have greater organization and provides a more systematic way of managing the student's behavior and stabilizing the classroom. The use of a token or point system also eliminates the vagueness of commands and reprimands. A token or point system will also relieve the teacher of constantly responding to the negative behavior of a student. As a result, a token or point system draws attention to appropriate behavior and compliance and decreased attention on negative behaviors. This intervention strategy is proactive (Hail, J. M., 2000).

Students must understand clearly what they must do to "earn" a token or point. Using the tokens system is appropriate for students from ages three to eight years. However, the point system is preferable for students ages nine years and above. Essentially, a point system allows students to earn points and record the points in some type of notebook or check registry. As the student accumulates and spends points the notebook is kept accurate to indicate the number of points that have been earned or spent. This approach is generally more useful and less offensive to students.

When developing a token or point system, there are several steps that will need to be followed. The following is a series of steps that will maximize the benefits of establishing a token system. (Gunter, P. L., Coutinho, M. J., and Cade, T., 2002).

1. When deciding to use a token program, it will be important to determine exactly what to use as tokens. A variety of objects ranging from plastic poker chips to buttons can be used. It is usually best if the teacher and students decide together what object to use as a token. When students are included in the decision process this allows them to have input and

results in greater compliance.

2. It is also important to discuss with students the specifics of the token program. This will ensure that they understand what is expected and what they may expect as a result of completing specific tasks or controlling certain behaviors.

3. There will be greater success if the teacher and students work together to construct a container in which the earned tokens will be stored. When there is a joint effort, students are more likely to see this new approach as a positive adventure, rather than as negative or punitive.

4. It will also be important to work with the students to establish a list of privileges or rewards that they can earn. Let students know how many tokens will be required to receive a specific activity or earn a particular reward. For example, the teacher and student may agree that it will take ten tokens to play for ten minutes on the computer, whereas only five tokens would be required to play for five minutes.

5. Decide with the students what targeted behaviors will result in an earned token or point. Targeted behaviors may be collective or individualized. For example, the teacher and students may decide that all students will receive three tokens when everyone brings his homework assignment to class. However, if the decision is to individualize the program, the teacher may give a student one for remaining in his seat, another for completing a task, still another for not interrupting the class.

6. Since some students may steal, cheat, or lose tokens, it is a good idea for the teacher to manage the "banks" for the students. For example, when the teacher sees a student seated and working on his assignment, they would simply walk over and give the student a token and tell him to go put the token in their bank.

7. Once these steps are completed, the token system can be implemented immediately. Give students a list of tasks or behaviors that are to be controlled or exhibited so they can see them on a regular basis.

8. Provide the students with feedback or allow them to count the number of earned tokens or points and how many more tokens or points are needed in order to receive the identified reward or privilege.

9. At the end of the day, the students may be allowed to use their tokens to purchase items from the treasure chest. However, they may wish to save their tokens to purchase items at the school store at the end of the week.

When establishing the point program with older students, this program seems to work best if the points are organized in a bank register, much like a checkbook. The teacher may wish to go to the bank where he or she does business and explain the program to the bank manager, and ask if they can have some bank books. This will save the teacher considerable time and money. However, if bank registers are not available, the program can be designed in columns in a notebook, marked with the dates, the deposits, the withdrawals, and the current balance. When students earn points, they are to be entered, along with the date, a brief notation as to the behavior or task performed and the new balance. When points are spent for a reward or special activity, enter the type of reward in the item column, enter the amount of points used under withdrawal, and deduct the amount from the balance. Using the point system is more successful when the teacher and student work together to keep the book up to date. It will be important to inform students that earned points and deductions can only be entered using the teachers' green flourescent pen. By doing this, teachers will discourage cheating.

Just as was discussed with the token system, when using a points program, it is important to construct a list of tasks or behaviors to be performed or corrected, along with a list of privileges and the number of points needed for the privileges. Obviously the privileges will need to be age-appropriate and the tasks to be performed can have greater flexibility. The number of points assigned to each task or behavior will need to be determined and agreed on by the teacher and students. The more difficult the task or behavior to be controlled the greater the number of points that should be received. Likewise, the more valuable rewards should require a greater number of points (Winter, T., and Haines-Burnham, J., 2005).

The point system operates identically to the token system. If the student has several teachers, it is important that everyone understands and uses the point system. This program works best when all of the teachers participate. However, one central teacher will need to be assigned to manage the program. The list of privileges and tasks should be reviewed periodically and changes made to keep the system current and interesting for students. If students are able to consistently complete a task or control the identified disruptive behavior for an extended period of time, other behaviors can be included. However, it should be noted, unlike the behavior modification program, this program starts the first day of school and continues until the last day. In addition, all students participate in the program. Of course, some students may not need this added incentive to control their behavior. However, remember, this program is used to stabilize the classroom. For those more difficult students, an adjunct behavior modification program will be implemented.

The token and point system is used only for rewarding positive behavior. The consequence for negative behavior is simply not receiving the token or point. Some teachers may have a tendency to use the program as a form of punishment by taking tokens or points away from students when they misbehave. The tokens or points earned belong to the student and should not be taken away. When earned tokens or points are taken away, students are likely to lose interest in the program and not be motivated to participate (Reitman, D., 2004).

On occasion students may need one or two tokens or points to receive a desired activity, and will attempt to get the teacher to give them an advance on future behavior. If teachers do this, students are less likely to complete the tasks since they have already received the reward or privilege. Allowing students to have tokens or points before they have earned them will sabotage the program and should never be done. If the students have not earned the necessary tokens or points, they should not be allowed to participate in the activity or receive the reward.

When administering tokens or points, be positive and acknowledge the student's successes. Remind students about what specific tasks were completed or behaviors that were maintained for the tokens or points. When a student is ready to purchase an activity or reward, allow him to take the appropriate number of tokens from the bank or deduct the number of points from the registry. If using the point system, make sure the student writes down the balance. If the student has a history of trying to cheat, it may be important for the teacher to check the token container or point book for correctness.

Tokens or points can be used to reward virtually any type of appropriate behavior or completed task, even if it is not on the list. A common mistake that many teachers make is to follow a token or point program too rigidly, thereby missing opportunities to reinforce appropriate compliant behavior that may not be on the list. Therefore, teachers may wish to provide bonus points for extra effort. While, the token economy program can also be used to reward any controlled behavior or independent decision-making, it is imperative that the tokens or points be administered immediately upon the completion of a task or compliant behavior. A delay in dispensing the tokens or points decreases the significance of the program and will result in limited motivation (Edelman, S.,and Clin, L. R., 2005).

Be sure to review the list of rewards, along with the tasks and/or behaviors every week or so with the students to determine if changes are needed. If the student becomes bored or is not willing to participate, this is an indication that either the student does not understand the program, the rewards are not important, or the expectations are too great. Initially, it is important to be patient as students adjust to the demands of controlling behavior or completing various tasks. While there will be some immediate successes during the first few days, as the weeks go by there will also be many failures.

One of the ways to keep students motivated with the token or point program is to include both short-term and long-term reinforcement for improved behavior. This can be accomplished by administering a token or point immediately after the task or controlled behavior has occurred and then, at the end of the day, students may use their tokens or points to buy a privilege or an item. Also, let students know that if they are able to accumulate a certain number of tokens or points by the week-end they can receive "bonus" tokens or points and spend the tokens at the school store. Reinforcements or rewards can include virtually any type of reward; tangible or intangible rewards, time rewards, social rewards, even homework passes.

A token or point system is an effective way to help students stay motivated to manage their inappropriate behavior. However, in order for this program to be effective, teachers must be creative. A token or point system is different from a behavioral modification program because it is used as a continuous part of the classroom discipline approach and it includes all students. The primary purpose of the token economy or point system is to stabilize a disruptive or chaotic classroom. This stabilization will allow for additional proactive interventions to be employed.

Establishing a Behavior Modification Program
Establishing a behavior modification program is for those students that are displaying some of the more challenging behaviors. In most cases

this program can work very quickly to produce changed behaviors. However, in some cases, especially for older students, a long-term process may be necessary. After all, many of these students have been exhibiting these chronic inappropriate behaviors for a number of years and it will take time to teach the student to effective self-regulate (Zanoili, Daggett, Ortiz, and Mullins, 1999). When a behavior modification program is not successful, it is usually because the program exists only in one domain, rather than using a multimodal approach. A well-designed behavior modification program will extend across several domains and will be in place for a specific period of time to assist a student in engaging in more appropriate behavior. One must approach a behavior modification program in much the same way one would work to provide assistance to a student with a learning deficit. The idea here is that intervention is a continual process of change and re-adjustment, and will need to take place across several domains, e.g. classroom, gym, art class, lunchroom, and the home. Barkley's (1997) research states that the most likely negative impact of a behavior modification program is to prematurely suspend the effort. When the program is prematurely suspended the student will often revert back to old behaviors of the failure cycle. Also, if a behavior modification program is limited to only one environment, it will be ineffective. Obviously, this calls for all school personnel to be involved with the student and work as a team to ensure success (McKinney, S. E., Campbell-Whately, G. D., and Kea, C. D., 2005).

Benefits of Behavior Modification:

Teachers will find many benefits to establishing a behavior modification program in their classrooms. Behavior modification does what the name implies; it modifies negative behaviors by rewarding positive behaviors. This is an excellent strategy for teaching students replacement behaviors while helping them become more responsible for their actions. Behavior modification provides students with success experiences rather than focusing on what they are doing wrong. In essence, behavior modification allows students to practice controlling their behavior, thereby teaching the art of self-discipline (Watson, T., Dufrene, B., Weaver, A., Butler, T., and Meeks, C., 2005). In addition, behavior modification empowers students by showing them how to control their environment, rather than reacting to the control of others. Behavior modification also allows teachers to better monitor classroom behavior and reinforce improved behavior. When a behavioral modification program is implemented at school and home, this allows teachers and parents to bridge their efforts. This cooperation serves as a powerful message to the student. Another benefit of a behavior modification program is that just as a letter grade provides students information about their progress, behavior modification lets students know how they are progressing behaviorally. When students feel hopeless because they seem to be in trouble all the time, the concrete evidence of their improvement will build their self-esteem and give them a sense of hope and motivation to continue controlling their behavior. It should be noted that a behavior modification program is an intense discipline intervention that is designed to quickly get a student back on track and teach the student more appropriate ways of behaving.

Implementing A Behavior Modification Plan:

A behavior modification plan is simply a systematic way of teaching students how to control their behavior in short increments (DeMario and Crowley, 1994). At the end of each interval, the student is provided a short-term reinforcement (reward).The theory is that when reinforcing positive behavior over a period of time, the student slowly learns to replace the old negative behaviors with the more positive ones. Teachers and parents have often used behavior modification in one form or another without realizing it. Behavior modification is a powerful proactive intervention strategy for students of all ages and has been used to modify the behavior of preschoolers as well as criminals in federal prisons.

A personal experience:

I recall using a simple behavior modification program with my daughter, Hillary, when she was about five years of age. At that time she had two frustrating habits. She would suck her thumb and play with her navel. I don't mean she would just suck her thumb; she kept her thumb in her mouth all the time. And I don't mean she would just play with her navel; she would pull her belly button inside-out and rub it. She rubbed her navel so much it would become red and irritated and I had to take her to the pediatrician to have it cauterized.

Since Hillary was five years of age, I was concerned that she was going to ruin her permanent teeth. So I decided to take her to see her dentist. I remember Dr. Davis, the dentist, being irritated that I was taking up his time to deal with such a trivial issue. He hurriedly took Hillary over to the medicine cabinet and placed some orange liquid on her thumb. He told me that the liquid was bitter-tasting and that if I would put this on her thumb every hour or so, she would stop sucking her thumb. As we stood there talking, Hillary returned her thumb to her mouth and continued sucking. After a minute or two, the dentist commented that Hillary must like sucking her thumb more than she dislikes the taste of the bitter liquid. He thought for a moment and called Hillary back over to the medicine cabinet. This time he placed a band-aid on both of Hillary's thumbs. I commented that her thumbs were not cut, so why the band-aids? Dr. Davis commented that the band-aids have sharp edges and mercurochrome medicine on them. The intent was for the band-aid to irritate Hillary's mouth, and the medicine would start to sting. Dr. Davis suggested that I make Hillary wear the band-aids every day for about two weeks and he was sure that she would stop sucking her thumb. I told Dr. Davis that I was impressed with his logic. I felt stupid for having not thought of using the band-aids. I left the dentist's office and was in the waiting room and thought of a possible problem. I returned to the office and as Dr. Davis was about to enter an examination room, I stopped him and commented that when I have on a band-aid and take a shower, sometimes it comes off in the water. I said, "I am a little concerned that Hillary might suck a band-aid down her throat." Dr. Davis looked alarmed and immediately grabbed Hillary's hands and removed the band-aids. I suppose he was concerned about a possible lawsuit.

At this point the dentist was not so eager to get me out of his office. In fact, he seemed somewhat perplexed. Dr. Davis called for his nurse to get him a pair of latex gloves. He put the gloves on Hillary's hands and told me to make her wear the gloves every day. He was sure that she would not like the taste of latex and would stop sucking her thumb. I resisted, telling Dr. Davis that it was not practical to have a five year old wear gloves for two to three weeks.

Even though Dr. Davis had a patient waiting, he asked me to come into his office. He said that he might have just what was needed. Hillary and I went into Dr. Davis' office and he showed me a contraption that looked a lot like a football helmet made of wire. The helmet-like object fit on the head and had a bar coming across the front that overlapped a person's mouth. He explained that the object was used for braces, but that he could use it to stop Hillary from sucking her thumb. Dr. Davis said he could design the device to fit very tightly against Hillary's mouth and he would add notches in the bar, so if Hillary tried to force her thumb into her mouth, it would scrape her thumb. Now, I was not going to buy something like this, but I was interested how much it would cost. So I asked Dr. Davis, *"How much is it?"* He responded without hesitation, *"It is only $1,300."* I said that I would have to think about it and we left the office with the thumb-sucking problem unresolved.

The next day I had an appointment with Dr. Crawford, Hillary's pediatrician. We were to have her little belly button cauterized. After the procedure was completed and as I was leaving, I turned to Dr. Crawford and asked if there was anything he could do to get her to stop pulling at her navel. I explained that my insurance did not pay for outpatient surgery, and that I was concerned that the continued cauterization would leave scarring on Hillary's stomach. Dr. Crawford thought for a moment and responded that he knew what was needed to stop the behavior immediately. He went over to a closet and got a roll of tape. He explained that it was not just any tape, but was the tape that adheres to the skin that is used to hold on prosthetics. Dr. Crawford said that once the tape adheres to the skin, it is almost impossible to remove without tearing the skin. He said a person would have to wear it off. I agreed to have the tape put over Hillary's stomach to cover her navel area. I thanked Dr. Crawford and we left the office. We walked down the hallway and out of the clinic to the parking lot. As we got into the car I reached over to put on Hillary's seat belt and noticed her shirt had blood on it. I thought that the stitches had come loose from the cauterization. As I pulled up her shirt to take a look, much to my surprise, I saw that Hillary had already pulled the tape off and her skin with it. Her stomach was bleeding from the skin being pulled off. I knew I had to do something!

The next day, I did not have to go to work, so I decided that I was going to help Hillary stop sucking her thumb and playing with her navel. I got out a flip chart and laid it down on the kitchen floor. With crayons I drew a grid to create a chart. The chart consisted of three vertical lines and two horizontal lines. At the top of the chart in each column I wrote the number 5 to represent five minutes. At the side, on the rows of the chart I wrote "TS" for thumb sucking and "BBP" for belly button pulling! I called Hillary into the kitchen and asked her if she would like to win some toys.

Of course she answered yes, and asked what she had to do. I told her that if she could just go five minutes without sucking her thumb we would put a big X in the grid where it says thumb sucking on the first row, and if she could go five minutes without pulling at her belly button we would put an X in the grid on the second row. I got the kitchen clock off the wall to show her what five minutes was. I told her that when she gets two Xs on each row, we would go to the store and get a toy. Hillary was very excited.

We sat down on the kitchen floor to watch the clock. With several reminders Hillary was able to go the full five minutes without sucking her thumb or playing with her belly button. I jumped up, told her how great she was, laughed, and gave her a big hug. I told her how proud I was, but that she needed one more X on each row. So we started watching the clock again. I had some clothes in the washer, and about that time the washing machine kicked off. I told Hillary to keep watching the clock while I went to put the clothes in the dryer. I was out the room for about one minute. When I came back into the kitchen, there Hillary was sitting on the kitchen floor watching the clock while sucking her thumb. I said *"Hillary, where is your thumb?"* She knew what she had done and started pleading and promising that she did not mean to put her thumb in her mouth. I reminded her of our agreement, and that she would have to start over with the thumb sucking task. She said she could not help it and started to cry. I told Hillary that she could play with her belly button, but she could not suck her thumb. She again insisted that she could not stop. I suggested that she just sit on her hand and play with her belly button with the other. So, we started over, and, with several reminders, Hillary finally got her second X. We got into the car and drove to the corner market about two blocks away and she selected a small inexpensive toy. As we drove to and from the market I noticed that Hillary continued to play with her belly button and suck her thumb. That was okay. As we drove into the driveway, I asked Hillary if she wanted another toy, and of course she said yes. She said, *"What do I have to do, daddy?"* I told her, *"Just the same thing, get your two Xs and we can go back to the store."* So we went into the kitchen and started set the clock again. Hillary had some failures and successes, but finally she got her two Xs again, so we again drove to the store to get another toy. We got back home and I asked her if she wanted another toy. So, we started over again.

After about two hours doing this program, with some minor reminders, Hillary could consistently go five minutes without sucking her thumb or playing with her belly button. I said to her that it was not fair that she was winning so many toys. I told her that if we increased the time to ten minutes, it would be fair. We increased the intervals to ten minutes and I showed her on the clock what ten minutes was. With the increased time intervals, Hillary initially had some difficulty mastering the task but, again with reminders, after about an hour she was able to consistently go ten minutes without engaging in either behavior. After returning home from getting a toy Hillary announced that she did not want any more toys. I asked her if there was anything else that she wanted. She said she would like to have some candy. I knew that it was almost lunch time, but I agreed with changing the reward. So, we changed the reward to be a candy bar and continued the game. Hillary was motivated enough to control the behavior, so we returned to the store and this time got a candy bar. Hillary asked if she could eat the candy and I told her that it belonged to her and she could do as she pleased. She eagerly ate the candy. (When I think about having done this with Hillary, if I was as smart as most teachers, I would have bought all these little toys and candy bars and put them in a closet. I was driving back and forth to the market all morning).

By this time it was almost noon and time for lunch. Hillary had almost completely stopped sucking her thumb or playing with her navel. I told her go to her room and play while I prepared lunch for us. I said that we could continue the "game" after lunch. During lunch I noticed that Hillary was still not sucking her thumb or pulling at her navel. She appeared to have mastered the task! However, I also noticed that Hillary was eating very little of her lunch. About that time, the cat came running through the kitchen, Hillary immediately jumped down from her chair and started chasing the cat. I yelled at Hillary in a firm voice to get back to the table and finish eating. She immediately put her thumb in her mouth and started pulling at her navel. What could have caused this return to the old behaviors? More than likely it was stress and anxiety. I realized that both behaviors were a means of providing her with comfort and security. Eating her lunch was not that important. After all, she had just eaten her candy bar. So, I asked her if she was finished. She said she was and I told her to go back to her room, and we would start the "game" again.

I got the chart, clock and markers and took them to Hillary's bedroom. I taped the paper to the wall and made a grid, and laid the clock on her bed. I told her that I was afraid that she might accidentally mark on the wall, so I needed to keep the markers. I told Hillary that since she was so good at ten minutes, I was going to make the time fifteen minutes. I showed her on the clock what fifteen minutes was and told her she should come out and tell me when fifteen minutes had past, then I would come and mark her chart. However, I told Hillary since she had to go so long to get her X, that instead of going to the corner market, when she got two Xs, we would go to the toy store. The first fifteen minutes passed and Hillary came to let me know that it was time to mark her chart. Then after another fifteen minutes, she again came to tell me it was time to mark her chart. We got into the car and drove to the toy store and Hillary wanted a big doll that was in the window. After making the purchase, I asked Hillary if she saw anything else that she wanted. She commented she needed a doll house for her doll. I reminded Hillary what she needed to do to earn the doll house.

We returned home and I reset the clock and returned to my desk to do some paper work. After about twenty minutes had passed I noticed that Hillary had not come out of her room to ask me to mark her chart. I went to check on her and she was busy playing with her new doll and had forgotten to watch the clock. I reminded her that she had to watch the clock and not suck her thumb or pull at her belly button and let me know when fifteen minutes was up to get the X. I returned to my desk and again waited for fifteen minutes, then twenty, and then twenty-five minutes. However, Hillary did not come out of her room to let me know that fifteen minutes were up. I returned to her room and she said she had forgotten again, but she was sure that it had been fifteen minutes. I again reminded her that she had to watch the clock and not suck her thumb or play with her belly button and let me know when fifteen minutes were up.

Well, Hillary is now a teenager and she certainly engages in some behaviors that I do not appreciate, but two of them are not sucking her thumb or playing with her belly button. Within six hours, we had been able to do what the dentist or pediatrician could not do. Her behaviors were completely extinguished! By late that afternoon, without any additional rewards or a chart, Hillary no longer engaged in these previously troubling behaviors. This is what a behavioral modification intervention program can do; it will change behaviors in the classroom. As was noted, a behavior modification program is an intense intervention strategy that is designed to change behavior very quickly.

Establishing a Behavior Modification Program:

When establishing a behavior modification program, there are several preliminary steps that must be taken before actual implementation. The following steps are designed to increase the potential for success (Long, J. D.,and Williams, R. L., 2005):

Step 1: Before developing a behavior modification program, it is important to take the time to monitor the student's behavior for several days or weeks. This will allow teachers to determine if there is a pattern to the behavior and to benchmark the frequency of the behavior. For example, one might discover that the problematic behavior occurs more frequently at a certain time of day, day of week, or under specific circumstances. If a pattern to the behavior can be established, a behavior plan may include modifying the environments or events to change the behavior. Also, the only way to tell if improvements are taking place is to have the benchmarks to refer back to.

Step 2: After collecting information via the observation, a meeting should be held with the student and parents to discuss the findings of the observation and the proposed intervention plan. In some cases, parents may be able to identify a reason why the behavior exists. For example, if a student's behavior appears more severe in the morning than in the afternoon, it might be because he is tired in the morning, has difficulty with transition, or is not receiving medication at the proper time.

Step 3: During the meeting with the student and parents discuss the behavior that is selected for improvement. Explain the behavior modification program and the benefits that can be gained from the program. Please note that the success of a behavior modification is more likely if the program focuses on only one behavior at a time or a few related behaviors. Trying to simultaneously address multiple or unrelated behaviors is fraught with disaster.

Step 4: Make sure that the proposed program contains short, medium, and long-term goals. The short-term goals will provide immediate reinforcement, the medium goal will allow for failure but not defeat, while the long-term goals will teach the student to maintain self-control and continue working toward the goal.

Step 5: When meeting with the parents and student make sure that everyone fully understands how the program will work. Discuss the purpose of the program, the expectations and the actual design of the program. Also, allow the student to select a series of rewards which he wants to receive. The parents are probably just as frustrated as the teacher, and this program should be presented with anticipated success. During this meeting praise the student and parents for their willingness to participate in the program.

Step 6: After meeting with the student and parents, the behavior modification program should be implemented immediately. Any delays will only reinforce the potential for failure. As the program is implemented, the consistent use of both the reinforcements and rewards is very important. Initially, the intervals should be set at a level that will ensure that the student will succeed. If the student is not able to meet the expectations from the beginning, he will become frustrated and refuse to participate.

Step 7: Once the program is implemented, keeping accurate records will allow the teacher, parents, and student to know how much progress or lack of progress has occurred. Record keeping also quantifies that behavior rather than allowing it to be subjective. If the student is unable to master the requirements for success, make adjustment to the intervals or to the rewards.

Step 8: Maintaining consistent contact with the parents and colleagues to provide feedback is another important factor that will contribute to the success or failure of a behavior modification program. Establishing and maintaining effective communications, controlling the level of demands, and making adjustments to the rewards, are crucial factors to the success of a behavior modification program.

Using Behavior Modification

When using a behavior modification program, students are able to manage the desired behavior for a certain period of time, until the goal has been achieved. At this point, the program can be discontinued or be started over with another troublesome behavior or task. For example, if the desired behavior is for a student to remain seated for twenty minutes, once the student has mastered this task for two weeks, he has essentially proven that they are able to accomplish this task. However, the teacher may discover that even though the student is remaining seated for a prolonged period of time, he is still not completing his assignment. The program can start over, with the desired behavior changed to the student completing a certain amount of their school work.

It may also be necessary to periodically change the reinforcement or reward that is being used. Students have a tendency to become bored or disinterested in a reward that does not change. When the reinforcement or reward is changed, especially if the student is allowed input, it will renew his interest and motivation. If changes are needed, it is important that students are involved in the decision making process. Involving students will help to avoid resentment and opposition and help to maintain the student's cooperation (McDiarmid, M. D., and Bagner, D. M., 2005). The number of behaviors to be included in a behavioral modification program should be limited. This is an intensive approach, and attempting to modify too many behaviors at the same time will lead to frustration and failure. Rather than working on three or four behaviors, master one then go to the next. If too many tasks are listed, the student will feel overwhelmed and simply give up or not try.

There are many different types of behavior modification programs. In fact, when it comes to establishing a program, teachers are only limited by their own creativity. The most important components to ensure success of a behavior modification program are:

1. Understand what specific behaviors are going to be targeted;
2. Set the demands so the student will initially succeed;
3. Make sure the rewards are important to the student;
4. Make adjustments to time demand intervals and rewards.

All successful behavior modification programs must provide immediate feedback, reinforcement and consequences. The following is a description of several behavior modification programs that have been implemented at various grade levels. It is important to note that these programs are practical, effective, and cost-efficient (Johnson, F., and Edmunds, A., (2006).

1. **Using a Timer:** One way to keep a student informed about his behavior is to use a kitchen timer. It is amazing what students will do for a timer and what they will not do for a teacher. A timer makes the sequence demands more concrete; whereas, a command by a teacher is conceptual. When using a timer, decide on an interval, such as five minutes, and every time the timer goes off the student is informed that his behavior is either acceptable or unacceptable. If the behavior is acceptable, the child receives

a small reward of some type, but if the behavior is unacceptable the student is told that he/she must try again.

2. **The Train Track:** This is a program that is effective for students in the third through eighth grades. The train track concept involves taking a piece of poster board approximately three feet by three feet, and covering it with green paper. Cut some brown felt to make the train tracks. Do not glue the tracks down, they will need to be moved later on. Next, cut out and laminate a picture of a small train engine and glue a piece of Velcro on the back of the train. Place the train track in the principal's office. Explain the program to the student and parents. Let the student know that if he can control a certain identified behavior for an agreed period of time (five minutes), he will get to go to the principal's office and move the train forward one track. Provide the student with a timer so he will know when five minutes is up. After moving the train, he is to return to the room and maintain his behavior for another five minutes to move the train again. When the student has moved the train enough to reach the end of the track, he receives a predetermined reward. The rewards remain in the principal's office until the end of the day when the student is allowed to go, just before the final bell rings, to pick up the rewards. This program serves several purposes.

a. It is visually concrete

b. By placing the program in the office, the student gets to go there for a positive reason, rather than a negative one.

c. By having the train track outside the classroom, it avoids other students' wanting to participate or tease the student.

d. By allowing the student to move the train every five minutes, he receives short-term reinforcement. It also encourages him to "stay on track" to get to the end (long-term goal) and receive a reward.

e. If the student fails to control the behavior, the consequence is simply not getting to move the train. The good news is that the student is allowed to start over and try again.

f. When the student reaches the end of the track, he receives a reward. This is the long-term reinforcement.

g. By allowing the student to go at the end of the day to pick up the rewards, the child is avoiding the transition of moving from the classroom to the bus.

h. The school principal and secretary can also offer reinforcement and encouragement to the student.

3. **Using a Recorder:** Another way to keep students with behavioral problems informed about their behavior without constantly having to call them down or supervise them is to have a recorder. The recorder will have a specific tone recorded that is emitted at random intervals. When the tone occurs, the teacher gives the student feedback about his behavior and provides the student with praise, a token or sticker, which he can use later to "purchase" certain privileges. However, if the student's behavior was inappropriate, he may receive a reminder about his behavior or simply not receive the token. When starting the program, keep the tone intervals short, but random. As the student learns to control his behavior, the time sequences between the intervals can be increased. This program can be used for students in middle school or higher. There are several ways to manipulate this program to strengthen the student's ability to self-control. When the tones are emitted at varying intervals, this forces the child to wait with anticipation for the sound. This process helps students strengthen the student's self-control.

4. **Using an Index Card:** Another behavior modification program that is effective for middle and school students is using an index card to teach self-control and self-monitoring skills. This program involves placing an index card on the student's desk with a line down the middle, one half for the morning and one for the afternoon. Then horizontal lines are drawn, indicating the class periods of the day. At the top of the card place a plus (+) sign and a minus (-). The card can be taped to the student's desktop. At the end of each class period the student places a plus or minus sign to indicate if he has maintained a certain behavior or completed a task. If the student changes classes, the card should be placed in a folder and brought back to the original teacher at the end of the day for review. Although teachers will need to check the card to be sure that it has been marked correctly, basically the student is able to manage the program. This program will teach the student both self-control and self-monitoring skills. Of course, as with any program, it is important that the student know specifically what behaviors are expected during the intervals. Equally important, the student and teacher will need to agree upon the resulting rewards.

5. **The Button Factory:** The Button Factory is designed to be used with students in elementary grades. It is a simple behavior modification program that can be used very effectively in both structured and unstructured locations. It is especially effective in the gym, on the playground, at the

cafeteria, or on a field trip. The Button Factory program is also less intrusive and is not so obvious to other students. The Button Factory program is implemented by placing a certain number of buttons in the student's left pocket. At certain intervals, (five minutes) if their behavior has been appropriate, they are to move one of the buttons to the right pocket. For example, during recess a student may play too rough. Tell the student that you will raise your hand every two minutes. If he has not tripped someone during the two minutes, he can move a button from his left to his right pocket. The objective is to move as many buttons as possible from the left to right pocket and receive some type of reward at the end of the activity. The reward is based on the number of buttons that have been moved. This type of behavior modification program is particularly effective when the student is sensitive about peers knowing that he is on a behavior modification program.

      6. **The Turtle Technique:** This program is especially effective for students in preschool through third grade. This program is similar to when teachers turn the light switch off and on to get the students' attention. To implement this program the teacher says to the students, *"What does a turtle do when there is danger?"* That is right; the turtle stops what it is doing and will pull its head in close to its body and stay really still. *"When we are in danger of not learning, I will say 'turtle time' and everyone is to stop what he is doing and pull his arms, legs, and head in, just like a turtle."* When using this intervention, following the activity, ask the students what behaviors they should be doing. This is a behavior modification approach that is to be used for all the students in the classroom. Even if only one student was misbehaving, the other students will be providing a reminder of appropriate behavior. Following the intervention, provide each student with a small treat for cooperating. If a student is not in compliance, that student does not get the treat and will need to repeat the classroom rule aloud. The students then return to the appropriate behavior and everyone begins adhering to the class rule or finishes the assigned task. This program essentially serves to redirect or break the cycle of disruption that is creating chaos in the classroom.

SUMMARY

Obviously there is no perfect behavior intervention plan. Each program will have its strengths and obvious weaknesses. What works for one student may not work for another. In fact, if someone ever says he has a perfect strategy that will work every time, he is either poorly informed or he is lying. This chapter has presented strategies for those students whose behavior results from poor impulse control. While the intervention strategies are designed to provide effective discipline, they also teach students self-discipline. After all, it is the lack of self-regulation of their behaviors that is getting them into trouble. It is important to note that each strategy has a systematic approach to completion. If any of the "systems" are not followed, the intervention may be rendered ineffective.

Chapter Nine

WHEN BEHAVIOR MANANGEMENT FAILS: RESPONDING TO EMOTIONAL AND BEHAVIORAL OUTLETS

Research studies have indicated, and teachers generally agree, that there is a general increase in the number of students exhibiting both behavioral and emotional problems. In addition, the severity of the emotional and behavioral issues has increased in recent years (von Tetzchner, S., 2004). This view is substantiated in research conducted by Barkley (2005) which found that there is a higher incidence of atypical students' involved in therapy and taking some type of psychotropic medication than there is of typical students. In fact, the research is clear that the rate of suspensions and expulsions is greater for atypical than typical students. From a school base prospective, there is data that suggests that more atypical students are receiving special educational services, are suspended more frequently, and drop out of school more often than do typical students. Specific behavior patterns have been linked to these atypical students. Among the more prominent behavior problems are: oppositional defiance, speech and language deficits, quasi-sexual issues, sleep difficulty, anxiety reactions, depressive symptoms, and difficulty managing anger. When dealing with these atypical students, it is not unusual for teachers to feel overwhelmed. However, it not just the teacher that becomes frustrated, these students and their parents are affected, too. Atypical students tend to experience a greater degree of conflict with their peers, siblings, and parents (Ramos, M. C., Guerin, D. W., Gottfried, A. W., Bathurst, K., and Olvier, P. H., 2005).

It is these above-mentioned emotional and behavioral characteristics which often cause teachers to refer to a student as being "difficult." Since many schools do not take the time to conduct a comprehensive behavioral and emotional assessment, it is important for teachers to take note of the behaviors that are associated with the atypical student. These difficult students are often defiant and argumentative. They tend to do whatever they want and will often ignore what their teachers say. In fact, these students will often do the very opposite of what their teacher tells them to do. Of course, teachers are trained to teach, not to deal with disruptive classroom behavior. When these students begin to interfere with the teaching process, teachers become frustrated and often react to the behavior, not the function of the behavior (Lopes, J. A., Monteiro, I. S. V., Rutherford, R. B., and Quinn, M. M., 2004).

Emotional Profile of the Disruptive Student

These students are often resistive to authority, and refuse to listen or follow directions. Therefore, as a consequence, efforts at discipline strategies are usually ineffective. When asked to complete a task, these students tend to be resistive, complain, and often make excuses for themselves. When the student does not get his way, he will argue with the teachers and will frequently refuse to take "no" for an answer. When teachers refuse to give in to these students, they will pout, withdraw, or become aggressive (Kaplan, A., 2000).

In many cases it is not unusual for these atypical students to be shy and timid. These students often exhibit poor social skills and as a result have difficulty making friends or participating in classroom activities. It is their timidity that causes teachers to put forth extra effort to involve the students. Students in lower grades will often cling to their teacher when a stranger enters the classroom, or when they are placed in a stressful situation. Students in upper grades will respond with *"I don't know,"* without trying to complete the task. Teachers may feel sorry for or pity shy students. However, when teachers feel sorry for or pity students, they are receiving more attention for their negative behavior and are being reinforced to continue the maladapted behavior patterns. Therefore, feeling sorry for or pitying these students only increases their disruptive behaviors and can destroy their self-confidence and self-esteem. It is this pitying and feeling sorry for students that results in the child's learning to be helpless (Mueller, Alison, 2005).

Students described as "difficult" often have numerous idiosyncrasies and tend to stand out among their peers. They can be very particular, adding to their disruptive behavior and peer conflict. New situations can provoke anxiety in these students, and they will often refuse to try what is not familiar; e.g. new foods, new activities, or even a new friendship. These atypical students only want things a certain way, and they can also be very hard to please. These students tend to notice what others have or what they do not have. As a result, these students appear to be constantly on the lookout for things they consider unfair. They will often blame their failure on the teacher and will accuse the teacher of not liking them (Johnson, F.L.,1996).

Another behavioral characteristic of atypical students is that they will frequently interrupt the classroom. These behaviors can be caused by a variety of reasons: Attention Deficit Hyperactivity Disorder, Oppositional Defiant Disorder, etc. These students will often break into others' conversations and demand attention from their teachers, especially when the teacher is involved in another activity. As a result of these behaviors, these atypical students often experience considerable peer conflicts and receive numerous reprimands from teachers. These students often perceive the peer conflict and reprimands as rejection and may become angry. As anger builds up, these students may begin to act impulsively and start yelling at others, become aggressive, and in general disrupt the classroom. During these anger outbursts, teachers may attempt to intercede only to be confronted with statements like *"You can't make me."* These students often call others demeaning names, make fun of others, or even try to hit peers and adults. These behaviors suggest that there is more going on than students' simply trying to get their way or wanting attention. These students are responding to a sensory issue. What this means is that once the student gets upset, he does not have the self-regulatory skills to calm himself down or control his behavior (van Grinsven, L., and Tillema, H., 2006).

These more challenging students often internalize their anger, which may cause the inappropriate behaviors to appear to just come out of no-where. For example, the student may become upset when someone across the room looks at him the "wrong" way. Teachers indicate that the atypical student's behavior often does not seem to fit with the circumstances surrounding the behavior. In some cases, these students will appear to overreact to events that may seem of little significance. However, considering their pent-up frustrations and high level of anxiety, these little events tend to exacerbate the student's overall functioning. It is usually these little events that are just enough to send a student over the edge. In order to deal effectively with these students, teachers must learn how to respond to their anger and pent up emotions. The wrong response may cause the students anger to become intensified, resulting in even greater behavior problems (Reid, R., Trout, A. L., and Schartz, M., 2005).

The Angry Student

Responding to anger can often be tricky for teachers. Teachers who are heavily invested in their students and profession may feel personally attacked by students' outbursts. On occasion, teachers be become inappropriate and respond back to the student in a similar manner. In either case, taking the anger personally or responding with anger is never professional or appropriate. It is important for teachers to understand the basic concepts of anger so they can determine how best to respond.

1. **Teachers must ask themselves what they feel when a student expresses anger?** If teachers take these attacks personally, there can be a tendency to respond back to the student in the same manner. However, anger is only a feeling about a perceived event. When anger is taken personally, it is assumed that it is being directed toward you. In reality the teacher is often only a convenient target.

2. **It is not healthy to repress feelings; they need to be channeled into a positive direction.** When students are not allowed to express their angry feelings, these emotions will become manifested in other ways. Instead of trying to repress students' feelings, help them find more acceptable avenues to express themselves. Taking time to teach students good skills will serve them for a lifetime. Students are often confronted with situations that evoke angry feelings. Teachers must help a student find ways to properly express his emotions. Drawing, writing, making, playing in water, or any activity that allows the student to express his anger is an excellent means of channeling the emotions in a positive direction. In addition, this process serves as a sensory outlet, which will reduce the stress, tension, and anxiety.

3. **Anger is associated with feelings of:**

a. Dependency: Anger often emanates out of feelings of hopelessness. When students see no end in sight or no way out, they become angry.

b. Sadness: Anger is often associated with a sense of loss. Young students experience loss differently than adults. While it may be a good thing that a family decides to purchase a larger home in a better neighborhood, a child only knows that he has lost his room, yard, neighborhood, and friends.

c. Depression: Depression has been referred to as "anger turned inward." When anger is associated with depression, the depression is only a symptom. One may treat the depression, but if nothing is done to help the student deal more effectively with anger, the depression will continue.

d. Powerlessness: Anger is often associated with feelings of powerlessness. This occurs when students feel that nothing can be done to change the situation. The goal of a teacher is to show students how they can have power over circumstances and everyday occurrences.

4. **Responding to Anger:**

a. Distinguishing between anger and aggression.

1) Anger is a feeling

2) Aggression is a behavior

While students may be given permission to "feel," they should never have permission to act out those feelings through aggression. This can be avoided by helping students express their feelings in more appropriate ways.

b. Appropriate response must teach, not punish.

The goal of discipline is always to teach students a more appropriate way of handling their anger. Punishment, while it may stop the inappropriate behavior temporarily, does nothing to teach students how to change their behavior over the long term. When teachers respond to students' anger with punishment, they are doomed to continue punishing students, and students are doomed to continuing to act out their anger.

5. **Techniques for coping with angry students:**

a. Catch students exhibiting positive behavior, and reinforce those behaviors rather than reacting to the negative behaviors;

b. Deliberately ignore inappropriate behavior that can be tolerated;

c. Provide physical outlets and other alternatives;

d. Control the surroundings to avoid students becoming angry;

e. Develop a relationship with students;

f. Express interest in students' activities;

g. Show affection and positive regard;

h. Use humor to ease tension;

i. Appeal directly to students with logic;

j. Explain solutions in concise simple terms;

k. Use physical restraints only if a student is about to hurt himself, hurt others, or is destroying school property;

l. Encourage students to see their strengths as much as their weaknesses;

m. Use praise, acknowledgement, ownership, and rewards as a means of motivating students;

n. Provide structure, be consistent, and set boundaries;

o. Take the time to talk with students about their feelings;

p. Build a positive self image among students;

q. Use punishment sparingly;

r. Model appropriate behavior;

s. Teach students to express themselves verbally;

6. Use appropriate discipline to deal with anger:

a. Be firm, but always be fair;

b. Be clear and concise with instructions;

c. Keep rules simple;

d. Don't ever be unduly harsh;

e. Don't belittle or call students names;

f. Don't embarrass a student in front of their peers;

g. Make sure any efforts at discipline teach self-discipline;

h. Use a discipline strategy that meets the student's needs

i. Never discipline in anger

ANGER: FACTS, THEORIES AND MYTHS

Anger is a feeling with physiological components

Anger is not a behavior, it is a feeling

Anger is universal among human beings

Non-expression of anger leads to increased risk of heart disease

What really matters is resolving the anger

Venting of anger sets the stage for working on a resolution

Anger is like a steam kettle; if left unexpressed it can build and explode

Depression and suicide are caused by unexpressed anger

Anger should always be expressed spontaneously and immediately

Anger should be contained until it can be expressed in a rational and calm manner

Anger is a secondary emotion with another real feeling behind it

Females are generally less able to express anger because they are socially conditioned

Aggressive behavior is a sure sign of anger

Humans are angry by nature

Venting by yelling or pounding on a pillow releases anger

Women are less angry than men

Some people never get angry

Males are able to express anger more easily than females

Anger is destructive, sinful and unhealthy

Angry outbursts lead to more problems

TV violence, sports, and video games release pent-up angry feelings

Behavioral Profile of the Challenging Student

It has been postulated that disruptive behavior occurs when students have difficulty regulating their behavior and emotions. These students will often have difficulty controlling their emotional response, remaining focused, or responding in an appropriate manner. These students often have low tolerance for frustration, appear disorganized or forgetful, or experience a sense of restlessness. These behaviors can result in any number of disruptive behaviors including, but not limited to: failing to complete homework assignments, losing homework that has been completed, having difficulty starting a task, or becoming bored in a classroom (Larson, J., 2005). There are several behavioral indicators of the atypical student.

Poor Adaptation: Students with these deficits are often poorly adapted and, as a result, will have difficulty during transition. This transition may be from place to place or subject to subject. This is why these students often have conflict in the hallway, changing classes, or starting a new task. These students simply do not handle change very well. These students often react to perceived changes and as a result will have conflicts with peers. Once these students are upset, they are hard to calm down. This difficulty is related to the student's inability to practice self-regulation.

Social Skills: Students with regulatory deficits will often exhibit poor social skills, resulting in additional peer and adult conflict. Since many of these students also have receptive or expressive language problems, their socialization skills are further hampered. As a result, these students often have difficulty understanding what has been said to them, or difficulty expressing themselves to others. Many people have experienced a time when they have forgotten what they were about to say or cannot think of the right word to use. They may say, *"It's on the tip of my tongue."* However, students with a language processing deficit may experience this difficulty throughout the day. This often results in students teasing the atypical student, causing more frustration in the classroom. These students often appear to be anxious and fearful. Most likely these students are afraid that they are going to be called on to answer a question. As a result, these students will do almost anything to get out of responding, including acting out, saying *"I don't know,"* or simply refusing to participate (Tsovili, T. D., 2004).

Intensity: These challenging students can also be very intense. In fact, it is not unusual for teachers to mistake this intensity for hyperactivity. While these two behaviors may manifest themselves in a similar fashion, they are vastly different. Highly active students can control their behavior when they want to, while hyperactive students cannot. However, both types of student may be referred to as being difficult. The intense student is often responding out of an emotional deficit, while the hyperactivity student's behavior is resulting from a sensory processing deficit. Teachers must be aware of these differences and respond accordingly. These challenging students can also be very unpredictable, making it difficult to know how to respond. On some occasions these students may be calm and practice self-control, while in other situations they may be easily agitated. This unpredictability makes it difficult for teachers to know exactly how to deal effectively with the atypical student.

Impulsivity: It is not unusual for these challenging students to exhibit a great deal of impulsivity and have a tendency to overreact to classroom stimulation. When these students overreact, it is often disruptive in nature. It is this overreacting that results in even more conflict with peers and teachers. These conflicts can also have a significant impact on the atypical student's self-esteem (Akos, P., and Galassi, J. P., 2004).

Poor self-esteem: When students have poor self-esteem they will often display a negative attitude and negative behavior. When students have a negative mood they often are argumentative and are seldom content for long periods of time. Therefore, teachers must work to keep the frustration levels in the classroom down, and the interest level up. Frustration and anxiety can be caused by a variety of factors, including a curriculum that is too advanced or non-stimulating; the classroom structure that is too rigid or too unstructured; or a teaching style that does not match the student's learning style.

As a result of the above-mentioned issues, a student's temperament characteristics will need to be understood in relationship to his behavior. Understanding such issues will allow teachers to develop and implement discipline strategies that are not only appropriate but also proactive. Behavioral and emotional problems found among these atypical students with additional emotional issues include excessive whining, stuttering, display of tics, and extreme fears and phobias.

A. **Whining:** Teachers complain that the atypical student often whines and this interferes with the teaching process. A variety of factors can cause a student to whine. The first consideration must be the student's health. When students have ear infections or allergies, they will often be more irritable and whine. In some cases, whining behavior may be a signal that the student is insecure and has low self-esteem. While it is important to not reward whining behavior, it can be difficult to ignore when it persists. If the whining is occurring for any reason other than physical illness, tell the student in a firm but caring voice that when he stops crying, you will talk to him about whatever is bothering him. If attention is given to the whining behavior, it will be reinforced.

B. **Stuttering:** Research has long supported the correlation between students with sensory deficits and language deficits. Language deficits can take on many forms. The behaviors can be receptive or can be expressive. In fact, in some cases students with significant emotional and behavioral regulation difficulties will stutter. Stuttering may be a symptom of a language processing deficit, a normal developmental process, or an anxiety reaction. When students struggle with speech or language skills it is important to have them evaluated as quickly as possible. Language is often an early indicator of more serious problems. However, if the stuttering exists secondary to a stage of development, it is important to not draw attention to the behavior. Stuttering is an involuntary muscle reaction resulting in a speech disorder. However, if repeated attention is drawn to this behavior, it can become habit-forming and can be very difficult to change. If the issue is related to age development, when students are allowed time to develop, the stutter will often correct itself (Daniels, D. E., and Gabel, R. M., 2004). If anxiety and stress are causing the stuttering, teachers will need to find ways to reduce stress in the classroom. When students stutter, encourage them to slow down without making it sound like they have a problem. A good way to do this is to say, *"I am not very good at hearing today, you will need to talk slower."* This makes the problem the teacher's, rather than the student's. Never become angry or tease students about their stuttering, it will only heighten the anxiety and make the behavior worse.

C. **Tics:** A tic is a behavioral characteristic that is both worrisome and difficult to understand. Tics can be caused by a neurological deficit or it can be related to undue stress in the student's life. Facial tics include rapid eye blinking, nose sniffing, throat clearing, head shaking and facial grimacing. When students display tics, it is important to not draw attention to the behavior. While the tic may be neurological in nature, undue attention will make the child more aware of the behavior and result in a habit formation. The primary effort must be to identify the cause of the tic. Therefore, it is important for the student to see a neurologist in order to rule out Tourettes Syndrome. If it is found that the tic is being caused by stress in the student's life, the teacher must find a way to reduce stress in the classroom. For example, the teacher may modify the classroom structure or make changes to the curriculum to reduce the child's stress level. In most cases, if the tic is being caused by stress, the tic will disappear once the stress level is reduced. In addition to neurological deficits and stress causing tics, such behaviors can be caused by a side effect from certain medications. For example, a stimulant medication for ADHD may often cause a child to start displaying tics. If the tics persist after the stress level is reduced, it will be important for the child to be evaluated by a physician to rule out a neurological deficit and determine the best way to treat the disorder (Packer, L.E., 2005).

Fears and Anxiety: Fears and anxiety can have many sources. Before teachers can start the process of helping students overcome these fears, they must have an understanding of why students have fears and phobias. In some instances fears and phobias may be related to students at an age and stage of development, or they may be caused by some event that has occurred. When students' fears exist secondary to a stage of development, these fears are usually of a short duration. However, if the fears have been caused by some traumatic event that has occurred such as divorce, death of a parent, displacement from their home, an automobile accident, or even exposure to abuse. These fears will take much longer to address (Weems, C. F., and Costa, N. M., 2005).

To help a student get past these overt fears, it is important to understand the types of fears that may be present.

1. **Fear of abandonment:** Fear of being left alone.

2. **Fear of the unknown:** This allows the students' imagination to take over and create all sorts of unreal objects and events.

3. **Fears of natural events:** Many students are afraid of thunder and lightning, have fears of someone breaking into their home, having an accident, or the school catching fire.

Excessive fears and phobias can be present in students at all grade levels. When these emotional reactions are present, they will often be disruptive to the classroom process. It is also important to note that while an event may not appear to be significant to an adult, it can be a major crisis for a student. In some cases, unresolved issues related to previous trauma may be exacerbated by the current minor event. For example, a student may have been in an area where a hurricane occurred, then two years later the student may be in a severe thunderstorm and become fearful that his family is going to be killed. To adults this fear may be irrational, but to the traumatized child the fear is very real.

Some fears and phobias may be associated with a student's anticipation of failure. When a student exhibits a fear of failure, it is usually because he has tried a new task and failed. When he failed, he may have been laughed at, ridiculed, demeaned, or rejected by his peers. When this happens, a student will become reluctant to take on a demanding task or volunteer in class. If discipline is associated with guidance, then teachers must recognize that dealing effectively with students' fears is an important part of the proactive discipline process. Teachers can help students deal with fears by providing time to express their emotions. This can be accomplished by setting aside time for students to talk, draw, write, work in clay, or engage in a variety of activities that provide an outlet for expression. When considering proactive discipline, it is important for teachers to not discount a student's fear and anxiety by telling him that he is being silly to feel a certain way (Floyd, M., Coulon, C., Yanez, A. P., and Lasota, M. T., 2004).

When a student appears to exhibit excessive fear and anxiety, teachers should not push a student into dealing with his emotions. Usually, a student will deal with the fear and anxiety when he is ready. Therefore, a student should not be confronted with a situation that will provoke his anxiety as a means of trying to get him to deal with his fear. Often when students are confronted or pushed into talking about their anxiety, the fear is exacerbated and it may make matters worse. Instead of confronting, accept student's fears, feelings, and reactions without belittling him. Talk honestly with the student about the truth of frightening events or situations. However, unless trained to provide psychological treatment, it is not the teacher's role to move the student to deal with his fear and anxiety (Muris, P., Meesters, C., and Knoops, M., 2005).

When talking with students about their fears and anxieties it is helpful to talk in the third person. For example, ask students what they would do to help a friend who is afraid of a certain event or situation. In addition, children are reassured when teachers share a personal story about a time when they were fearful or anxious. This sharing helps to connect the teacher and students, and lets them know that everyone experiences fears on occasion.

When teachers share information of a personal event or situation that caused them to be fearful, it gives students permission to accept their own fears and anxiety, rather than deny them. There are many resources available for students to read or watch that can help them find practical solutions for dealing with fears and anxiety. However, as was previously noted, one of the most important things teachers can do is lower the overall stress level in the classroom. This may mean making accommodations in the curriculum and classroom structure (Leen-Feldner, E. W., Zvolensky, M. J., and Feldner, M. T., 2004).

Often students in elementary grades will experience a fear of abandonment. When a student is fearful of abandonment he will often cry when he gets on the school bus or enters the classroom. Since young children are more concrete than conceptual, if they cannot see the parent, they allow their imagination to take over. While fear of abandonment may exist secondary to an emotional trauma or loss, it can also result when students have experienced enmeshment with their parents. This is usually referred to as separation anxiety. For example, a separation or divorce of parents; displacement within the family; death of a grandparent or pet; or a move to another part of the city can cause children to experience loss, which will manifest as fear of abandonment or separation anxiety. The underlying thought is, *"If Dad could leave us, so could Mom."* When students experience fear of abandonment, their anxiety is increased and they often become disruptive. It is important that these reactions are not dismissed or approached in such a way that it does not create even more anxiety (Mayselessx, O., 2004).

There are several things that teachers can do to help a student overcome separation anxiety or fear of abandonment. When a student exhibits these emotions and behaviors, it is usually because he feels that the situation will never return to the state with which he is familiar. For example, the student may be afraid that his parent will not be home when he returns from school. In some situations *"magical thinking"* may take over. For example, magical thinking occurs when the student is afraid the parent will be killed in an automobile accident if they are not with them. The child honestly believes that as long as he is with the parent, the parent will be safe. It is magical thinking to assume that one's presence will prevent an accident. One technique that teachers can use to help students experiencing fear of abandonment or separation anxiety is to ask the parent to give the student an item or object that personally belongs to the parent. For example, the parent may take off a bracelet and say to the child, *"I want you to keep this bracelet for me today. It is not your bracelet to keep, but only for today. When you return home, I want you to give it back to me."* The transference effect of the object to the parent is often just enough to give the child sufficient security to know that the parent will be home when they get there. When using this technique, be sure to stress that the item is not the student's to keep, but only to take care of so he can give it back to his parent. While it is not the teacher's role to bring about therapeutic change, if nothing is done to help the student move beyond his fear and anxiety, one can anticipate continued disruptive behavior in the classroom (Bernstein, G. A., Layne, A. E., Egan, E. A., and Tennison, D. M., 2005).

Strategies for Helping Students Deal With Fears and Anxiety:

1. Help students identify the emotion associated with the fear.

2. Lower the demands in the classroom to lower the general stress level for students.

3. Modify the external sources of the fears, such as if the student is afraid to read out loud, suspend or reduce this activity for a time.

4. Don't exaggerate the student's fears or under-estimate the importance of the fears.

5. Allow students plenty of time to express their fears and provide numerous creative outlets.

6. Accept the fears as a reality to the student. This means that the importance of the student's fears is not diminished.

7. Tell the student the truth about frightening events. Accidents can happen, buildings can catch on fire, peers to make fun of each other.

8. Help students improve their decision-making skills.

9. Have plenty of resources available for the student to read or watch that give practical solutions for dealing with fears.

10. Suggest ways the student can cope with the fear. As the student gains security and makes progress, then the reality of the fear can be addressed.

Behavioral Outlets:

One of the ways students often express themselves emotionally is through behavioral outlets. A common behavioral outlet is a temper tantrum. The way a student handles conflict will also help to differentiate between a student that is being manipulative (typical) and one that lacks self-regulation skills (atypical). While some people assume that only infants have temper tantrums, elementary, middle and high school students can have a temper tantrum. In fact, some say even teachers and administrators have temper tantrums! The first objective when confronted with a tantrum is to determine if the outburst is a form of manipulation or is related to the student's lack of self-control. It is not unusual for a temper tantrum to be a source of emotional and behavioral outlets for students. These students are often seen as being reactive and disruptive to the classroom.

Temper Tantrums: The differences between a typical and atypical temper tantrum are obvious. If the temper tantrum is related to manipulation, it is usually of a short duration, two to five minutes. The typical temper tantrum will often start, then stop for about fifteen seconds and then start back. Essentially, the student is stopping to see if he is getting his way. This temper tantrum is about getting something. It is manipulative, and the student can stop if he wishes.

However, if the temper tantrum is atypical it is being caused by a lack of self-control. Essentially, once the temper tantrum starts, a student cannot stop himself. These temper tantrums usually last between five and fifteen minutes. The temper tantrum goes on and on; and finally stops when the student has literally worn himself out physically and emotionally. Following an atypical temper tantrum it is not unusual for the student to fall asleep. He may wake up in about ten minutes and go join his peers as if nothing happened. Remember, discipline is related to learning. Most often no learning takes place when a student has an atypical temper tantrum. This means that the behavior will re-occur. As was previously discussed, two of the primary reasons for typical misbehavior is to get attention and gain power. If the purpose of the temper tantrum is to get attention or gain power, these goals can be met and the behavior dealt with positively or negatively in a variety of ways. When teachers give attention to the student during an outburst or give in and allow the student to have his way, the behavior is being reinforced. If the temper tantrum subsides after the student gets attention or is given what he wants, then it is apparent that the behavior is related to manipulation. If the behavior stops after the student gets his way, then we can assume that the student has self-control. In contrast, atypical temper tantrums indicate that the student has difficulty with self-regulation. Intervention must be provided to teach the student in small incremental steps how to self-control. It is imperative that the atypical temper tantrum is not reinforced (Stoolmiller, M., 2001).

Responding to a temper tantrum:

When dealing with temper outbursts, teachers will need to be firm and not feel sorry for the student. Feeling sorry for a student, or giving in, will only make matters worse. If possible, teachers should try to ignore a temper tantrum and continue with classroom activity. Any response to a temper tantrum must be consistent. When the student is calm, let him know what he must do to get what he wants. Once the temper tantrum has begun to subside, try to provide a distraction to further reduce the behavior. Once a temper tantrum is over, later in the day, talk to the student about the misbehavior and try to appeal to his logic.

If the temper tantrum is related to an inability to self-control, it is very different from the tantrum that is for purposes of manipulation or power. When a typical student has a tantrum to manipulate, he knows exactly what he is doing and he is engaging in the behavior for a specific purpose. In contrast, when a tantrum is related to a lack of self-regulation, these students cannot control their behavior. Once the tantrum starts, they do not know how to pull it back. While the manipulative student has control, the atypical student loses all control.

The tantrum by a typical student will usually last for two to seven minutes, while the atypical student's tantrum may continue for ten to twenty minutes. These more difficult temper tantrums will subside only as the student becomes physically exhausted. Since these more difficult tantrums are not related to manipulation, they obviously will be more difficult to stop. When the atypical student is having a temper tantrum, move the student to an area so he will not hurt himself. If the student may injure himself by thrashing about, put a towel under his head or move him to a carpeted area and away from sharp corners or a hard floor. As the temper tantrum runs its course, try to comfort the student by rubbing his back or hair, while talking in a very calm and soothing voice. After the temper tantrum is over, talk to the student about his out-of-control behavior and offer alternative ways of handling a difficult situation.

Since the prognosis of helping an atypical student with these difficult tantrums is so minimal, one may ask, *"Why try?"* Consider the previous discussion of a student who graduates from a school district and fails to learn self-regulatory skills. They find themselves in a situation which calls for self-control, e.g. confronted by an aggressive drive, or an irate supervisor. If the student has not learned how to control his temper, he may get into a fight with the irresponsible driver or get fired from his job. Research has suggested that most young men between the ages of 18 and 25 in prison are there, not because they have a criminal personality, but because of a lack of self-regulation and self-control. They get themselves into a situation and do not know how to get themselves out. All this occurs because the student did not learn adequate self-regulation or self-control. Temper tantrums may be one of the early warning signs of a student that is not developing in the skill to practice self-control. This is why proactive discipline must teach self-discipline, self-control, and self-regulation. Proactive discipline is designed to teach students skills that they can use today, tomorrow, and a lifetime.

SUMMARY

Proactive discipline involves not only specific intervention strategies but also an understanding of emotional and behavioral outlets. When teachers make decisions about discipline, it is important to understand what might be causing a student to be disruptive. Some behaviors occur because the student is trying to manipulate, while others result from an inability to regulate emotions and behavior. When students are unable to regulate emotions and behavior, they may exhibit a variety of disruptive behaviors in the classroom. Such emotional deficits will be manifested as excessive fear, anxiety and anger, while behavioral outlets may include stuttering, tics, and tantrums. Responding to students who display emotional and behavioral issues will require more than typical intervention strategies. Discipline strategies for these students must also teach students self-regulation.

Chapter Ten

BEYOND DISCIPLINE: TEACHING
SELF-DISCIPLINE SKILLS
TO STUDENTS

The way teachers apply a consequence may be just as important as the consequence itself. It is not enough to simply know what consequence to use; a teacher must also know how to apply the consequence. In fact, how a consequence is applied will determine success or failure. Very often oppositional behaviors in the classroom are the result of teachers being inconsistent in the way consequences are applied. When inconsistencies exist, students view the consequences as punishment, rather than something that is designed to help them learn a more appropriate way of behaving.

A consequence should always be presented as an option of choices. As a result, students have a choice to continue the misbehavior or to accept the consequence of the inappropriate behavior. When consequences are used appropriately, they increase students' awareness of their present and future behavior. This awareness is accomplished when students are provided with a reminder of their behavior and the resulting consequence. In essence, a consequence will always provide students with choices. When applying a consequence which provides a choice, students are able to internalize the meaning of their behavior and gain greater insight into how their behavior resulted in the consequence (Marshall, M., 2005).

This method works to increase students' awareness of their

responsibility and provides them with choices. As a result of these choices, students are empowered. Students have the power to choose either to continue or discontinue their inappropriate behavior. It is this reminder and choice that provides students with a continuum from the present behavior to the future behavior. In addition, since choices empower students, their self-esteem is enhanced and this helps them become more responsible (Bernstein, D., Marx, M. S., and Bender, H., 2005).

Punishment:
Providing consequences is an alternative to punishment. Punishment tends to decrease self-esteem, while consequences are designed to build self-esteem. Punishment tends to emphasize power that one has over another, while a consequence places emphasis on students' right to choose. Punishment makes a demand of students and, in many cases, the demand is not logically related to the situation. In addition, punishment implies a moral judgment, and since most responses are to negative behavior, the judgment is, *"You are bad."* Since punishment equates the misdeed with the person, punishment is personalized. This suggests that the student is bad, instead of the behavior being bad. It is important for teachers to learn how to send a message that says, *"Although the behavior may be inappropriate, this does not mean that the student is bad"* (Moorefield, L., 2005).

In some cases teachers may attempt to apply a consequence but, because of the way it is applied, it ends up being a punishment. When teachers take actions that are related to past behavior instead of present or future behavior, the actions become a punishment. Since learning is an important component of proactive discipline, if learning does not take place, then the action is not a consequence. The purpose of a proactive discipline strategy is to enhance a student, not to destroy his self-esteem. Since punishment is personal attack, there is a tendency for such actions to put students down and show them disrespect. In some cases, punishment can be a demand for obedience under the threat of physical pain or the loss of a personal privilege. When decisions are made under the veil of threat, such decisions are not made out of respect and cooperation, but rather out of fear. A choice made under such circumstances is not a choice at all. Proactive consequences will teach students a more appropriate way of behaving while at the same time build their self-esteem.

As indicated, the problem is not always that the consequence is inappropriate, but the way in which the strategy is implemented makes it inappropriate. For example, you may recall in Chapter Six the discussion about how using time-out can be an effective consequence or it can be an ineffective punishment. Any discipline strategy must focus on the present and future behaviors, enhance the student's self-esteem, provide the student with a choice, teach the student an alternative behavior, and it must be logically related to the behavior. An alternative to punishment is to alter or withdraw a privilege until the student is better able to handle the activity in a responsible manner. While this book certainly does not endorse any type of physical restraint, in some cases teachers may need to gently guide a student to where he needs to go, or to remove an object from the student's hand. In the event that a student or an object must be physically removed, do so in a manner that conveys that you are not trying to hurt the student. If physical action is required, do not give the student attention or engage in discussion. In many situations, students will want to talk to the teacher once action is being taken. When this happens, their real effort is a ploy to manipulate or delay the teacher, and to get out of the consequence. However, regardless of the strategy selected to implement, it is always necessary to incorporate these five components mentioned above: 1) focus on the present and the future, 2) enhance the student, 3) provide a choice, 4) teach the student an alternative way of behaving, and 5) it must be logically related.

Making Reactive Discipline Proactive:

As previously mentioned, it is not that time-out or taking away a privilege or any other approach is not an effective consequence, it is the way these strategies are implemented that causes them to become a form of punishment. The following are steps that will help ensure that a discipline strategy will be proactive and will prevent it from becoming a punishment.

1. **Make sure students know what behaviors are required.** Making sure that students know the rules and expectations means to involve them in decisions about what is expected. Teachers will receive greater cooperation if students have been consulted about what they consider to be appropriate rules and expectations.

2. **Always provide reminders.** This recognizes that students often have short attention spans and a reminder will provide them with a "choice" to stop the behavior or face a consequence. It is another way to give students power.

3. **Take action consistently.** If misbehavior occurs after the reminder, take action immediately. Do not talk with the students while taking action. When teachers continue to give reminders they are being inconsistent. The objective of the student is to talk the teacher out of taking action. If you feel you need to talk with the student, simply let him know that you will talk with him when the consequence has been completed. If students are allowed to talk, it is not unusual for them to beg, plead and pester, until they are given what they want.

4. **Know the location or action you plan to take.** For example, if you are removing an object, know where you are going to place the object, or if you are removing the student from the situation, know where the student is to go.

5. **Talk to the student.** Once the consequence has been completed, and the student is calm, talk to him about the behavior. Avoid saying, *"Why did you do that?"* The word *"why"* is far too subjective for students to comprehend. In fact, many adults cannot adequately explain "why" they behave inappropriately. Instead of using the why word, use *"what."* Ask the student, *"What happened that caused you to have to be placed in the hallway?"* If the student acts as if he does not know, remind him of the classroom rule that was violated, and the reminder that was given.

6. **Re-establish a positive relationship.** Any type of consequence is an act of rejection. Therefore, following the completion of the consequence, it is important to re-establish the relationship with the student. This involves turning the liability that has occurred into an asset. As the student completes the consequence, find something positive to say about his behavior during the consequence. For example: *"I am really proud of you for being able to stand out in the hallway. Two weeks ago when you had to come out to the hallway, you made noise and kicked the door constantly. But today you stood here quietly. I can tell you are taking responsibility for yourself. I am proud of the maturity you are showing."* Give the student a pat on the back as a sign of approval.

7. **Provide a replacement behavior.** In order for an intervention strategy to be a proactive consequence, a replacement behavior must be provided. This becomes the teaching component of the discipline process. For example, ask the student what was going on that caused him to behave in such a manner. Make a suggestion of a different way the situation could be handled. This approach will "teach" the student an alternative way of

handling a problem.

8. **Provide a choice and reminder.** At the conclusion of the consequence ask the student if he wants to return to his previous activity, or do something else. For example, *"Do you want go back to your seat, or sit somewhere else?"* This provides students a choice to anticipate, predict and control their future. The reminder part focuses on the present and future by informing the student that if he engages in the behavior again, he will have to return to the consequence.

Some teachers may think the above steps are too extensive and will distract from the other students. However, if done properly, these steps should require no more than two to three minutes away from instruction. This is minimal, considering how much time is lost on inappropriate and ineffective attempts to change student behavior. In contrast, when students are sent out of the room and there is no follow-up discussion, no reestablishing of the relationship, no replacement behaviors taught, and no choices provided, the action becomes a punishment rather than a consequence.

Talking to Students:

Talking to students about their behavior can also be an effective discipline strategy. However, most teachers talk with students about their behavior when they and the students are upset. Talking to students when everyone is angry or frustrated is not helpful. Even adults have a hard time talking rationally when they are upset, so why would we expect a student to do so? Teachers are often surprised when they talk with their students during periods of calmness and discover that they are able to come up with acceptable alternatives to their misbehavior. When talking with students before the misbehavior occurs, it is much easier to establish acceptable rules of discipline. In addition, it is during this time of calmness that consequences can be discussed and cooperation sought. However, it is important to know when, where, and how to talk to students about their behavior problems.

1. Talk to students when there is not a problem. This will ensure that students are calm and they will be more receptive to the discussion.

2. Talk to students privately, away from their peers. When teachers attempt to talk with students about their behavior problems in front of their peers, students will often be embarrassed and will probably try to save face. They may start "fronting" the teacher and generally react negatively.

When teachers talk with students in the presence of their peers, they should not be surprised when the student denies the behavior or becomes defensive. After all, saving face in front of peers is usually more important than cooperating with a teacher.

3. **Make the timing convenient.** When talking with students, make sure it is a time that is convenient to you and the student. It is not a good idea to try and talk to a student about a problem in the hallway, between classes. Also, don't pull the student out of his favorite class to talk with them. Make sure that you have the time for the discussion and that it is not a time when the student would rather be somewhere else. For example, you may want to use your time for prep time to talk to a student. However, this is the time when the student has P.E. and P.E. is the only class the student likes.

4. **Keep the conversation informal.** Don't make the discussion a big deal. This is a time to get the student to talk a little about what is going on in his life. Let the student know that you just want to get to know him better.

5. **Appeal for assistance.** Tell the student that you really need his help. Let him know that he has great leadership skills; however, sometimes the leadership is negative. Inform the student other students often do whatever they do. They are not "making" students misbehave and it is not their fault. Instead place emphasis that they have the capacity to lead students to behave appropriately or inappropriately. Ask the student to help you by leading students toward positive behavior. Be sure to inform the student that no one knows about the discussion. Seek the student's cooperation and commitment to help you. This will empower the student and encourage more positive behavior.

6. **Avoid the shame/blame game.** Don't blame the student for the behavior of the other students. Instead, let the student know that the other students seem to follow him regardless of his behavior. Also, don't try to shame the student into cooperation. Students usually will rebel against shame and blame and often become more oppositional.

7. **Ask for feedback.** Asking for feedback can be as simple as asking, *"What do you think about what I have said?"* Allow the student time to respond. If the student is hesitant to cooperate, ask him if he is willing to try being more positive just for a couple of days to see how it works. When a student takes on this new role and the teacher provides plenty of praise and

recognition, in most cases the positive behavior will continue.

8. **Seek cooperation and agreement.** Conclude by asking the student again if he is willing to help you with the class. Remind the student that no other students know about the agreement. Be sure to shake hands as a seal of agreement. If the need for behavior is severe, the teacher and student might want to sign a contract for change.

Providing Choices:

On several occasions, the point has been made to provide students with choices. Some teachers may be wondering why choices are so important. Choices help students accept responsibility for their behavior while at the same time empower them to improve. In previous chapters it was suggested that these more challenging students often exhibit varying degrees of low self-esteem. Most teachers will agree that discipline should never be a contributing factor to student's low self-esteem. However, when effective discipline incorporates a choice, it empowers students and will enhance their self-esteem.

By providing choices, students will feel important knowing that they have some power over what happens to them. Therefore, when applying consequences, choices are essential. When students are given choices, teachers are essentially suggesting an alternative behavior. Once a choice is given, teachers will need to accept the student's decision. The student may choose to discontinue the inappropriate behavior or accept the consequences that have been presented. When giving students a choice to either discontinue their misbehavior or accept a stated consequence, there really is no reason to pity or feel sorry for the student. After all, they have made the decision to choose the consequence. However, very often teachers will continue to give one reminder after another rather than taking action. This inconsistency is confusing for the student (Havill, L. K., 2004).

When students choose to continue their inappropriate behavior, they are essentially deciding to accept the consequence for their behavior. When applying a consequence, be sure to remind the student that following the consequence, there will be an opportunity for him to make a better decision and change his behavior. Even if the student seems genuinely sorry for the inappropriate behavior, do not acquiesce and allow him to get out of the consequence. To do so would be inconsistent and will show the student he can talk his teacher out of the consequence. If, following the consequence, the student continues the inappropriate behavior it is apparent that the consequence used was not effective. Either the same consequence will need to be discontinued, or a different strategy implemented.

A part of the overall discipline process is to understand what the behavior is saying. Therefore, if the inappropriate behavior continues, try to determine what is causing the misbehavior and determine if the consequence is appropriate for the student. The teacher may discover that the consequence is not age-appropriate for the student, or perhaps the teacher may have been inconsistent in the past and the student did not realize that this time the teacher was serious.

Teachers must constantly be looking for ways to improve their use of consequences. It is not as simple as just applying consequences. Many factors are involved in changing behaviors from negative to positive. There are many subtle attitudes, feelings, and actions that can turn the best-intended consequences into punishment and render them ineffective (Rogers, W. A., 2002). The following are some of the most frequent attempts that result in consequences being ineffective.

1. **Being Inconsistent:** One of the major difficulties teachers encounter when applying consequences is being inconsistent. Obviously, no one is totally consistent; teachers are also human. However, teachers must work to respond to students in a consistent manner. If a behavior is ignored one day and then punished the next, students never know where they stand. In fact, this inconsistency is confusing when it exists from classroom to classroom. For example, if a student in seventh grade math class gets in trouble for talking, and then in his science class the behavior is allowed, it becomes confusing for students. Consistency is needed with individual teachers, but also throughout the school. It is strongly recommended that, at a minimum, all seventh grade teachers on a specific team get together and decide jointly what behaviors will be acceptable and unacceptable, and what consequences will be utilized.

2. **Pitying Students:** Another common mistake that teachers make when using consequences is to pity or feel sorry for their students. Over-protective teachers often have a hard time following through on consequences. They feel sorry that their students are "suffering" the consequences. Pitying a student can damage his self-esteem because it suggests that the student is too inadequate to live with the decisions he makes. Pity implies that students cannot handle life's requirements. Pitying often does

not stop with teachers but can lead to learned helplessness in students. When students learn to feel sorry for themselves they have a tendency to give up when they encounter difficult situations. These are the students who often respond, *"I can't," "I don't know how,"* or *"I don't want to."* Empathy is different from pity, in that empathy is an expression of concern by the teacher. The teacher is sorry that the student must experience the negative consequences of his behavior. Empathy allows teachers to express confidence that their students' will learn from the experiences. However, empathy does not negate the fact that the student must accept the consequence for the behavior.

3. **Concerned About Impressions:** Another mistake that some teachers make is to become concerned about what others (students, parents, colleagues, and administrators) may think of them. These teachers often fail to follow through on consequences because they fear that others may judge or blame them. This can be especially true for new or insecure teachers. Teachers must realize that there is no such thing as a "perfect" teacher. Just as with any area of life, teachers will make mistakes when using consequences and discipline. Teachers must realize that, in most cases, they have not been trained to manage classroom behavior. It is interesting that even though classroom behavior is one of the major issues teachers face, most college education programs do not require teachers to become skilled in this area. However, on a positive note, when teachers are concerned about improving their behavior management skills, they usually find a way to do so. Attending seminars, reading books, or taking a refresher course are all ways to improve these skills.

4. **Talking Too Much:** Another common error teachers make when implementing consequences is talking too much to their students. Usually the first thing that a teacher will do when a student misbehaves is to talk to him. Students expect to be lectured to or nagged. When teachers do exactly what students expect, it only reinforces the negative behavior. Most people do not listen or think rationally when they are angry or upset. Therefore, if students are not listening, there really is no reason to talk to them. Instead, replace the talking with action. If the situation does not require immediate attention, teachers may choose to follow the "silence is golden" rule. However, it is important to discuss the situation later when the student has calmed down and there are no conflicts. When deciding which situations require immediate attention, look realistically at the problem behavior. In most

cases talking to a student can be delayed. If the situation needs immediate attention, choose words wisely. Make sure that the discussion does not take place in front of his peers, do not belittle, blame, or engage in name-calling. If you decide that you must talk to the student during a point of conflict, be brief. Too much talking can lead to hints, reminders, and threats, all of which ruin what is trying to be accomplished. Once a student has been informed of an impending consequence, and he chooses to continue misbehaving, take action then talk with the student after the consequence.

5. **Use Appropriate Timing:** The effective use of consequences also requires appropriate timing. Appropriate timing is one of those factors that can cause what appears to be a proactive discipline strategy become ineffective. It is important that teachers choose the right time to talk to the student. As was previously discussed, most talking can be delayed until a time when both the teacher and student are calm. Talking during a conflict will often only produce hurt feelings and usually does not result in a lasting agreement. Most students will agree with just about anything when they are upset, anxious, or angry. Just as the timing of talking is important, the timing of a consequence is equally important. This is why it is important for teachers and students to decide in advance on the consequences that will be used for a specific behavior problem. Making these decisions when everyone is calm will prevent future classroom disruption.

6. **Avoid Hidden Motives:** In some situations teachers may have hidden motives when giving a consequence. This is especially true when teachers first learn about using consequences as a disciplinary tool. Consequences may be seen as a new trick to make the student behave. Consequences should never be used as a means of controlling students, but rather to teach them more appropriate way of behaving. For example, a teacher may assign a student the task of writing one hundred sentences just to keep the student busy. In every discipline strategy there should be an academic or behavioral objective. However, if consequences are given to control or keep a student busy, the motive will come through loud and clear. Also, never use a consequence to get even with students. When teachers feel like getting even, they are better off considering the potential negative results of revenge, than trying to use a consequence. Remember the old saying, "*If you are trying to get even, you will never get ahead!*"

7. **Don't Play Detective:** Another common mistake made by teachers is when they attempt to play detective, trying to find the guilty

party. While it may seem appropriate to discipline only the student you feel has caused the problem, this is actually an ineffective approach. To play detective and find the guilty party will increase classroom misbehavior. It is very common for such an approach as being a detective to result in competition and rivalry among students. Such an approach will help one student maintain his "good" student status, while making the other student look "bad". If this should happen, don't be surprised when the student who got into trouble seeks to get even with the other student, as well as with their teacher. In situations when there are multiple students involved in disruptive behavior, everyone will need to receive a consequence. This approach may seem unfair, but remember, going after the guilty student only adds a little more shine to the "good" student's halo.

8. **Rejecting the Student:** Another mistake that some teachers make is to reject their students instead of students' behavior. Proactive consequences do not focus on the student but rather the student's behavior. Everyone acts inappropriately at times, but this does not make everyone a bad person. If teachers believe that their students are basically worthwhile and that all behavior has meaning, then they are in a position to separate the student from the behavior. Students will need to understand that while their teacher may reject their behavior, they are not personally being rejected.

Before deciding what specific type of consequence to apply, it is important to understand that the benefit of a consequence is directly related to how the consequence is applied. A consequence may be rendered ineffective if applied inappropriately. The following are some suggestions that will enhance the effectiveness of a consequence (Brady, K., Forton, M. B., Porter, D., and Wood, C., 2003).

1. **First, try to determine what the student is attempting to communicate through his inappropriate behavior.** After considering what might be causing the student's misbehavior, decide if a consequence is needed and if so, what type. Based on what has been discovered, it may be appropriate to not apply any consequence, and allow a natural consequence to occur. Natural consequences occur without a teacher's involvement. However, some misbehavior may require a logical consequence. Misbehavior often occurs secondary to a need for attention, power, revenge, or to display his inadequacies. When students seek attention through misbehavior, it is best to avoid giving the attention that is being demanded. If power appears to be the goal, it is best to withdraw from the conflict. If seeking revenge is the

goal of misbehavior, try to avoid feeling angry, and do not respond back to the student with revenge. Instead, focus on building a trusting relationship with all students. Last, never allow students to display their inadequacies. To do so is to agree that they are indeed inadequate. Typical ways students display their inadequacy is by failing to complete an assignment, saying they don't know how to do the work, or in general they refuse to try.

2. **Another important consideration before giving a consequence is to determine who owns the problem.** Who could possibly own the problem? It could be a teacher problem. The curriculum may not match the student's learning style, the presentation of material may be boring or meaningless to the students, the classroom could be disorganized or messy, or the teacher could have a personality conflict with the student. Of course, the problem may belong to the student. Usually when a student owns the problem, natural or logical consequences will follow. For example, if a student refuses to complete his class assignment, he receives a failing grade. However, if as a result of the failure the student does not qualify to participate in a sporting event, a natural and logical consequence has occurred. A logical consequence is directly related to the student's misbehavior. In order to avoid being part of the problem, teachers need to make sure that the material is relevant and applicable, the classroom is well organized, and that the material is presented in such a way that it matches students' learning styles.

3. **The purpose of proactive discipline is to teach students more appropriate ways of behaving.** When using consequences, it is important to provide students with alternatives to their misbehavior. This will allow them to make better decisions in the future. When allowing the student to make choices, be prepared to accept whatever decision he may make.

4. **If a student decides that he would prefer to experience the consequence rather than amend his inappropriate behavior, or to complete the assigned task, a consequence is appropriate.** Once a consequence has been given, following through is imperative. When the consequence is over, the student may wish to change his behavior or complete the task. Even though the student may promise to amend his behavior, the consequence must still be given. An example of this process can be demonstrated through a common experience that most teachers have encountered. It is not unusual for students to interrupt their teacher while they are talking to another student, parent, or even an administrator. When this happens the appropriate response is to give the student a choice of

either stopping their interruption or receive a consequence, such as to go to a certain location in the room until you are finished. When the reminder is given, most students will stop the interrupting momentarily, and then will interrupt again. When the student interrupts again, the appropriate response is to send the student to a specific location in the room for a short period of time. By telling the student to go to another part of the room, "until" you are finished, you imply that he may return at a later time (when you are finished). Teachers must also consider the student's goal for the behavior. Be sensitive to any behavioral and emotional issues that may contribute to the student's disruption behavior. However, regardless of the causation for disruptive behavior, students must learn to practice self-control.

5. **When dealing with students displaying disruptive behavior, avoid using words such as "should," "ought," "must," or "have to."** These words are judgmental and convey that the teacher has power over the students. Many disruptive students have a tendency to be oppositional, and these types of messages may lead to more conflict. Also, avoid using phrases that students may perceive as sarcasm or put-downs. An example of a simple phrase that could be received as a put down is, *"I have told you a hundred times to stop."* This simple statement suggests that the student must be stupid and should know better. Teachers will forget these little throw-away lines within a few minutes, but students may remember them for hours. When a student has been hurt by such statements, the natural tendency is to "get even" with the person that hurt them. Rather than using words or phrases that may offend students, focus on their inappropriate behavior and the alternatives that are presented. An example of how to respond to the difficult student is as follows: *"Either you change your behavior or you will have to ... you decide."* Other examples of appropriate responses are, *"You have a choice, you can either stop or...." "I am sorry, but...."* and *"You may as long as you...."*

6. **It is best to focus on what is positive about students, rather than what is negative.** In other words, catch students being good instead of catching them being bad. When teachers focus on students' positive behaviors, there is a greater opportunity to reinforce the positive, rather than giving attention for the negative behaviors. When a consequence must be provided for negative behavior, as soon as the student engages in some appropriate behavior, seize the opportunity to provide praise. This approach will help students separate their behavior from themselves personally. It makes clear that while the behavior is unacceptable, the student is still cared about.

7. **There are several advantages to talking with students about the classroom rules and resulting consequences.** Students are far more committed to consequences when they are involved in the decision-making process. Also, when students are involved in the decision-making process they are empowered. However, there will be certain times when negotiation is not appropriate. It is during these times when teachers will need to assure their students that they are sorry, but the consequence will have to be applied. When this situation occurs, let the students know why they are not being allowed to have input into the consequence. In times when the situation does not allow for negotiation, or if the students prove they are not ready to handle a situation, it will be important to be fair but firm with the student. Also, guard against the consequence that may become a punishment. Punishment is related to revenge or anger toward students, rather than a proactive effort to correct or teach students more appropriate behaviors.

The objective of any discipline program is to assist students in changing inappropriate behaviors to appropriate behaviors and to ensure that the changed behaviors are integrated to last a lifetime. Most students can adjust their behavior for a short period of time. However, the objective of a proactive discipline strategy is to teach students to maintain positive behavior over a long period of time (Walker-Dalhouse, D.; 2005). In doing so, students will become more responsible in their actions throughout their lives. Another objective of proactive discipline is to help students stop engaging in the same inappropriate and often destructive behaviors over and over. Teachers must ask: *"How can I bring about long-term change in my students?"*

One of the most powerful ways to encourage appropriate behavior in challenging students is by modeling positive responsive behavior. When teachers are angry and say hurtful things to students, students are likely to become angry and say hurtful things to each other, and to their teacher. Teachers must realize just how much power they have in the classroom. Students will often respond in a similar fashion to their teacher (Lasley, T. J., II, Siedentop, D., and Yinger, R., 2006). I recall when I was in private practice seeing a mother who was complaining that her three-year-old child often hit her. During the session the child was playing, making a little noise that was typical for three-year-olds. Without even thinking, the mother reached down and slapped the child on the leg. Several minutes later the mother was ready to leave and the child was enjoying playing with some toys. As the mother insisted that the child put the toys away, the child stood up and hit the mother in the face. The mother turned to me and said, *"See how aggressive he is?"* This mother did not realize how much she had influenced her child's behavior.

Instead of allowing disruptive behavior to continue, teachers can help students make changes by teaching them alternative ways of behaving. This can often be accomplished by talking with the student and modeling appropriate behaviors. However, if a teacher tells students how to stop a certain behavior, then the students see their teacher engaging in inappropriate behavior, it sends a confusing message. The old saying, *"Actions speak louder than words"* is truer than we often realize.

As teachers implement proactive discipline strategies classroom behavior problems will decrease. As this is occurring, the previous ways the students had used to get their needs met will slowly discontinue. However, teachers must realize that the same needs that were causing the misbehavior will still be present. In other words, while the misbehavior may decrease, the needs remain the same. As a student's misbehavior decreases, it is important to find ways to meet the student's needs in positive ways. This may be accomplished by providing the student with praise and attention when positive behaviors occur. The response is to help students get their needs meet in a positive rather than negative manner. When positive consequences are applied to appropriate behaviors, the changed behaviors are strengthened. However, if teachers fail to provide positive reinforcement to positive behaviors, students will revert to their old ways of getting their needs met (Oswald, K., Safran, S., and Johanson, G., 2005).

It is not unusual for the more challenging students to have some sensory issues that can prevent them from understanding instructions. Difficulty expressing oneself or taking in information is related to an inability to process information. Therefore, when teachers give instructions that are vague and non-specific, this will increase the potential for disruption and noncompliance. Vague instructions such as, *"Johnny, stop disrupting the class,"* does not adequately describe what the student is doing or is supposed to do. Instead, state specifically what the student is doing that is disruptive to the class. Instead say, *"Johnny, stop talking while others are reading!"* This statement is a detailed description of the inappropriate behavior being exhibited by the student. Instructions should always be as specific as possible so students know exactly what they are doing, and what you want them to do, or what you want them to do differently (Lenze, L. F.,1996).

Another common mistake teachers make is to give instructions that are a polite request rather than a statement of fact. Using the above-stated example, the teachers may state, *"Johnny, will you please stop talking while others are trying to read?"* This statement is a polite request and it gives the student a choice ("will you") and it is like begging the student to cooperate ("please"). While the statement does not need to be a polite request, neither does it need to be authoritative or negative. When statements are made negatively, students tend to respond negatively. The statement must be firm, while telling the student exactly what he is doing that he needs to do differently. For example: *"Johnny, I want you to stop talking out loud while others are reading."* This may sound like a minor issue. However, you will be amazed the difference in how students respond when the statement is made specific and firm.

Teachers must decide if they want to give students choices about disrupting their classrooms, or to provide a direct command to stop. If the student has a choice, then a polite request would be appropriate. However, if the objective is for the student to stop interrupting the class, to say, *"Will you please stop interrupting the class?"* would not be appropriate. When giving students a polite request, the student has to option of saying, "Yes" or "No." When students are given a choice to continue or discontinue disruptive behaviors, don't be surprised or frustrated when they choose to continue. The question is not, *"Will you stop interrupting?"* The response must be a polite statement with a fact. Saying, *"Johnny, I want you to stop interrupting now,"* is a polite statement of fact, and does not give the student a choice (Hampel, P., and Petermann, F., 2005).

Behavior can also be changed by making situations consistent and routine. Students with processing deficits tend to respond better to situations that are structured, rather than unstructured. Fewer behavior problems will occur in the classroom if there is an established routine that is followed every day. Students with sensory issues often have difficulty handling transition. They do not like surprises. Having routines in the classroom allows students to know what is going to happen and what is expected. These routines provide predictability and consistency for the student. Routines may exist of rules, the way the classroom flows, the way material is presented, and when certain events will occur (Sheinman, A. J., 2000).

When students are trying to learn new ways of behaving, it would not be fair to expect them to do everything correctly immediately, or without help. Just as when students struggle with reading they are provided academic assistance, students must also receive help behaviorally. Sadly, some people only consider student failure from an academic standpoint. However, students can experience failure emotionally, socially, and behaviorally. Therefore, don't give up on students when they fail behaviorally. These students will need constant reminders about their behavior and will need to be taught the tools to guide them toward more appropriate classroom functioning. A consequence is defined as a reaction resulting from a student's behavior. To increase success, a consequence must occur immediately after the student's behavior and should result in a learning experience. Consequences can be natural or logical, and positive or negative (Deroma, V. M., Lassiter, K. S., and Davis, V. A., 2004).

Natural Consequences:

Natural consequences are those consequences that occur without a teacher's involvement. In essence, the consequence is a direct result of the student's behavior. Some of the most powerful lessons learned are those that result from natural consequences. An example of a natural consequence might be when a student loses his homework assignment and he receives a zero for a grade. This consequence is further strengthened because the parents are informed and may take some type of punitive action. As a direct result of not taking care of the homework assignment, the student experiences failure, and possible parental rejection. After experiencing the natural consequence, the next time the student will take care to place the homework assignment in a location where it is safe. Natural consequences are also beneficial because they take the teacher out of the role of giving the consequence. Essentially, nature takes care of the consequence. However, if the student has difficulty with organization skills, it is imperative that the overall discipline strategy includes giving suggestions on how to be better organized (Stichter, J. P., Conroy, M. A., and Boyd, B. A., 2005).

Logical Consequences:

Logical consequences are consequences that are applied by the teacher. The word "logical" comes from the fact that the consequence is somehow logically related to the student's misbehavior. When consequences are given that are unrelated to the inappropriate behavior, students may become confused as to why they are receiving a consequence. For example, if a student is acting up in class and he loses recess, he will not draw a connection between his behavior in the class and the lost activity. Such a consequence is in no way related to the misbehavior. Therefore, for the consequence to teach the student a new way of behaving, the consequence will need to be related. An appropriate logical consequence or response to the above-stated conflict would be to remove the student from the classroom for a period of time. Unless consequences are logically related to misbehavior, there is little chance that students will improve their behavior (Charney, R. S., 2002).

A natural consequence represents a violation of the "natural order" of relationships, while logical consequences represent a violation of the "logical order." Logical consequences are effective only when they are logically related to the misbehavior, presented as a choice, and administered in a firm but fair way.

SUMMARY

Proactive discipline is not only doing something to students, it involves the way interventions are implemented. In many cases, well-intended strategies become acts of punishment because of the way they are applied. This chapter deals with those issues that can be used to ensure that discipline strategies are proactive and effective. The five most important factors that render strategies ineffective are: being inconsistent, failing to talk with students after the consequence is completed, not re-establishing the relationship with the student after the consequence, failing to provide the student with a replacement behavior, and failing to provide students with choices.

Talking with students can become an effective discipline strategy. The important thing to remember when talking with students is to follow some strategy. For example, talk with students in private and away from their peers to avoid embarrassment. Always make sure you have time to talk to the student. This means pulling the student aside to talk just before class is to start would be inappropriate. So, choose a time that is convenient. Keep the conversation informal and seek the help of the student. Never talk to students about a behavior problem when they are angry, it will only make it worse.

Another way to move beyond discipline is to always provide students with choices. Choices empower students and help them take responsibility for their behavior. When students make a choice to continue with their misbehavior after a reminder has been given, they are choosing to receive a consequence. A consequence may be either natural or logical. A natural consequence occurs without the help of a teacher, while a logical consequence is given by the teacher, but it is logically related to the behavior. In essence, it makes sense.

Chapter Eleven

PROACTIVE DISCIPLINE MEANS BUILDING AND MAINTAINING SELF-ESTEEM IN THE CLASSROOM

Teachers may question their role in building self-esteem. A point has been made that teachers are responsible for teaching an academic curriculum and for students' safety. Are they also responsible for building and maintaining their students' emotional well-being? In relationship to proactive discipline, building self-esteem and maintaining student self-esteem is an integral part of the total process. Research has suggested that when students have a high self-esteem they are less likely to misbehave or act out (Cramer, P.; 2006, Gendron, M.; Royer, E.; Bertrand, R.; and Potvin, P., 2004, Lopez, Cristy, and DuBois, D. L., 2005). However, in order to build self-esteem, it is important to have an understanding of how self esteem can impact behavior. Obviously, one's self-esteem is crucial to the overall development of a child. The following is a list of characteristics that are usually present when students are experiencing high self-esteem (Johnson, F., 1996).

1. Students feel that they are important to someone who is important to them.

2. Students feel special even though they are unable to put into words why they are special.

3. Students feel that they can accomplish things and have the

confidence to try new experiences.

A student's self-esteem will be demonstrated more through their behavior than their words. Research suggests that when students brag on themselves, it is an indication that they are attempting to compensate for having a low self-esteem. In fact, when students exaggerate their abilities or brag on themselves, they may be attempting to compensate for feelings of inadequacy. Self-esteem is best observed in students by how they behave, especially in times of conflicts (Delisle, J., and Galbraith, J., 2002).

Most students with high self-esteem are able to handle conflicts that come their way. When students with high self-esteem are unable to succeed they will seek alternatives or accept the situation. However, when students are experiencing low self-esteem they tend to allow the stress of life to pull them down. These students tend to respond to stress much like a poorly insulated building in the middle of a winter storm. When the stress is too great they must exert considerable energy to maintain homeostasis. Students with low self-esteem are often afraid of failure and of what others might think of them. As a result they will often simply give up rather than face the possibility of failure (Rogers, Bill, Ed., 2004).

It is important to remember that self-esteem is expressed by how one acts, and not necessarily by what one may say. Self-esteem is different from self-concept. Essentially, self-concept is what students may "believe" about themselves, while self-esteem is the behavior that one exhibits. In some situations a student's self-concept (belief) may not match his behavior (self-esteem). An example of this is when a student states that he is the most popular student in school, but receives few invitations to social events, or a student may state that he is one of the best basketball players in school, but does not attempt to play on the high school team.

Self-concept and self-esteem are similar in that both will enhance a student's sense of personal satisfaction:

1.   A student has successfully expressed his self-concept and self-esteem when he sees themselves as being good at athletics and trys out for the basketball team.

2. They live up to their own expectations or the expectations of someone they value, such as receiving a compliment for a job well done.

3. The student's self-concept (self-belief) is confirmed by others, such as when he is praised.

An important quality for a proactive teacher is to know how to tell when a student has high or low self-esteem. There are numerous test instruments available to measure a student's self-esteem. However, before rushing off to have a students' self-esteem evaluated, review the statements below which are paired with the behavioral characteristics of both high and low self-esteem. Remember, exhibited behaviors are the best indicators of self-esteem. These characteristics will provide a general idea of how self-esteem is manifested (Spooner, Andrea L., Evans, M. A., and Santos, R., 2005).

Signs of High Self-Esteem

Behavior	Statement
Students take pride in accomplishments	"I really like this project I worked on.
Acts independently and assumes responsibility.	"I can finish this by myself" or "I'll take that to the office for you."
Tolerates frustration well.	"Boy, these practices are hard, but I can do it."
Approaches new challenges with excitement.	"Man, tomorrow we are going to start learning math divisions."
Feels capable of influencing others.	"Here, let me show you how to do it."
Exhibits a wide range of emotions	"It is a great feeling to win, but lousy to lose."

Signs of Low Self-Esteem

Behavior	Statement
Tends to avoid situations that provoke anxiety.	"I don't want to read aloud, I'll just mess up and everyone will laugh."

Discounts own talents and accomplishments.	"My project looks like crap."
Feels that others don't like him.	"Everybody on the team hates me."
Blames others for own mistakes	"You didn't tell me to do the math problem using fractions."
Is easily influenced by others.	"I know I should not have gone along with them, but they dared me to."
Becomes defensive or easily upset.	"It is not my fault I missed the shot. I'll just quit the team."
They feel powerless.	"I'll never finish this assignment. Everybody else is using the markers."
Exhibits a narrow range of emotions.	"I don't care."

Because self-esteem is related to self-concept, students are motivated to act in ways that demonstrate both. There are three major factors that affect the behavior of students and influence how they feel and think about themselves.

1. Students will act in ways that will increase their sense of self-worth and satisfaction. Most students seek praise.

2. Students will act in ways to confirm how they perceive others' view of them. An example: If students think their teacher views them positively, they will act appropriately. However, if they think their teacher sees them as being negative, they will seek criticism and punishment.

3. Students will act so as to maintain a consistent self-image, even if their environment changes. An example: If students feel badly about themselves, they will perform badly even if they are capable of performing well. This becomes very frustrating for teachers and administrators because they know if they can change the classroom or curriculum for their students,

it will change the student. However, in these situations even when classes or curriculum changes are made and schedules are modified, without something happening to change the student's self-esteem or self-concept, he will continue to misbehave.

Manifestations of Low Self-Esteem:

In psychology we know that the body will always let you know about your emotions. When students have low self-esteem, their behavior will reflect it. Students do not have adequate verbal skills to express their emotions; therefore, they often will "show" a teacher how they feel. Students will express their feelings about themselves through their behavior. When students have experienced low self-esteem for a long time, negative behaviors tend to become habits, and habits are very difficult to change. This becomes cyclical. A student may experience something that is interpreted as being negative. He feels badly, then he behaves in ways to match his feelings. As this pattern continues, a student's sense of self-worth, self-image, self-esteem and self-concept all become increasingly negative and this ensures continued failure (Michie, F., Glachan, M., and Bray, D., 2001).

Low self-esteem impacts on every aspect of a person's life. It is important for teachers to understand how low self-esteem can affect a student. Self-esteem will impact students emotionally, socially, academically, physically and even psychologically. The following list indicates some of the ways in which each of these five areas is affected by low self-esteem.

1. **Emotionally:** Students with low self-esteem tend to become upset easily, are usually very sensitive, they will often have many unpredictable temper outbursts, and may become aggressive, verbally and physically.

2. **Socially:** Students with low self-esteem often experience peer rejection and conflict. They are often withdrawn or become isolated. They tend to have difficulty relating to others or participating in groups.

3. **Academically:** Students with low self-esteem often have trouble concentrating, they tend to perform poorly, and will often exhibit a great deal of anxiety when trying to complete a difficult task. While these students may be fairly intelligent, their academic performance is often far below their capability. (These students are often misdiagnosed as being ADHD).

4. **Physically:** Students with low self-esteem often complain of stomach aches, headaches, and may have some nervous habits; e.g. frequently biting their nails. These students often suffer from allergies and frequent

infections. (Experiencing low self-esteem can be stressful and it is this stress that often breaks down the immune system, resulting in a greater number of illnesses).

5. **Psychologically:** Students with low self-esteem will often act in an aggressive or bizarre way. These students may on occasion display signs and symptoms of suggesting neurotic or psychotic features.

Students with low self-esteem often do not feel that they are important to people who are important to them, such as teachers, certain peers or parents. In some cases, these students report that they feel that their teacher does not like them. As a result, students with low self-esteem often feel that people are against them and looking for things that are wrong. However, most often they cannot explain exactly why people don't like them. Because of the low self-esteem, these students often feel incapable of handling stressful situations, and various classroom challenges will often provoke anxiety. These students experiencing low self-esteem will often expend great energy and effort trying to avoid challenging tasks. This approach to avoidance indicates that these students would prefer not trying a particular task than face the possibility of failure or rejection. Low self-esteem can cause students to show little interest in accomplishing various tasks and have no special goals. Students with low self-esteem are often mistaken as being lazy or unmotivated when, it fact, it is their emotional state that is causing the behavior (Watkins, D. E., 2005).

Students with low self-esteem will often express little self-satisfaction and tend to blame others for their mistakes. These students often make excuses for themselves and refuse to accept responsibility for their own mistakes. It is not unusual to find students with low self-esteem being jealous of others, noticing what others have and what they do not have. These students will often accuse their teacher of having favorites or treating other students better than they treat them.

Students exhibiting low self-esteem are often dependent and will try to get their teacher or peers to complete things for them that they can do for themselves. For example, a second grade student may ask his teacher to tie his shoes. Dependent students tend to be followers instead of leaders, and are easily influenced by their peers. These students also tend to have a low frustration tolerance. They allow little things in the classroom (someone looking at them) to upset them. Making matters worse, these students will often refuse to talk about their feelings and may even deny that they have feelings. Much of the disruptive behaviors that occur in classrooms are related to this problem. This unwillingness to address feelings can become a significant problem. When students refuse to talk about their feelings, they will usually end up acting them out (Akos, P., and Galassi, J., 2004).

When students have low self-esteem they often experience considerable stress. It is fairly easy to identify students under stress. Stress will be manifested in a variety of ways. Students under stress experience increased physical symptoms such as stomach aches, headaches, diarrhea, and on occasion, vomiting. In addition to the above-mentioned physical symptoms of stress, teenagers may also experience an increased heart rate and poor circulation in their hands and feet, causing both extremities to be cold. Stress can also cause students to experience chest pains, dizziness or fainting spells. It is not unusual to find students with low self-esteem experiencing asthmatic discomforts, allergic attacks, difficulty breathing, increased respiratory infections, and tightness in the chest. Other symptoms teachers often observe in students during times of stress include nail-biting, thumb-sucking, incontinence, disturbed sleep patterns, nightmares, and even facial tics (Fredriksen, K., Rhodes, J., Reddy, R., and Way, N., 2004).

Psychologically, low self-esteem can cause a student to exhibit increased irritability. When students are under stress, minor things will cause them frustration. These students tend to become more dependent on their teachers, and may engage in more arguments with adults and peers. Students under stress will also experience increased temper tantrums and appear to lose control more easily (Gendron, M., Royer, E., Bertrand, R., and Potvin, P., 2004).

From a social standpoint, students with low self-esteem may have problems relating to their peers. Teachers report that students with low self-esteem are more withdrawn or socially isolated. Peer conflict seems to occur more frequently. Stressful students will often respond with sarcastic statements about themselves and others. In many instances these students seem to delight in belittling or teasing other students or may fabricate stories and go to great lengths to tell bizarre or exaggerated tales to gain attention (Brasler, C. E.,and Laursen, E. K., 2005).

While most teachers are able to identify students experiencing low self-esteem, just identifying the issue is not enough. Educators have principles to live by. One such principle is that any action must be both necessary and sufficient. While being able to identify low self-esteem is necessary, it is not sufficient. Proactive teachers must also know how to build positive self-esteem in their classroom. Building self-esteem is perhaps more important than recognizing self-esteem. Research has suggested that inadequate self-esteem appears to be lacking more often in students who display challenging behaviors than in the general population. Self-esteem is a serious issue and should not be taken lightly. For example, Hunsucker (1976) reported that low self-esteem is related to numerous social problems such as increased drug use among teenagers, promiscuous sexual behavior, destructiveness, vandalism, and dishonesty. However, there are some myths related to self-esteem that can cause teachers to misunderstand self-esteem or to respond to it inappropriately.

Myths of Self-Esteem

Don't despair—there are several actions that can be taken to increase students' self-esteem. However, first a teacher must recognize the various myths that exist regarding self-esteem (Cokley, K. O.2003).

1. **Some people feel that self-esteem is a function of lower socio-economic status.** This is blatantly untrue. Low self-esteem is found in students of every socio-economic level. Rich kids and poor kids alike experience low and high self-esteem.

2. **A second myth is that good behavior is an indicator of high self-esteem.** Good behavior can be deceiving. Some students exhibit compliant behavior, yet take little pride in their accomplishments or themselves. Students with low self-esteem may accomplish a great deal, but still continue to think of themselves as failures. Psychologists refer to this phenomenon as the "imposter syndrome." These students tend to feel that even though they accomplish certain goals, they are unworthy and feel as though they are "imposters." When students fail to take credit for their accomplishments or discount their successes, it is important to teach these students not only to take responsibility for their failures but also to accept their successes.

3. **A third myth concerning self-esteem is that when a child is loved they will naturally develop a healthy, high self-esteem.** Obviously, all children need to be loved and cared about, but to assume that love will cause a student to overcome low self-esteem is an excessively simplified answer to a very complex issue. Self-esteem is complex because no one thing leads to a healthy self-esteem. Loving children is important, but other factors must be present in order to build and maintain a student's self-esteem.

Formula for Building Self-Esteem in the Classroom

In addition to understanding what contributes to students' self-esteem, there are several things that can be done proactively to build and maintain self-esteem in students. It is important for teachers to spend time building students' self-esteem. Research by Storksen, I., Roysamb, E., Moum, T., and Tambs, K. (2005) suggests that two consecutive years of low self-esteem will become manifested as depression. Of course, self-esteem is a state of being. That is, self-esteem can be increased or decreased depending on the events that occur. However, depression is more problematic and can be more difficult to change. There are several things that a teacher can do to build self-esteem in the classroom. When implementing strategies to building self-esteem, however, there are certain factors that must take place in the classroom (Johnson, F. 1996).

1. **Warmth and Caring:** The first step in building students' self-esteem is to provide them with a classroom that communicates warmth and caring. Acceptance and praise says to students that they are cared about and that their teacher enjoys being around them. There are several ways teachers can show students that they are cared about. Doing something special every once in a while for students tells them that they are special. This can sometimes be as simple as bringing in a special treat for students or going outside to play basketball with them. When teachers do these things it sends the message that their teacher enjoys spending time with them. If fact, the message is, *"There are many things that I could be doing, but nothing is more important than spending some time with you."* Doing something special for students is different from helping students with an assignment. While it is important to help students with their assignments, this is a part of the teacher's job, and does not communicate that the students are special and important.

2. **Encouragement:** An environment that provides warmth and caring is a healthy start toward encouraging students. Providing encouragement is one of the necessary ingredients for building students' self-esteem. Students will need to receive encouragement to do things that are difficult or which might result in failure. It is important for students to at least try to complete a task. Without trying there can be no learning. Teachers must help students understand that there is no such thing as failure. Failure only means that the students have not yet mastered the task. They

must be willing to try and fail in order to learn. Students who are not afraid to try new things tend to have higher self-esteem than students who are afraid of new experiences.

3. **Decision Making:** After providing students with warmth, caring and encouragement, teachers will now have the opportunity to teach students how to make positive decisions and to be held accountable for those decisions. A real weakness in decision-making skills exists in our society, from political leaders, company presidents, to drug users. People need to learn to make difficult decisions in their everyday life. Unless students are given choices, they will never learn to make good decisions. Students that grow up in an environment where they are not allowed to choose or be held accountable are more likely to become irresponsible and dependent. When teachers are inconsistent and fail to hold their students responsible for their choices, they contribute to their students' low self-esteem.

4. **Positive Expectation:** The next ingredient to building students' self-esteem is to have positive expectations. However, having positive expectations of students without providing them with the other necessary ingredients can result in undue pressures and lead to self-destructive behaviors. When positive expectations are balanced with warmth and caring, encouragement, and the opportunity to make decisions, students will strive to develop their positive self-esteem.

5. **Be Firm, But Fair:** The final ingredient for helping students develop a positive self-esteem has to do with being firm, but always fair. Being both firm and fair can be difficult to accomplish. In addition to determining how high the expectations should be for students, teachers must also decide how firm they should be. However, if teachers have a good understanding of students' goals and motivations for their misbehavior and discipline is coupled with warmth, caring, encouragement, the opportunity to choose, and positive expectations, firm but fair discipline will come more easily and lead to positive self-esteem in students. Firmness refers to being consistent and providing structure. Fairness, however, is not treating every student the same. Fairness is treating each student according to their special needs. For example, it would not be fair to expect an ADHD fifth grade student to remain seated for fifty minutes completing a math assignment. However, this may be a behavior that a typical student could accomplish. Fairness is treating each student differently, based on their individual needs.

Proactive discipline is not "doing something" to students, but rather it is a multi-modal approach that involves everything that goes on in the classroom. Building students' self-esteem is an important part of a total discipline process. While most teachers understand the importance of meeting the physical, academic and social needs of their students, meeting students' emotional needs is just as important. As with any academic or discipline intervention, when building students' self-esteem teachers must develop and utilize specific strategies. While previous chapters have stressed the importance of providing positive reinforcement and communicating effectively with students, it is equally important to help students by showing empathy, helping them learn to accept compliments, and teaching them how to handle criticism and conflict. When these areas are not appropriately addressed, students will struggle with their emotional development in relationship to self-esteem and will have more classroom behavior problems.

While teachers are responsible for maintaining a safe learning environment, they cannot possibly watch every student every minute of the day. Students must learn how to handle conflicts on their own. It is not unusual for students to experience teasing, bullying and rejection at some point when at school. If students can learn the skills necessary to manage these difficult situations on their own, there will be fewer behavioral conflicts in the classroom. While there is currently a great deal of discussion and research focusing on bullying, the emphasis has been on the bully, not the victim. While it is important to understand why some children become bullies, it is also reasonable for teachers to understand what students may be doing to invite bullying. This does not mean that we need to re-victimize or blame students that are being bullied but rather to consider what these students may be doing to unconsciously invite such behavior.

Teasing and bullying often occur when students react to the behavior of others. Since it is a reaction that the teaser is trying to get, when the student reacts, he is essentially reinforcing the bully's behavior. One skill that students must be taught is how to control their reactions. In most situations, the teasing or bullying will discontinue when this occurs (Gropper, N., and Froschl, M., 2000).

There are several ways to teach students how to not react to teasing. Students must learn that name calling or putting others down is one of the ways other people compensate for their own low self-esteem. This information will help students understand that the real problem is not with them, but rather with the bully (Dufresne, J., 2005). Therefore, when students are called names, it really indicates that the other person has low self-esteem and is only trying to put someone down to feel bigger. Since teasing does not signify anything about the victim, the victim does not have to react. In fact, when students react to name calling, teasing, or bullying behavior they are actually giving significance to the behavior. When teasing and bullying cause a reaction, this empowers the teaser or bully and empowers them to repeat the behavior (Sprague, J. R., and Walker, H. M., 2004).

There are several techniques that can be taught to students that will help them learn how to take power away from the teaser or bully.

1. **Agreement:** One such technique is to agree with the statement.

This is accomplished when the teased student simply agrees with the teaser. For example, if a student is being made fun of because he is not very good at basketball, he may agree, saying; *"You may be right, but I still enjoy playing basketball."* If the teaser sees that his comments are not getting a reaction, the put-downs will probably stop.

2. **Emotional Shrug:** Another technique is the emotional shrug.

This technique can be used to take the sting out of name calling or put-downs. The emotional shrug teaches teased students to shrug their shoulders and say, *"So what."*

Some teachers have attempted to teach their students to ignore or just walk away when they are being teased or called names. While this may work sometimes, at other times it may indicate to the bully that the student is weak. To ask a student to ignore or walk away when he is being teased is asking a lot. It is usually best to respond in a way that suggests that the teasing really does not matter. The opposite of a conflict is not avoidance, it is indifference (Damiani, V. B., 2006).

When building self-esteem in students it is just as important to avoid being negative as it is to be positive. While it takes a great deal of time and effort to build a student's self-esteem, it will only take a moment to destroy it. There are a variety of things teachers should and should not do when building students' self-esteem.

1. **Learn to offer encouragement that is helpful and specific.** Tell students specifically what you like about their behavior or acknowledge their accomplishments in a very specific way, such as, *"I really liked that you helped with the lunch count today."*

2. **Another important factor for building self-esteem involves learning to effectively communicate with students.** Teachers must learn

to listen closely to students' words and pay attention not only to the words that are being said, but also to the feelings behind the words. Effective communication means to maintain eye contact and posture in a way that indicates interest in what students are saying. This action will build self-esteem.

3. **Building students' self-esteem involves providing them with opportunities to develop their creativity.** When students are allowed to solve problems through their own creativity they feel better about their accomplishments. However, if the student fails to solve the problem correctly avoid criticizing him. This will hurt his self-esteem even more.

4. **Another important way to build students' self-esteem is to teach students good social skills.** It is not unusual to find students coming from home environments where poor or limited social skills are practiced. Research has pointed out that students who exhibit poor social skills tend to have greater peer conflict. Therefore, it is important to teach students appropriate social skills, then to allow them to practice them. Of course, one of the best ways to teach good social skills is to modeling them in the classroom.

5. **Another important way to increase students' self-esteem is to encourage them to share their feelings.** When teachers communicate that what students have to say is important, students are encouraged and feel that they are persons of worth.

6. **Equally important is for teachers to accept students for who they are, not for what they can become.** If students sense that they are not living up to their teacher's expectations, they will feel defeated and this will lower their self-esteem. This is not to suggest that teachers should accept inferior work for which the student is capable, but they should rather accept students for who they are.

7. **Just as it is important for teachers to give students specific compliments, it is equally important for teachers to not praise students in overly broad ways.** That type of praise fails to acknowledge a student's uniqueness.

8. **Obviously insulting the student or using sarcastic statements will cause him to feel negative about himself and will probably result in greater classroom conflicts.** If teachers label, compare, or call students names, this will lower their self-esteem and destroy their sense of self-worth. These things are often done in the classroom without the teacher even

realizing it. When teachers say things like; *"Don't go thinking you are all grown up, young man," "Why don't you sit still like Sara," or "I had your sister in my classroom two years ago and she was really nice little girl, what happened to you?"* they are using sarcasm, name calling, put downs, and comparing students.

Sadly, some teachers attempt to control their students by using sarcasm, name calling, comparing, etc. Such a statement hurts the student's self-esteem and creates resentment between classmates. Focusing on students' faults will cause them to feel belittled and will lower their self-esteem. Using criticism with students may work well to get them to stop their misbehavior for the moment but does nothing to bring about long-term change. Criticism and negativism toward students is one of the main reasons why students express low self-esteem in the classroom.

In an effort to build self-esteem in the classroom, teachers must ask themselves several questions: *"Do I communicate faith and trust to my students?" "Am I proving support and confidence?" "Do I give more attention to the negative behaviors of my students than to the positive behaviors?" "Do my students feel free to take risks and learn from their mistakes?"* These questions contain several of the factors that must be in place before effective discipline can take place or self-esteem can be enhanced. Students need to experience faith, trust, support and confidence from their teacher to think and feel positively about themselves. When the classroom is one designed to build self-esteem, proactive discipline has a much greater opportunity of making a difference in a student's behavior (DeRosier, M. E., and Marcus, S. R., 2005).

If the answers to any of the above-mentioned questions suggest that you may be contributing to students' low self-esteem, all is not lost. There are several very specific things that can be done to change the course of the relationship, and to begin building students' positive self-esteem and implementing proactive discipline. In order for students to grow healthy and strong physically, they must receive plenty of nutritious foods, peaceful rest, plenty of exercise and plenty of fresh air. Likewise, students will also grow healthy emotionally when teachers take specific actions to nurture their students emotional well-being.

Ingredients for Building Self-Esteem
1. **Unconditional Acceptance:** Unconditional acceptance indicates

that teachers care about students for who they are, not for what they can · become. That is, teachers will care about their students regardless of their behavior (Bettmann, J., 2000). Unconditional acceptance also communicates to students that they do not have to do anything special to receive a teacher's care. Teachers acknowledge that all of their students have special attributes. Unconditional acceptance will show students that they are important to the overall classroom functioning. This approach also communicates to students that they matter to someone (their teacher) who is important to them.

2. **Approval:** All students need to feel they are liked for themselves, just the way they are. When providing approval teachers demonstrate care and concern all the time, not just when students behave appropriately. Approval can be provided even when teachers do not especially like the way students are behaving. Providing approval does not mean that students' misbehavior will not be met with a consequence, it only means that teachers continue to find value in students, even when their behavior is inappropriate.

3. **Security:** Providing students with safety and security is one of the main roles of teachers. Every student needs to know that his teacher will keep him safe and secure. However, security and safety is not just physical safety, but emotional safety as well. Emotional security is present when students feel confident that what they say will not be met with ridicule, embarrassment, put downs or punishment, especially in front of their peers. When students do not feel safe and secure they will experience fear and anxieties. Students with exceptionalities are accustomed to being the butt of many comments and jokes. These students may need an even greater sense of security and protection. However, all students need to feel that they belong and fit into the classroom. Therefore, in order to build self-esteem in the classroom, teachers must provide physical and social safety and security.

4. **Independence:** When teachers provide students with independence they empower them to try new things, even if the effort results in failure. Allowing students as much independence as possible in the classroom indicates that the teacher has confidence in the students' ability to do things on their own. This action is designed to enhance the self-esteem of students. The opposite of providing independence is to create dependency. Unfortunately, when teachers control their classrooms they cause students to develop greater dependency. When students are dependent, they begin to look to their teacher to tell them what to do and become hesitant to try new things. It is this dependency that lowers students' self-esteem.

5. **Structure:** Providing structure in the classroom comes in several forms. Structure is related to the actual physical organization of the classroom, the curriculum, and the organization of how the material is presented. Most importantly, students must be provided the boundaries that allow them to know the limits to which they are allowed to function. It is structure that results in security, and security translates to self-esteem. Curriculum structure means that materials are organized in such a fashion that makes sense to students. It makes the material easier to follow and is more meaningful and applicable. Organizational structure means that the classroom is organized in such a fashion as to decrease disruptive behavior. A cluttered and disorganized classroom will always lead to greater disruption and behavioral conflicts. It is within the context of structure that students can be confident of their actions and function knowing that they are responsible for their actions (Johnson, F. and Edmunds, A.; 2006).

6. **Guidance:** While teachers may not realize it, guidance actually means discipline. Guidance is provided when teachers gently, but purposefully, guide students in gaining a positive self-confidence, self-image and self-concept. Another way in which teachers provide guidance is to teach students about concepts of kindness, courage, honesty and fairness. In essence, when teachers provide students with guidance, they are helping them learn effective life-coping skills. These skills will help students live in a greater society.

7. **Faith:** Students need to know that their teachers have faith in their abilities and decisions. However, faith goes beyond simply expecting students to complete a task. It suggests a belief in the students' decision-making skills. Having faith in students will help develop a set of values by which students can live and will serve them for a lifetime.

Some teachers take the approach that it is not their responsibility to teach these social and value skills to students. There is a resounding view on both sides of the spectrum that teachers should not involve themselves in such actions with students. For example, some people state that it is a parent's responsibility to teach such values and schools need to stick to academics. In addition, others suggest that teaching values is essentially establishing some type of moral judgment. However, a lack of values is one of the greatest weaknesses in the educational system today. Parents are busy with work and other responsibilities and often do not take the time to provide their children with value clarification. In some situations family dysfunction is so prevalent that children do not receive guidance at home. Therefore, the responsibility falls to educational institutions to provide this information. The reality is that teachers teach values every day, whether they want to or not. Values are taught when teachers show kindness, acceptance, approval, and recognition. The lack of value clarification can be seen in the attitudes of many who feel that their behavior is wrong only if they are caught. When students are not provided this guidance they will often lack confidence and will express limited respect for the natural social order. The best way to provide students with guidance is to model how to treat others.

When teachers take on the task of understanding their students' development and their goals, learn how to speak the language of encouragement, and work at implementing strategies to build self-esteem; they can be assured that their students will have a far greater chance of developing into healthy, emotionally well-adjusted students. As a result, students will experience fewer behavioral problems in the classroom and in life (Johnson, F., 1996).

SUMMARY

An important aspect of proactive discipline is building the self-esteem of students. During this chapter we have pointed out that there is a direct correlation between students' self-esteem and the behavior that is exhibited in the classroom. Just as with any strategy to address an academic deficit, teachers must provide strategies to build students' self-esteem. There are specific actions that can be taken to increase students' sense of self.

During this chapter we have been able to identify specifically the behavioral and emotional indicators of low and high self esteem and discuss how these factors are manifested in misbehavior in the classroom. Specific suggestions were made in relationship to how teachers can enhance students' self-esteem. Evidence was also presented to help teachers set up a classroom environment where positive guidance can be provided.

Chapter Twelve

USING GUIDANCE WITH DISCIPLINE: ENHANCING SELF-ESTEEM THROUGH EFFECTIVE DISCIPLINE

Teachers must recognize just how much power they actually have with students. How teachers respond will significantly impact how students feel about themselves. When discipline actions are directed toward the person rather than the behavior, students receive the message that they are "bad." The theory of Self-Fulfilled Prophecy and the Pygmalion Effect both suggest that students tend to become what they are told. Therefore, if the classroom discipline says, *"You are bad,"* then students will act in ways to correlate their behavior with the message. In essence, students work to make their teacher correct. In contrast, if the discipline says, *"You are a good person, but your behavior is bad,"* students will feel that they are good and will strive to behave in such a manner. These theories point out just how important and powerful teachers really are (Rowe, W. G., and O'Brien, J., 2002).

Some teachers have the mistaken notion that it is not possible to discipline students and build their self-esteem at the same time. However, there are many ways to help students have positive thoughts and feelings, while at the same time maintaining effective discipline. In order to accomplish this, teachers will need to examine how they respond to students and determine if their discipline strategies encourage or discourage students' self-esteem.

201

Students will be discouraged when the discipline strategies being used result in feeling rejected or generally put-down. When students feel put-down or rejected they will often seek attention and recognition in those areas where they are most certain to receive these needs. One only has to look around their school to gain insight into how this process works. Each day in schools throughout the United States teachers deal with students fighting, cheating, using profanity, making smart remarks, talking back or, in general, being disruptive. Since the emergence of student development there has been great controversy regarding the appropriate use of disciplinary technique. While some school districts, with parental permission, continue to use corporal discipline, others have completely rejected the idea of using physical means to respond to behavior. At some point, even the most skilled teacher has become frustrated enough to where they feel that physical punishment may be the only means of managing a student's behavior. Even though most teachers reject the idea of using corporal punishment, they often fail to realize that their use of "emotional" punishment is just as damaging (Cast, A. D., Schweingruber, D., and Berns, N., 2006).

When teachers have a limited knowledge about child behavior, effective classroom management or hidden agendas, it is not unusual to find discipline becoming more like "emotional punishment." In many cases these responses occur when teachers have become frustrated or simply do not know any other way to get students to behave.

Teachers are often influenced in their teaching style and the manner in which they respond to students based on the experiences they had as students. When teachers have had a positive experience during their own elementary, middle, or high school experience, they will often strive to become much like the teacher that so influenced them. Likewise, if the experience was negative, teachers will exhibit some of the same behaviors that they experienced. For example, if one's teacher or parents used sarcasm or emotional distress as a means of controlling behavior, there is a greater likelihood that the individual will also use these techniques. However, this is not always the case. Such experiences can also have the opposite effect. Some teachers recall being treated poorly in school and they seek to correct the wrong by becoming a positive, caring and proactive teacher. When this occurs, there can be a tendency for teachers to overcompensate and become too lenient with their students (Rubin, R., 2005).

When emotional punishment is used to control behavior, students will often respond by avoiding the teacher or seeking revenge. When this happens it is not unusual for teachers to encounter verbal aggression or passive resistance from their students. In essence teachers receive from their students essentially what they give them. Considering the almost-daily news of chaotic episodes in our schools, one may question why any teacher would ever use emotional punishment as a means of trying to control students. It seems that these responses occur most often when teachers feel overwhelmed. This frustration can relate back to some of the original discussions in this book. Society has changed, family systems have changed, students have changed, and the government is more active today in regulating education than at any time before. Teachers seem to have more to do with fewer resources than ever before (Skiba, R., and Peterson, R., 2003).

Today schools function under federal mandates of "No Child Left Behind" legislation and IDEA '97 and '04, while at the same time demands of state assessment have increased. Teachers often say instead of "No Child Left Behind", it should be "No Teacher Left Behind!" As a result of these increasing demands, teacher burnout occurs. In some cases, teacher shortages have caused school districts to accept teachers who are not certified in their specific area of instruction or who are teaching on an emergency certificate. In order to compensate for these shortages of specialized teachers, universities and colleges have established a post-career certification education track for individuals who are seeking a teaching certificate as a second career. In addition, universities continue to require prospective teachers to take courses in history of education, philosophy of education, methods of education, but not courses in behavior management. However, it is precisely classroom behavior that teachers seem to struggle with the most. While theory, history, and philosophy of education are all important to know and understand, theory, history, and philosophy of education are not going to help a teacher when a student is tearing up the classroom. As a direct result of their lack of knowledge related to effective classroom management, and their heightened frustration, teachers often resort to techniques to control students. Using emotional punishment to control students may serve to stop the misbehavior for a short duration, but it has little lasting positive effect. In fact, using emotional punishment ensures that the misbehavior will reoccur. Responding to students in such a way violates the very definition of proactive discipline. It fails to teach, it does not enhance the student, it is not focused on future behavior, it does not provide a choice, and it is not logically related (Long, J. D., and Williams, R. L., 2005).

When teachers attempt to control students with emotional punishment, they drive their students away and make it impossible to have a positive relationship. In addition, using sarcasm as a means to control students contradicts the objectives of proactive discipline—to "teach." When a particular punishment becomes ineffective, teachers must either find a different means of controlling, increase the severity of the emotional punishment or lower the expectations for the student. Herein lies the greatest harm, the student ends up with low self-esteem, feelings of inadequacy and a sense of rejection (Sutton, R. E., 2005).

It may sound ridiculous, but it is not unusual for emotional punishment to become the preferred consequence by students. Some students grow to expect adults to reject them, and may even set up the situation where rejection is likely to occur. These students would rather be sent to the principal's office than stay in the classroom to complete the assignment. If we agree that the purpose of discipline is to teach, then we must also agree that any effort to control students is an ineffective and inappropriate means of discipline. Emotional punishment tells students that they did something wrong, but it does not respond to students with dignity or provide them with an alternative behavior. In fact, emotional punishment teaches students that sarcasm, put-downs, and making fun of others is an acceptable way of getting what they want. One of the goals of this book is to help teachers develop a more positive relationship with their students. Using emotional punishment will greatly reduce the opportunity for teachers to establish and maintain any ongoing positive involvement with their students. Therefore, if teachers use sarcasm, name calling, comparisons, and general put-downs in an effort to shame and blame students into behaving, they should not be surprised when students recall them as a negative experience. While students may not always remember what you teach them, they always remember how you treat them (Gnezda, N. M., 2004).

When using positive discipline strategies, teachers are rewarded in several ways. In contrast, when they use emotional means to control students, teachers become frustrated and often do not enjoy teaching. Being frustrated can cause one to experience a variety of emotional conflicts. When teachers are frustrated they may experience stress, which in turn can lead to both emotional and physical concerns. When emotional punishment is avoided and other more positive discipline techniques are utilized, problem behaviors can be changed without damaging the relationship with students, and teachers tend to feel more positive. Proactive discipline will help students become more cooperative and they will see their teacher as a positive adult role model. As a direct result of positive discipline, students develop a greater sense of self-worth and more positive self-esteem. Proactive discipline is a win-win situation for everyone (Rubin, R., 2004).

Punishment, in general, is a personal, negative attack on students. Since punishment is personal, it can teach students that they are failures rather than that their behavior was a mistake. Such feelings will often cause students to feel discouraged and it is this discouragement that appears to be at the root of much of the inappropriate classroom behavior. Discouragement seems to occur when students feel that they are inadequate or feel that they cannot meet the standards set up by their teacher. Also, when teachers respond to students with punishment, students often feel that their teacher does not value them. When students are discouraged by their teacher, they will often gravitate to a negative peer group to receive the attention, power, recognition and acknowledgement that they desire. In fact, research by Marshall (2005) has suggested that when students feel rejected by teachers and peers, they will slowly move to gang affiliation to receive this sense of belonging and ownership.

Teachers must try to determine how their students may be discouraged in the classroom. One of the more common ways that students are discouraged is when more is expected from them than they can perform. For example, when an eighth-grade student is required to complete three projects at the same time for one class, he will become discouraged. The student begins to feel that the teacher has assigned the projects to avoid teaching. He may not be able to see the light at the end of the tunnel, and as a result simply gives up. Just as a teacher would not expect a dyslexic learning disabled student to read fluently, he must be sensitive to other expectations he has for students. Some students are simply not capable of achieving what is demanded of them. In addition, some teachers may communicate negative expectations to their students. When teachers communicate that they expect their students to fail, these feelings will cause students to doubt their own ability and consequently they will fail or refuse to try. Teachers must understand that this failure by students is only an effort by them to match their behavior to what they perceive the teacher expects (MacKenzie, E. P., Fite, P. J., and Bates, J. E., 2004).

Without realizing it teachers can intimidate their students.

Intimidation will result when teachers fail to develop a positive relationship with their students. When teachers are insecure, they will often attempt to intimidate students and find themselves involved in continual power struggles. The message of intimidation or a power struggle is, "I must win." In response, students often rebel against their teacher or may just give up. Effective discipline works best when teachers communicate that while it is important to do one's best, it is not necessary to always win or be right.

Since discouragement has been linked directly to students experiencing academic and behavioral failure, it is important that teachers learn to encourage their students, rather than discourage them. Teachers can build encouragement in their classrooms by giving students permission to take risks. How can teachers encourage? Encouragement is provided when teachers focus on students' successes and give them positive recognition for their efforts. This action will build a student's self-esteem, self-concept, and sense of self-worth. Students can be discouraged or encouraged with words and behaviors. For example, positive recognition can be given to any ability or behavior demonstrated by students at any time. When encouragement is applied consistently it will result in a more positive teacher/student relationship. When a positive teacher/student relationship exists, students are less likely to act out in class. It is interesting that a student may misbehave in one teacher's classroom, but will not in the classroom of a teacher they know respects and values them (Lawrence, S. M., 2005).

Students are encouraged when teachers focus on positive behavior, rather than negative. Positive expectation and encouragement go hand-in-hand. Using encouragement means that teachers value their students for who they are, not what they can become. Therefore, it is important that teachers not burden students with negative messages that they must improve before they are accepted. When teachers place demands or have unrealistic expectations, students will begin to believe that they are not good enough until they reach the standards set by their teachers. Some of the most effective methods for encouraging students are having faith, recognizing effort and improvement, and focusing on strengths and assets.

Encouraging Students

Faith:

Having faith in students is one of the most important ways teachers can offer encouragement. Teachers can demonstrate faith in their students without requiring them to prove that the faith is deserved. A lack of faith can also be demonstrated in various ways. When teachers fail to trust their students, they are showing a lack of faith. Faith is most clearly demonstrated when teachers allow students to take responsibility for their behavior. This is not to suggest that teachers should not watch after students or set limits and restrictions. Students need guidance and supervision, and teachers are responsible for providing safety for students. However, once rules have been established, teachers need to let students know that they expect them to follow the rules. If it is discovered that a student is not following a class rule, faith is not warranted and the rules will need to be renegotiated.

When students fail to follow a specific rule that they have participated in developing and fully understand, using a consequence means that the students have made a decision to violate the rule. In such cases a consequence is required. However, more importantly, teachers will need to understand the student's goals for the misbehavior, ask who owns the problem, present choices to the student, allow the student to choose the consequences, follow through, refocus on the positive behavior, re-establish the relationship, teach a replacement behavior, and then renegotiate additional guidelines, if needed (Schubert, J. L., 2004).

Recognizing Effort and Improvement:

Proactive teachers are those who recognize effort and improvement in their students. It is easy to give encouragement and praise to students for accomplishing a task or maintaining their behavior. However, students are not going to accomplish a task or maintain behavior every day. If encouragement is restricted to only a completed task, there will be fewer opportunities to encourage students. If, however, teachers can learn ways to encourage student's efforts, rather than just their achievements, students will be encouraged to find value in their efforts and improvements as well as their accomplishments. Recognition can be given to any evidence of improvement that students may exhibit. For example, a student may come and tell the teacher that another student will not let them play a game. The teacher may respond, *"I am glad you came and told me about the problem instead of getting angry and hitting someone. However, you need to tell him how you feel."* It is this recognition that allows students to feel accepted as they are, and will motivate them to try harder to achieve. However, when teachers demand more than a student is capable of providing, they feel that they are not adequate or acceptable. Just as applying pressure to an infected sore creates more soreness, applying emotional pressure to students will cause them to be even more disruptive. Teachers can be assured that applying such pressure to students will result in either rebellion or resignation.

Focus on Strengths and Assets:

In an effort to provide students with encouragement, teachers must find ways to focus on strengths and assets of the student. Of course, we have been conditioned to focus on negatives rather than positives. Society places greater attention on mistakes than on successes. For example, consider a Friday night football game. A player on a football team has played very well throughout the game. But near the end of the final quarter, a student fumbles and the other team picks up the ball and runs it all the way back for a touchdown. Everyone in the stands jumps to their feet and screams or boos the poor student. They completely ignore the positive plays the student has made throughout the game. This same process occurs with teachers. Who are the teachers that receive national exposure? Is it the teachers who work day in and day out, making a difference in students' lives? Of course not; it is those teachers who engage in inappropriate behavior with the students. Just as teachers are frustrated with the lack of positive support they receive from society, so are students that do not receive positive support from their teachers.

Teachers can encourage students by recognizing their assets and then commenting on them. Assets can be found in almost any behavior or action. If a student feels inadequate, looking for something positive and then commenting on him will tell the student that he has many positive attributes. This may require teachers to look diligently to find strengths and assets. However, it really does not matter how big or small the attribute is, as long as it is recognized. Things that teachers may recognize as an asset are: helping in the room, working on an assignment, getting along with others or any other specific activity, even those where discipline has been required. For example, if a student is placed in time-out an asset can be commented upon. The ability to complete the consequence is an asset. When teachers comment on students' assets, students are encouraged and will be motivated to continue improving (Bradford, M., 2005).

Encouragement is one of the primary ways teachers can build students' self-esteem. When teachers encourage students, it serves as a foundation for building a relationship based on equality and mutual respect. Encouragement will help students discover their own personal self-worth and grow in their self-esteem.

Praise:

Praise is another building block for building self-esteem. Praise should not be mistaken for encouragement—they are very different. Praise will result in a different response from students than encouragement. Praise is a reward from someone in authority for a job well done. Praise suggests that students will receive this verbal reward only as long as they complete a task or behave a certain way. Since praise is a reward, obviously students will not deserve a reward every day (Weisser, S. O., 2005).

Encouragement:

In contrast to praise, encouragement can be given even when a student is not successful. Encouragement recognizes effort, improvement and the student's interest. Encouragement shows students that they are appreciated and it recognizes their assets, personal resources and contributions, as well as their achievements. Encouragement is not a reward, but rather recognition of the students' self-worth. When encouragement is given, students feel acknowledged and recognized for their efforts.

When using encouragement, avoid using such words as "good," "great," or "terrific." Instead use phrases that demonstrate acceptance, show confidence, and recognize student's efforts and improvements. This can be accomplished by focusing on students' strengths, contributions, and assets.

A. **Acceptance:** Simply asking a student, *"How do you feel about this?"* shows that the teacher accepts the student and is interested in the student's opinion.

B. **Confidence:** Making a statement such as, *"I believe you can handle it,"* will demonstrate to a student that you have confidence in his abilities.

C. **Recognize Improvement:** Teachers can recognize improvement by making a statement such as, *"I can see you have made a lot of progress."*

D. **Appreciation:** Saying, *"Thank you for helping"* will demonstrate that you appreciate students' assistance.

Building self-esteem requires that teachers have a positive relationship with their students. Therefore, it will be important for teachers to conduct a self-assessment of their abilities to relate to students. One of the most important components of building self-esteem is for students to feel that their teacher has faith in them. Teachers must ask: *"Do I tend to communicate faith and trust in my students?"* Also, students need to receive support and confidence from their teachers. When students receive support and confidence from their teachers they feel a sense of freedom to try new things, even though their efforts may result in failure. A failure within itself should never be considered bad. However, do not make the mistake of thinking that failure only refers to academic efforts. Failure also occurs in regard to socialization, emotions and behavioral issues. In classrooms there should be no such thing as failure. In fact, failure only means that the student has not yet mastered the task. If he just keeps trying, he will eventually master the task. However, when students have low self-esteem they will often try and fail, then give up. This is another reason why encouragement of students is so important (Gartrell, D., 2002).

Proactive encouraging teachers will also look for ways to be excited about their students' interests and the things in which they are involved. While encouragement is a part of the total proactive discipline process, it should not be viewed as a way to get students to do whatever their teacher wants, but rather as a way to help students fulfill their potential. Although teachers may want their students to adopt our values and interests, it would be inappropriate to try to force students to do so. However, teachers can recognize a student's interests even when they are different from the teacher's. While teachers may influence students, students are independent thinking people who will make their own choices about interests and values. Therefore, it seems reasonable to give students as much freedom as is age-appropriate in an atmosphere of acceptance and openness. Such an approach will help students grow in their confidence and self-respect. Over time students may well take on their teachers' values, but trying to force such values upon students will surely lead to greater conflict and rebellion.

Another important aspect of encouraging students is to avoid comparing them to their peers. Comparisons can be a slap in the face, and demoralizing to students. There is no reason to mention how well another student is doing or pointing out how well other students are behaving. Comparisons reduce students' self-respect by devaluing their efforts and will most often result in resentment. Rather than comparing students to others, much will be gained by encouraging students by accepting them and their individual differences.

Because of certain personality traits, especially challenging students are often very critical of themselves when they have difficulty achieving a certain goal. These students will often make self deprecating statements, calling themselves "stupid" or other such names. When these students do not reach the level of achievement they expected, they often feel stupid or that they are not as good as others. In essence they see themselves as failures. While it is important to encourage students to reach for their goals, it is equally important not to place undue pressure on them to achieve more than they are capable. When pressure is applied, these more difficult students often feel that they are inadequate. Feelings of inadequacy can result in fear and anxiety about failing, and this leads to greater failure (Gerber, M. M., 2005).

There are ten strategies that can be used to encourage students and help them develop their self-esteem (Johnson, F., 1996):

1. **Give responsibility:** When students are given responsibility they are encouraged. Take the attitude that students are responsible people and expect them to take responsibility for their actions.

2. **Show appreciation for contributions:** When students are willing to complete a chore in the classroom or to help another student, be sure to give recognition for the action and effort. Tell the student that you appreciate his positive efforts.

3. **Ask students for opinions and suggestions:** Teachers are often surprised to find that students know far more than they may have anticipated. In some cases, students may even know information that their teacher does not know; this is especially true about such things as sports, music and movies.

4. **Encourage students to participate in decision-making:** When making classroom rules or other decisions that involve the entire class, encourage students to participate. This will indicate a level of trust and respect for students' opinions and decisions.

5. **Accept mistakes of students:** Remember, without mistakes there can be no learning. Few people are able to accomplish a task when they first try. Try not to overreact to mistakes. In essence, create an atmosphere in which it is safe to make mistakes, discuss the mistakes, and learn from them.

6. **Emphasize the process, not just the end product:** This means to pay attention to the effort, progress or improvement of students, not

merely what they accomplish. The end product is seen as an achievement of a goal or an accomplishment. By recognizing the effort and progress, teachers help students increase their self-confidence and sense of motivation.

7. **Turn liabilities into assets:** Become an expert in scouting for positive potential in students. Recognize any behavior that is an improvement, such as staying in time-out, asking for help, completing a task, or making a good decision.

8. **Show confidence in students' judgment:** Students will not exercise good judgment unless their teachers have confidence in their ability. Show confidence by accepting students' decisions about such things as use of free time and decisions about improving behavior, or even continuing with the misbehavior. In essence, this means that when students make a decision to continue misbehaving, teachers should be confident that they are ready to handle the consequences.

9. **Have positive expectations of students:** If teachers expect the worst of students, there is a good chance that is what they will get. The opposite of expecting the worst, however, is not expecting the best. If teachers demand perfection, they will be disappointed and students are bound to have doubts about their abilities. Instead of expecting perfection, expect effort and improvement from students.

10. **Develop alternative ways of viewing a situation:** Use your own creativity to discover ways to see the situation from students' perspective. When students come to you with a discouraging problem, ask, *"What is it about the situation that is encouraging?"* For example, if a student is discussing a conflict, the very fact that they are willing to talk about the problem, rather than becoming aggressive, is encouraging.

It has been suggested several times throughout this book that students often do not have the cognitive or conceptual processing skills to match their feelings with their words. As a consequence, students will often "show" teachers how they feel rather than "tell" them. But, if all students could conceptualize and put into words what they feel and think, teachers might be very surprised. The following is series of statements that teachers might well hear from students if they could express themselves:

1. "Don't spoil me. I know quite well that I ought not to have all that I ask for. I'm testing you!"
2. "Don't be afraid to be firm with me. I prefer structure and it

212

makes me feel more secure."

3. "Don't let me form bad habits. I have to rely on you to detect them in the early stages and teach me more appropriate ways of getting my needs met."

4. "Don't make me feel smaller than I am. It only makes me angry and gets me into more trouble."

5. "Don't correct me in front of my peers. I'll take much more notice if you talk quietly with me in private."

6. "Don't make me feel my mistakes are unforgivable. It upsets my sense of values."

7. "Don't protect me from consequences. I need to learn the result of my behavior."

8. "Don't be too upset when I say, *"I hate you,"* or *"You are mean."* It isn't you I hate, or that you are mean. It only means that what has happened in the classroom is important to me, and I want you to feel badly."

9. "Don't nag at me. If you do, I will protect myself by not listening."

10. "Don't forget that I cannot explain myself as well as I would like. This is why I'm not always very accurate or I say, *"I don't know."*

11. "Don't break your promises. I feel let down when you fail to do what you promised."

12. "Don't tax my honesty too much. I am easily frightened and when I am upset I will say anything to get out of trouble."

13. "Don't be inconsistent. Inconsistency completely confuses me and makes me lose faith in you."

14. "Don't tell me my fears are silly. They are terribly real and you can do much to reassure me if you try to understand."

15. "Don't put me off when I ask questions. If you do, you will find that I will stop asking and seek my information elsewhere."

16. "Don't act like you are so perfect. It seems like you are saying you are better than me, and it gives me a shock when I discover that you are not perfect."

17. "Don't ever think it is beneath your dignity to apologize to me. An honest apology makes me feel surprisingly positive towards you."

18. "Don't forget I learn best with creativity. I cannot learn as much without it, so please be creative and enthusiastic."

19. "Be organized. When you are disorganized I get confused and it is easier for me to get into trouble."

20. "Remember that I have bad days. Sometimes I come to school tired or even sick. My parents argue because we don't have enough money and I worry about them."

SUMMARY

During this chapter self-esteem and the behavioral components have been clearly identified. In addition, specific information was presented to demonstrate how self-esteem impacts student behavior. However, just knowing this is never enough. Teachers must also know how to build self-esteem in their students without losing focus on proactive discipline. A foundation was laid that suggested how to develop a classroom where positive self-esteem can be developed, then specific suggestions were made to actually build self-esteem.

However, when teachers respond to students in certain ways, students' self-esteem can be destroyed. Not only must teachers know what to do, they must also know what not to do. Additional information has been provided to help teachers avoid the unintentional actions that will destroy a student's self-esteem. When students are not allowed to or cannot express themselves, they often begin to act out their feelings. However, if students could adequately express themselves, they might well be able to tell teachers what to do and not do. In many cases, the thoughts of students might be surprising to teachers.

Chapter Thirteen

MOVING BEYOND TRADITIONAL DISCIPLINE STRATEGIES: NEGOTIATION, BEHAVIOR CONTRACTING, AND CLASSROOM MEETINGS

The objectives of proactive discipline include creating a positive learning environment, teaching students more appropriate ways of behaving and improving teacher/student relationships. Rather than providing students with attention in times of conflict, more will be accomplished when students are recognized for their positive behaviors. When students receive attention for positive behaviors, they are much more willing to deal with problems before they occur. As the teacher/student relationship improves, teachers are able to assist students with making positive decisions and learning skills that will lead to self-control (Doveston, M., and Keenaghan, M., 2006).

Before any proactive changes can be made teachers and students must agree that a smoother-functioning classroom is beneficial to all concerned. However, this desire for a smoother functioning classroom will not be the goal of a student when he can get his needs met through his misbehavior and disruption in the classroom. When students disrupt the classroom one can be assured that they are getting their need for attention, power, or avoidance. Therefore, one of the first things to be accomplished is to engage students in the decision-making process and discuss how needs can me met positively. This can be accomplished by modeling respect, and encouraging all students to be involved in the decision-making process concerning classroom rules, expectations, and consequences. In order to accomplish this, teachers must learn to negotiate and establish behavioral contracts with students, while implementing a process whereby regular classroom meetings are held.

Negotiation:

Many teachers take the approach that they must be dictatorial with students. However, when teachers approach their classroom management with an attitude of control, it often backfires and results in additional conflict, while decreasing the opportunity to form positive relationships with students. In contrast, teachers need to engage students in the negotiation process. Some students do not know how to negotiate, so teachers will need to model for students the process of negotiating. Once learned, these skills will help students with situations and circumstances throughout their lives.

Negotiation is the process by which a teacher and students find areas of agreement concerning a variety of behaviors, tasks or other activities. When first introducing the concept of negotiation, attention will need to be paid to voice tone, as well as circumstances surrounding the time of the negotiation efforts. Make sure there are no distractions to interfere with the negotiation process. It is never a good idea to try to implement negotiations at a time when there is conflict. While most topics can be negotiated, there are some that cannot. This process is so delicate that it must be presented at a time when everyone is willing to listen, participate and recognize that this process empowers everyone (Hobday-Kusch, J., and McVittie, J., 2002).

When talking with students about behavior problems that need to be changed, begin the negotiation process by providing a descriptive praise or an expression of affection, such as, *"I really appreciate your willingness to talk about how things are going in the classroom."* If the behavior that needs to be changed involves a safety issue or other school policy issues, the amount of input allowed will be limited. However, regardless of the situation, it is important to remain calm and rational and avoid making critical comments, accusations or judgments about students. Instead of making critical statements, simply describe the negative behavior and contrast it with the desired behavior. Also, teachers will need to identify the consequences of the negative behavior and the rewards that will occur from the positive behavior. The following is a step-by-step process for using the negotiation process (Dalke, A., 2004):

1. **Introduce the subject in a pleasant and calm manner.** First

provide praise or an expression of affection, empathy, appreciation or concern: Example: *"I am so glad that you are in my room. There are a few things I'd like for us to talk about."*

2. Describe specifically the inappropriate or problem behavior. Example: *"I've noticed lately that you are not turning in your homework. I am afraid that this may cause you to fail."*

3. Describe the appropriate or alternative behavior and any unusual circumstances. Example: *"I know you work a part-time job, and I understand that there is often no one at home to help you with the homework assignment. However, the work is designed to help you learn the skills that will allow you to move on to the next grade."*

4. Describe the natural consequence of the behavior and what happens when the behavior occurs. Example: *"If you do not get these skills and pass, you will just have more problems next year."*

5. Ask for acknowledgment, feedback, and input. Example: *"Have you thought about this?"*

6. Negotiate a possible solution with the student. Ask the student if they have any suggestions or options of how to handle the problem. Example: *"What do you think we could do to help you finish your homework?"* If the student cannot come up with any suggestions, provide a few possibilities. Once a suggestion has been made, reach an agreement with the student. (It is important to ask the student how all this sounds. This will identify the level of agreement or disagreement. If the student seems hesitant, ask if he is willing to give it a try for a week).

7. Come to a final decision together. If a decision can be made, it is probably a good idea to write it out and sign the agreement in order to make it formalized or, at a minimum, shake hands on the agreement. Do something to indicate a concrete agreement.

8. Provide encouragement through praise and other rewards. Praise the student for any appropriate behavior he displays during the negotiation process. Some examples of things to praise are eye contact, not arguing or complaining, not making silly comments, not denying that there is a problem, and not blaming someone else for the problem. Example: *"Thank you for taking the time to talk with me about this. I realize it may seem like just more work to you, but it is really important to me that you are prepared for the next grade. I appreciate the good suggestions that you made and the fact that you didn't argue or make any excuses. Your response shows me that you are* *developing a lot of maturity and becoming more responsible."*

9. **Keep track of the student's agreed-upon change and provide feedback.** One of the ways to keep record of the agreement is to ask the student how it went with the assignment. Also document when the student turns in each assignment. Each week talk with the student about how well he is doing or if there are any problems getting the work done. Again, ask the student if he needs any help. Be sure to note any progress being made and perhaps compare previous efforts to current efforts.

Almost anything can be negotiated. When students want a specific item or privilege, a procedure can be negotiated that will determine what will be expected to receive the item or privilege. When teachers negotiate with students, it teaches them that they have the ability to achieve whatever they want by working to improve a specific behavior or to meet certain criteria. This process will help students experience success, will build the self-confidence of students, and show them that they have the power to achieve.

Negotiating consequences or privileges with students has many benefits. It teaches them skills that they will use throughout their lives. It helps them learn skills required to live a more productive life, get the things that they want, and in general, to get along in the greater society. In addition, this process teaches students the art of compromise, positive decision making and deferred gratification. In fact, many people in our society are unable to put off for today so I can get what I want tomorrow. These skills will help students become more independent and responsible citizens. When teachers negotiate with students, it builds and improves their self-esteem while enhancing the teacher/student relationship. As a result of being included in this process and feeling a sense of power, students are less likely to view their teacher as arbitrary or unfair. Lastly, when teachers negotiate with students, they are showing respect for students and the students will feel that their views are important and valued. Everybody wins in the negotiation process (Bullock, C., and Foegen, A., 2002).

Behavior Contracting:

Once a process of negotiation has been successfully implemented, a natural progression is to move to the stage of behavior contracting. Developing a contract with students does not suggest a lack of trust. In fact, behavior contracts serve as a tool to ensure clarity of expectations.

Many students with exceptionalities appear to have a greater chance at success when the classroom provides structure. A behavior contract is designed to supply this needed structure to students. Structure allows students to know specifically what is expected and what will happen if they violate the established structure. Without adequate structure students do not know what they should do, when they should do it, how they should do it, or what will happen if they do not complete the task (De Martini-Scully, D., Bray, M. A., and Kehle, T. J., 2001).

Regardless of how well or how poorly the classroom functions, there are some specific actions that can be taken to prevent conflict within the classroom. If conflicts already exist, it will be important to establish some type of behavioral agreement between the teacher and students. To establish an effective behavioral contract, the students' needs must be identified. In other words, ask the students, *"What needs to happen in order for you to get along in the classroom?"* This will require the teacher and students to talk about the behaviors that need to change and how this can be accomplished. At this stage of the discussion, information is somewhat general and non-specific. A more thorough discussion of how to manage a classroom meeting will be presented later in this chapter. When discussing topics that are possibly volatile it is important to remain as calm and objective as possible. It is through this calmness and objectivity that teachers will remain fair and have realistic expectations of students. Without this calmness and objectivity, teachers may become upset and say something to create even more conflict (Martin, J. E., Mithaug, D. E., Cox, P., Peterson, L. Y., Van Dycke, J. L., Cash, M. E., 2003).

A behavioral contract will provide students with specific rules and consequences which will give the students the structure to function within the classroom environment. Remember, structure provides security and security is one of those variables that build self-esteem. When students know what is expected, there is a greater change of compliance. Designing a behavioral contract may include such things as: behavior in the classroom, when to turn in homework, how to treat others, use of appropriate language and any specific behavior that needs to be addressed. However, teachers should not assume that behavior contracts are only applicable to students. Don't be surprised when students also want the teacher to follow certain rules. If students suggest that the teacher should also follow rules, do not view this as opposition or defiance, but rather their way of showing acceptance. In fact, such suggestions are reassurance of fairness, and give teachers the opportunity to serve as a positive role model (Wilkinson, L. A., 2003).

An additional benefit of the behavioral contracting approach is that it provides students with a sense of empowerment. Most students who consistently misbehave do so because they feel powerless, and their misbehavior is a way to escape from such feelings and gain control in the classroom and power with their peers. When teachers and students establish and agree on a behavioral contract, negotiation becomes an important part of the process. As was previously noted, an important part of the negotiation process is to ensure that each student has the opportunity to participate and provide input. Therefore, establishing a behavioral contract provides for structure, empowers students, enhances trust, and helps students learn how to establish and maintain a positive relationship with peers and adults.

Developing a behavioral contract requires teachers to be specific, clear, concise, flexible and, above all, an effective communicator. In order for a behavioral contract to be successful, the benefit received by the student from cooperation must be equal to or greater than the needs being met by the negative behavior. Therefore, teachers will need to properly identify needs and goals of students in order to communicate what benefits will be derived. Some students have a need for attention, while others may desire power and control. The goal for the teacher will be to achieve a more smoothly-functioning classroom, while the goal of the student may be more personal. However, it is the ability to meet these needs that will motivate everyone (teacher and student) to work at establishing a behavioral contract. When attempting to determine the goal or benefit for students, remember they often live in a perpetual state of immediate gratification. Therefore, don't be surprised if they want a reward that will meet an immediate personal need (Xin, J. F., and Forrest, L., 2002).

In order to increase the opportunity for success, a behavioral contract must contain short-term and long-term benefits. A short-term benefit may be given at the end of the class period or at the end of the day. Short-term rewards or benefits seem to work best when they have a cumulative effect. This accumulation process allows students to reach their long-term goal. A short-term reward may be ten minutes of free time at the end of the class period. The cumulative effect may be that if the entire class follows the contract for a month, they receive a pizza party at the end of the week.

A behavior contractual agreement will work only when all parties are able to follow through with that which has been agreed upon. That includes both rewards and consequences. However, it is not unusual for teachers to fail to follow through with the contract because they get busy and forget, feel sorry for the student, or just don't see any benefit to the program. It can be difficult to inform students that they have failed to live up to their end of the agreement and at the same time keep them motivated to continue following the contract. When teachers, for whatever reason, fail to follow through on the agreed behavioral contract, students are sent a double message. The primary message is that the behavioral contract is a serious program. However, the secondary message is that it is acceptable to violate the agreements. If behavioral contracting is going to be successful, rewards and consequences will need to be applied on a consistent basis, yet leave room for negotiations. In order to ensure success of the contract and make it easier to deal with failure when it occurs, it is vital that everyone agree upon the rewards and the resulting consequences. If this agreement is not established initially, the behavioral contract is doomed to failure (Laursen, E. K., and Peterson, D., 2005).

When establishing a behavioral contract, it will be far more productive if students have had input into deciding the expectations and the rewards. Also, make sure that the rules are concise, specific, and attainable. When students understand the expectations and they are specific, they will know immediately when they have accomplished a goal or failed to reach the goal. By stating clearly the expected changes, students are given a sense of power and security. Students will often verbally agree with almost anything when they feel pressured. During these times students will make verbal agreements and have every intention of keeping them. However, when the expectations are left as a verbal agreement, they are more conceptual. Because of students' impulsive nature, such agreements are often broken. It is usually a good idea for the behavioral contractual agreement to be written down. By writing the contract it becomes more formal and is made concrete. Writing the agreement allows the contract to serve as a visual cue and constant reminder for students, instead of the teacher having to constantly remind or nag the students. Also, when agreements are only verbal, students can make excuses that they did not understand or claim that that is not what they agreed to (Kuh, G. D., Laird, T. F. N., and Umbach, P. D., 2004).

Classroom Meetings:

Another important technique for making classroom function more smoothly is establishing and holding classroom meetings. Many conflicts in a classroom can be avoided though this process. These are meetings that are regularly scheduled (usually once per week) in which all class members are invited to participate. The purpose of these meetings is to inform students of upcoming events, make plans and decisions, provide encouragement, and solve problems. While an emergency meeting may take place when there is a problem, the regularly scheduled classroom meeting assures each class member that he will have an opportunity to voice his concerns at a definite time each week. Unlike negotiations, class meetings serve to do more than just solve problems. In fact, if such meetings focus only on problems, interest is likely to dwindle rapidly. Feldhusen, J., and Feldhusen, H., (2004) state that holding regular class meetings provides opportunities for each person to:

1. Be heard
2. Express feelings about the class
3. Give and receive encouragement
4. Agree or disagree on assignments that are distributed
5. Express concerns or complaints
6. Settle conflicts or deal with recurring problems
7. Participate in class planning

To make classroom meetings productive there are several steps that will need to be followed:

1. **Establish a specific time for the meeting to be held**

The entire class should reach a consensus about when the meetings should be held. This process will also give teachers the opportunity to explain the meaning of consensus. Although every student may not fully agree, the consensus process teaches the art of negotiation. If fairness and decision-making can start in the planning stages, all students will feel their opinions are important. Keeping the time of the meeting consistent from week to week will establish the meeting as a regular part of the classroom activity. If some students decide not to participate, the meeting should continue and decisions can still be made by those who do participate. As the resistant students see that decisions are being made without them, they will be motivated to participate.

2. Each student should be given the opportunity to lead

Students should decide together how to rotate the leadership role. When discussing this with students, suggest that it be done by alphabetical order or by drawing names out of a hat. Even students with exceptionalities have the ability to lead and should be given the opportunity to do so, even if they require assistance. Basically the leader keeps track of when the meeting starts, the time limits for discussion, and when the meeting should end.

3. Establish and stick to time limits

Teacher and students should agree on time limits and they should be followed religiously. Time limits should be applied to how long the meeting will last and how long one student will be allowed to talk. Without such time limits, one student may try to dominate the meeting, or the meeting may drag on until other students lose interest. The leader of the weekly meeting is responsible for keeping track of the time limits and ending the meeting.

4. All students should have a chance to offer ideas

It is usually best to allow the students to speak first, thereby the teacher will be able to add ideas or offer more appropriate alternatives if necessary. Depending on the age of the students, it may be necessary for the teacher to develop a general agenda and include any specifics that need to be discussed. However, if the teacher leads off with lots of ideas, the students will feel that the real purpose of the meeting is for the teacher to impose his views on the students.

5. Encourage everyone to bring up issues

If class meetings are to going to be successful, all students must have the opportunity to have their concerns discussed. Therefore, the leader should go around the room and give each person a chance to speak. This can be handled before the meeting starts by asking each student if he has anything that he wants to bring up at the meeting. Remember, when a student is talking he cannot be interrupted unless he asks for feedback.

6. Meetings should not become gripe sessions

Constant complaining can destroy the purpose of the class meeting. To make the meeting productive, it must be agreed that if anyone wants to complain about something, they should be prepared to offer and work toward a solution. Ask the students, *"What can be done to solve this problem?"*

7. Use the class meeting to discuss school assignments

When students forget or refuse to do school or homework assignments, it is usually a sign that the work is either too difficult or is not fully understood. This problem can be solved by asking the students what additional information is needed. After deciding what additional help is needed, a plan should be established to make sure each student is able to complete the tasks. This may involve peer tutoring, or providing additional assistance from the teacher. If a new project is being introduced, discuss the details and allow the students to decide how best to approach the project.

8. Class meetings are not just for problem solving

Weekly or monthly fun activities should be planned by the class. These activities may include watching a movie together, taking a field trip, having a pizza party or having an activity outside. While some students may think that these meetings and the activities are silly, allow each student to make his own decision, but make sure that everyone feels invited to participate.

9. Teach good communication skills

The class meetings allow teachers to make use of reflective listening skills and to show students that their feelings have been understood. If needed, ask for clarification. Use open-ended questions to encourage students to contribute. Be sure to remember to send "I messages" and to express positive feelings to students.

10. Make decisions by consensus

This does not involve voting, but rather general agreement. Voting creates winners and losers and can cause resentment and interfere with cooperation. Therefore, simply ask if everyone agrees. If all students do not agree, ask those who do not agree if they would be willing to try that which was decided for a week and review the decision at the next meeting. If general agreement cannot be reached, then the discussion will need to be continued until consensus is reached or postpone the decision. This may be a time to move into a negotiation phase.

11. Evaluate the classroom meetings

At the close of each meeting, ask students how they feel about the meeting and what suggestions they have for improving the meetings in the future. If they are becoming simply a time for complaints, allow for some ventilation and then try to address the purpose of the meeting.

12. Evaluate decisions at the next meeting

It is important at the beginning of each classroom meeting to review the commitments or decisions that were made at the previous meeting. In this way, students can decide whether to keep the decisions or change them.

If some students refuse to participate in the classroom meetings, the meetings can continue and decisions can still be made. Communicate clearly that each student has equal influence, and therefore if one student chooses not to participate, he forfeits his input. In many instances, when a student chooses not to participate, he will join in after seeing how the rest of the students are responding to the meeting. Don't be surprised if some students hold off for awhile and then join in the classroom meetings. After all, it is not very comfortable to be on the outside of something others seem to find rewarding. Initially these students may join in by making a silly comment. Thank the student for the comment and ask him how he would change things.

SUMMARY

This chapter has focused on what it takes to move beyond traditional discipline strategies. Some teachers may think that negotiation, behavior contracting and class meetings have little to do with proactive discipline. However, if everything a teacher does in the classroom impacts on the overall behavior of students, then each of the above items is relevant.

The three primary areas that were discussed were negotiating with students, establishing behavioral contracts, and holding regular classroom meetings. The benefit of each of these approaches is to move beyond the traditional methods of behavior intervention and to begin empowering students to take responsibility for the behavior that occurs in the classroom. As a direct result, teachers begin to establish a powerful relationship with students that will provide them with skills that will last a lifetime. These students will find that they can get their needs met in positive ways, rather than resorting to negative behavior to get the same needs met.

Overview of the Best Practices and Principles of Proactive Discipline

1. **Concentrate on reinforcing positives:** This will help build students' self-concept and feelings of worth. Use praise and other rewards freely.

2. **Establish a positive relationship with students:** Make learning fun. Work at involving students in tasks that they enjoy and in which they find meaning.

3. **Give students honest choices whenever possible:** Avoid direct orders and commands. Allow students to have as many choices as possible.

4. **Let the student know how you feel about his behavior:** Use "I-Messages" by saying, *"I don't like what you are doing,"* rather than, *"You are really making me so angry."*

5. **Always refer to students' behavior, not their personality:** *"You are behaving inappropriately,"* not *"You are bad."*

6. **Try to give students their way whenever possible:** If a student's behavior is not infringing on your right to teach, other students' right to learn or safety in the classroom, then the behavior may not need to be responded to.

7. **Encourage students to express their feelings:** Feelings cannot be dealt with when they are suppressed. Therefore, encourage students to express their feelings such as anger, sadness, fear, or joy. Let students know what the limits are of their expressions. Limits should be fixed and known and not vague and stated after the fact. If students have difficulty expressing themselves appropriately, help them find alternate means to express their feelings that are more acceptable to others.

8. **Develop a specific agreement with students:** Spell out specifically what behaviors will be allowed and those that will not. Offer alternative behaviors that they can use instead of the inappropriate

behaviors that are to be changed. Specify what will happen if the inappropriate behaviors continue.

9. **Remain calm and objective at all times:** Discipline should never be implemented when a teacher is frustrated or upset. When frustrated or upset, it is better to make note of the behavior and deal with it when everyone has had a chance to calm down.

10. **Never use threats:** Pointing out natural and logical consequences to behaviors in a non-judgmental manner can be helpful; threats never are.

11. **Be on the offense rather than defense:** Arguing with students or trying to bargain with them to avoid a confrontation will only make the situation worse. Be proactive to avoid conflict.

12. **Allow students to express their feelings:** Acknowledge their feelings and their right to feel a certain way. This does not mean that you agree, only that they have a right to feel that way. Also, students do not have the right to act on their feelings.

13. **Take action to clear the air:** When signs of tension begin to appear in the classroom, be proactive to deal with the issues. Avoid confrontations when tension is present. It may be necessary to suggest alternatives for the student to release the tension, such as going for a walk. This is not the time to lecture. Back off from demands if necessary in order to head off a major confrontation.

14. **Give as much freedom as possible to students:** Giving freedom will help students develop their own controls within the classroom. If possible allow students the opportunity to go for a walk or utilize other methods that will help calm them down. Avoid setting arbitrary time periods to cool off. Allow the student to resume normal classroom activity when he is ready.

15. **Watch for signs of disruption at all times:** Symptoms which might indicate a lack of interest in the classroom include boredom,

restlessness and aggression. When these signs are present, set some activity in motion rather than allowing the tension to build.

16. **When acting-out behavior occurs, don't react:** Use a soft voice and manner. Shouting and yelling will only increase the behavior.

17. **Avoid the use of punishment:** Using punishment to control students only creates additional problems. Make sure that any action taken is proactive discipline that teaches students more appropriate ways of behaving.

18. **Avoid a "gang mentality:"** When temper tantrums and other hostile behaviors occur, remove the student from the situation. Never deal with problem behaviors in front of peers. If possible take the student outside the classroom in order to avoid an audience.

19. **Sometimes it is wise to ask for assistance:** If a student has not responded to normal behavioral management, it will be wise to ask for assistance. *No Child Left Behind* legislation requires schools to have intervention teams to deal with problems related to academic performance and behavioral issues. There is a saying that five people can come up with more ideas in one hour than one person in five hours. Asking for help is not a sign of weakness; it is a sign of courage!

20. **When problems occur, return to normal functioning as soon as possible:** After a student has calmed down from the acting-out behavior, return them to the classroom as soon as they are ready. If the student has had a crisis (particularly in front of other students), help him or her save face. Do not make a big deal about the return.

21. **Do not punish students:** Taking action that is emotionally painful or unrelated to the behavior of the student is seldom helpful. Any actions taken must help students learn from their behavior. Therefore, consequences of a behavior should be pointed out and then students are made responsible for the results of their behavior. When using consequences, make sure you also use interventions to change the behavior.

22.**Do not take any action that has not been spelled out previously:** If consequences or actions need to be taken, they should be specific to thebehaviors that are expected. A student should not be held accountable forinfractions of a rule that was not written until after the act occurred. Once it is determined what action will be taken for a specific behavior, consistent follow-up will be needed.

23. **Do not moralize or lecture students:** Help students identify the behavior that was inappropriate and how the behavior impacted on the individual and theentire classroom. Do not try to deal with "why." That is far too complex.

24.**Get to know your students:** Become knowledgeable about all students, their past experiences and behaviors so you can understand them. This may require you to read their school records or make home visits. Understand that while past experiences may be an indicator of future behaviors, it is not the only determinant. One cannot predict what will become of a student when he receives appropriate discipline, creative instruction, and develops a positive relationship with the teacher.

25. **Do not expect miracles:** Changing behavior takes time and strategic plans must be carried out consistently over a long period of time.

26. **Benchmark students' behavior:** Keeping a record of behavior will reveal specific patterns to the behavior and will provide information related to the antecedents and consequences of the behavior.

27. **Remember, all behavior is meaningful:** It is difficult for students to change behavior patterns which are meeting their needs. Change will only occur when students have had an opportunity to develop a new behavior pattern to meet those needs. The secret is to remain proactive, be persistent, and find ways to help all students succeed.

CONCLUSION

Obviously there is no one perfect way to teach or deal with students. While teaching subject matter may be a science, dealing with student behavior is, at best, an art. Teachers must remember that they are human beings, not a human doing. Being human suggests that one is experiencing a process. Most teachers will agree that teaching is an experience! What works for one student often will not work for another. What worked yesterday probably will not work today. This is why it is important for teachers to understand that discipline is not doing something to students, it is a way of interacting throughout the day. This book is dedicated to helping teachers develop a proactive approach to classroom management that will help teach self-discipline to all students. While it is normal to become frustrated or lose focus of what is being accomplished through the teaching process, teachers must continue to remember that they really are changing the world, one child at a time.

I recall being in the third grade when an event occurred that has helped me stay focused throughout my career in education. One Monday morning I was walking down the hallway at Priceville Elementary School and as I looked up I saw a poster beside the principal's office door. The poster announced that a circus was coming to town. The poster grabbed my attention because it reminded me of a *National Geographic* cover. I would often work at getting kicked out of class because my teacher would send me to the library to complete my school work. But, instead of doing the assignment I would sneak a *National Geographic* magazine just to look at the beautiful photographs. I loved those pictures of a lush green forest, yellow giraffes, orange tigers, gray elephants! I thought about that circus coming to Priceville all day long. When I got home that afternoon I ran to my father and told him that a circus was coming to town and asked if I could go. He immediately asked, "When is it?" I responded, "Saturday." Then he asked the question that I dreaded: "How much is it?" I said, "It is only $2." He reminded me that he was a sharecropper and only worked when the crops were in season and the weather allowed. He said he just could not afford for me to go to the circus. I begged, pleaded, and pestered and he reminded me again that he just did not have the money. He could see the disappointment on my face, and after a few minutes he came back to me and said if I would do my chores for the rest of the week without

230

complaining, he would get the money from somewhere and I could go to the circus.

Now some of you will know what I am talking about, and others will not have a clue. I was so excited that I took off running and ran straight to the wood pile and cut my kindling and took it into the house (chore #1). Then, I ran to the coal pile and loaded my bucket up and took the coal into the house (chore #2). Next, I ran to the well and drew the water out, placed it into the water bucket and took it into the kitchen (chore #3). Then, I ran to my father to ask how I had done and asked if I was going to get to go to the circus. He laughed and reminded me that it was only one day. I had four more days to go. On Tuesday I got off the bus and ran straight to the wood pile and got in the wood. I then got in the coal, and then the water. Again, I went to my father and asked, "Daddy, did I do my chores all right?" He responded, "Yes, you did a fine job, keep it up." Wednesday, I did the same thing. I got off the bus and got in the wood, coal, and kindling without being asked. I went to my father and asked, "Daddy, did I do my chores all right? Am I going to get to go?" He responded again, "Fred, I am a little surprised how well you are doing." My father was not known for encouragement. I did not care; all I wanted was to go to that circus. On Thursday the same thing occurred. I got off the bus and, without stopping, I went to the coal pile and got in the coal, to the wood pile and got in the wood and to the well and got in the water. Again I went to my father and asked, "Daddy, am I doing alright, do I get to go to the circus?" He reminded me that I had one more day to go.

Friday finally came. I was so excited to get my chores done I could hardly wait to get home. That old school bus came rambling down the dirt road toward my house. The bus was about ten yards from the bus stop when the driver opened the bus door. Even though the bus had not stopped rolling, I jumped off the bus to go do my chores. As I jumped from the bus, I fell down and got dirt and gravel all over me. I had gravel sticking in my head and I was bleeding. The bus driver slammed on his brakes, jumped off the bus cursing saying; "You little so and so, you are going to get me fired." My father came running to see what all the commotion was all about. I did not care. I jumped up and ran past both of them and ran to the wood pile and got in my kindling. I ran to the coal pile and got in the coal. Then I ran to the well and drew the water out and ran it inside the house. Then I ran to my father and asked; "Daddy, daddy, have I done my chores good? Do I get to go to the circus?" He responded, "Yes, you have done your chores very well." I responded, "So, Daddy, do I get to go to the circus tomorrow, do I, do I?" He said, "Yes, I have your money and tomorrow morning I will give you the $2 and you can ride your bicycle into town to see the circus."

I could hardly sleep that night. I tossed and turned and finally got up around 6:00 a.m. I got dressed and waited for my father to get out of bed. I went around the house kicking coal buckets and moving furniture, trying to wake up my father. My father finally got up around 7:00 a.m. and I asked him for the money. He laughed and told me that I would have to wait; he would tell me when I could go to the circus.

I think it was about 11:00 a.m. my father called me into the house and gave me the $2. He told me to ride my bicycle into town and go only to the circus and when it was over to I needed to come straight home. He did not want me hanging out in town with my friends. I got on my bicycle and rode the six miles into Priceville to see the circus. Now, Priceville was just a small town with one street. No one actually lived in town. There were only businesses along the main street. I was riding my bike into town and just as I got there, I saw people crowded along the main street; they were lined up six and seven deep. They were all screaming and hollering. I quickly laid my bicycle down (I did not have a kick stand). I pushed my way through the crowd, knocking down a couple of smaller children in order to get to the front. I finally got to the front and could not believe my eyes. Everything that was on the poster was right there in front of me. In fact, many of those animals I had seen in those *National Geographic* magazines were right there in a procession going down this little main street. There were lions, tigers and bears in cages, elephants and giraffes being guided down the street, and a host of other strange-looking animals.

I was so excited. I had never seen anything like this before. At the end of this procession of animals was a dancing clown throwing candy out of a bag to the crowd. That was what all the people were yelling about. They wanted him to throw them some candy. I am sure many of you have been to a parade in some small country town. The people were picking candy up off the ground and grabbing it out of young children's hands. But, I did not care about the candy. I was excited to just be seeing these wild animals.

Well, the dancing clown made his way down the street and finally got to where I was standing. Thinking back, I guess he saw the excitement on my face and, wanting me to feel special he stopped right in front of me. The clown bent over, took a bow before me, and tipped his hat. I was so excited, I was all giggly. I did not know what to do. Well, let me tell you, my mother may have had only a second grade education, every time that little Baptist church door opened, she took me to church. Now, if you have gone to church as much as I did, if you don't know anything else, you know that if someone puts a hat or plate in front of you and you have some money, you had better put it in. So, I took $2 out of my pocket and dropped it into the clown's hat. The clown paused for a moment and looked confused. He looked around at the crowd gathering candy. No one was paying any attention to the clown. He stuck his hat out again to me. I did not have any more money. In the meantime the procession was moving on without the clown. The clown turned and saw the precession leaving him behind. With my money inside, he placed his hat back on, turned and started walking down the street and throwing candy out to the crowd.

Soon the animals and clown disappeared down the street headed to the outskirts of town. The crowd dispersed and I went and picked my bicycle and rode the six miles back home. I guess it was about 1:00 p.m. when I got home. My father said, "Son, you are home awfully early, did you go to the circus, did you see it?" I responded, "Daddy, it was great! It is the best thing that has ever happened to me." "I promise if you will let me go next year I will start right now doing my chores."

I will never forget, it was two years later, I was in the fifth grade and we were in Ms. Speak's social studies class. The teacher was using a slide projector to show us some exotic animals on the screen. I leaned over to my best friend and asked where these pictures had come from. My friend, David told me to be quiet. He said, "Don't you remember that circus that was in town two years ago, Ms. Speak took pictures and made them into slides." As I sat there and watched that slide show, it dawned on me. I had not gone to the circus. I had only seen a parade going down a main street on its way to become a circus.

I share this experience with you because it is possible that many of us have only been in the parade of the kind of teacher that we are capable of being. But, I dare say to you, if you will work on differentiating between typical and atypical behavior patterns; do a self assessment; ask, *"How may I be contributing to the behavior problems in my classroom?"* Set up your classroom to support positive discipline, then develop discipline strategies that not only provide discipline, but actually teach self-discipline and build relationships. You will not only become the kind of teacher that you want to be but, more importantly, the kind of teacher that your students desperately need you to be.

It is my sincere hope that this book will serve as a vehicle that will enhance your knowledge of student behavior, improve your relationship with students, and encourage you to remember that you really are changing the world, one student at a time!

INDEX

References

Ainsworth, J. W.; and Roscigno, V. J. (2005). Stratification, School-Work Linkages and Vocational Education. *Social Forces*, v84(1), p257-284.

Akin-Little, K. A.; Eckert, T. L.; Lovett, B. J.; Little, S. G. (2004). Extrinsic Reinforcement in the Classroom: Bribery or best practices. *School Psychology Review*, v33(3), p344-362.

Akos, P.; and Galassi, J. P. (2004). Gender and Race as Variables in Psychosocial Adjustment to Middle and High School. *Journal of Educational Research*, v98(2), p102.

Anguiano, P. (2001). A First-Year Teacher's Plan To Reduce Misbehavior in the Classroom. *TEACHING Exceptional Children*, v33(3), p52-55.

Anstine, J.; and Skidmore, M.; (2005). A Small Sample Study of Traditional and Online Courses with Sample Selection Adjustment. *Journal of Economic Education*, v36(2), p107.

Arnold, Elizabeth Mayfield; Goldston, David B.; Walsh, Adam K.; Reboussin, Beth A.; Severity of Emotional and Behavioral Problems among Poor and Typical Readers. *Journal of Abnormal Child Psychology*, v33 n2 p205 Apr 2005

B.F. Skinner, (1957). *Schedules of Reinforcement*. Charles B. Ferster, New York, NY.

Baldwin and et.al. (1990). Evaluation of Alcohol and Drug Use Attitudes and Behaviors in Pharmacy College Faculty. American Journal of Pharmaceutical Education, v54 n3 p233-38.

Barkley, R. A. (1997). *ADHD and the Nature of Self-Control*. Guilford Press, New York, NY.

Barkley, R. A. (1998). *Attention Deficit Hyperactivity Disorder: A Handbook for Diagnosis and Treatment* (2nd ed.). Guilford Press, New York, NY.

Barkley, R. A. (2000) *Taking charge of ADHD: The Complete, Authoritative Guide for Parents* (2nd edition). Guilford Press, New York, NY.

Barkley, R. A. (2005) *Taking Charge of ADHD: The Complete, Authoritative Guide for Parents* (3rd edition). Guilford Press, New York, NY.

Barton-Arwood, S.; Morrow, L.; Lane, K.; Jolivette, K. (2005). *Project IMPROVE: Improving Teachers' Ability to Address Students' Social Needs*. Education and Treatment of Children, v28(4), p430-443.

Baw, S. S. (2002). Transforming the Whole Class into Gossiping Groups. *Forum*, v40(1), p44-49.

Beachum, F.; and Dentith, A. M. (2004). Teacher Leaders Creating Cultures of School Renewal and Transformation. *The Educational Forum*, v68(3), p276-286.

Belvel, P. S.; and Jordan, M. M. (2003). *Rethinking Classroom Management: Strategies for Prevention, Intervention, and Problem Solving.* Corwin Press. Thousand Oaks, CA.

Bernstein, D.; Marx, M. S.; and Bender, H. (2005). Disciplining the Minds of Students. *Change*, v37(2), p36.

Best, W. (2005). Investigation of a New Intervention for Children with Word-Finding Problems. *International Journal of Language and Communication Disorders*, v40(3), p279-318.

Bettmann, J. (2000). Nurturing the Respectful Community through Practical Life. *NAMTA Journal*, v25(1), p101-16.

Bilynsky, N. S.; and Vernaglia, E. R. (1999). Identifying and Working with Dysfunctional Families. *Professional School Counseling* v2(4) p305-13.

Bippus, A. M.; and Young, S. L. (2005). Owning Your Emotions: Reactions to Expressions of Self-Versus Other-Attributed Positive and Negative Emotions. *Journal of Applied Communication Research*, v33(1), p26-45.

Black, L. (2000). Teacher-Pupil Talk in Whole-Class Discussions and Processes of Social Positioning within the Primary School Classroom. *Language and Education*, v18(5), p347-360.

Black, L. (2004). Teacher-Pupil Talk in Whole-Class Discussions and Processes of Social Positioning within the Primary School Classroom. *Language and Education*, v18(5), p347-360.

Bolger, K. E.; and Patterson, C. J. (2001). Developmental Pathways from Child Maltreatment to Peer Rejection. *Child Development*, v72 n2 p549-68.

Boreham, N.; and Morgan, C. (2004). A Sociocultural Analysis of Organizational Learning. *Oxford Review of Education*, v30(3), p307-325.

Botting, N.; and Adams, C. (2005). Semantic and Inferencing Abilities in Children with Communication Disorders. *International Journal of Language and Communication Disorders*, v40(1), p49-66.

Boyd, J.; and Boyd, S. (2005). Reflect and Improve: Instructional Development through a Teaching Journal. *College Teaching*, v53(3), p110.

Bradford, M. (2005). Motivating Students through Project-Based Service Learning. *T.H.E. Journal*, v32(6), p29.

Brady, K.; Forton, M. B.; Porter, D.; Wood, C.; (2003). *Rules in School. Strategies for Teachers Series*. Northwest Foundation for Children, Greenfield, MA.

Brasler, C. E.; and Laursen, E. K. (2004). Strengthening Controls from Within: Manipulated by Peers. Reclaiming Children and Youth: *The Journal of Strength-based Interventions*, v13(2), p110.

Brinker, S. R.; Goldstein, S. E.; and Tisak, M. S. (2003). Children's Judgements about Common Classroom Punishments. *Educational Research*, v45(2), p189-98.

Brock, B. L.; and Grady, M. L. (2002). *Avoiding Burnout: A Principal's Guide to Keeping the Fire Alive.* Corwin Press, Inc., Thousand Oaks, CA

Buehl, D. (2001). Classroom Strategies for Interactive Learning. Second Edition. *International Reading Association*, Newark, DE.

Buerk, D. (2000). *What We Say, What Our Students Hear: A Case for Active Listening. Humanistic Mathematics Network Journal*, v22(2), p1-11.

Butt, G.; Lance, A.; Fielding, A.; Gunter, H.; Rayner, S.; and Thomas, H. (2005). Teacher Job Satisfaction: Lessons from the TSW Pathfinder Project. School Leadership & Management, v25 n5 p455-471.

Byo, J. L. (2004). Teaching Problem Solving in Practice. *Music Educators Journal*, v9(2), p35.

Call, N. A.; Wacker, D. P.; Ringdahl, J. E.; and Boelter, E. W. (2005). Combined Antecedent Variables as Motivating Operations within Functional Analyses. *Journal of Applied Behavior Analysis*, v38(3), p385.

Campbell, E.; (2003). Moral Lessons: The Ethical Role of Teachers. Educational Research and Evaluation: An International Journal on Theory and Practice, v9 (1) p25-50.

Cast, A. D.; Schweingruber, D.; and Berns, N. (2006). Childhood Physical Punishment and Problem Solving in Marriage. *Journal of Interpersonal Violence*, v21(2), p244-261.

Charney, R. S. (2002). *Teaching Children To Care: Classroom Management for Ethical and Academic Growth, K-8*. Northeast Foundation for Children. Greenfield, MA.

Chory-Assad, R.; and Paulsel, M. (2004). Classroom Justice: Student Aggression and Resistance as Reactions to Perceived Unfairness. *Communication Education*, v53(3), p253-273.

Church, E. B. (2005). Building Language Through Conflict Resolution: Discussing Problems Enriches Language While Leading to Solutions. *Early Childhood Today*, v20(3), p48.

Codding, R. S.; Feinberg, A. B.; Dunn, E. K.; Pace, G. M. and Schunk, D. H. (2005). Effects of Immediate Performance Feedback on Implementation of Behavior Support Plans. *Journal of Applied Behavior Analysis*, v38(2), p205.

Cokley, K. O. (2003). What Do We Know about the Motivation of African American Students? Challenging the "Anti-Intellectual" Myth. *Harvard Educational Review*, v73(4), p524-58.

Cook, J. (1996). The Curriculum Conundrum. *Teaching PreK-8*, v26(6), p60-61.

Cooper, L. J. and et.al. (1992). Analysis of the Effects of Task Preferences, Task

Demands, and Adult Attention on Child Behavior in Outpatient and Classroom Settings. *Journal of Applied Behavior Analysis*, v25(4), p823-40.

Covington, M. V. (2002). Rewards and Intrinsic Motivation: A Needs-Based, Developmental Perspective. *Eric Document*, ED471686.

Cramer, P. (2006). *Protecting the Self: Defense Mechanisms in Action*. Guilford Press, New York, NY.

Cross, T. L. (2005). Nerds and Geeks: Society's Evolving Stereotypes of Our Students with Gifts and Talents. *Gifted Child Today*, v28(4), p26-27, 65.

Curwin, R. L. (1993). The Healing Power of Altruism. *Educational Leadership* v51(3), p36-39.

Dalke, A. (2004). The Grace of Revision, the Profit of "Unconscious Cerebration"; or What Happened When Teaching the Canon Became Child's Play. *Journal of General Education*, v54(1), p58-82.

Damiani, V. B. (2006). *Crisis Prevention and Intervention in the Classroom: What Teachers Should Know*. Rowman and Littlefield Publishing, Lanham, MD.

Daniel, S. S.; Hickman, E.; and Wood, F. B. (2005). Severity of Emotional and Behavioral Problems among Poor and Typical Readers. *Journal of Abnormal Child Psychology*, v33(2), p205.

Daniels, D. E.; and Gabel, R. M. (2004). The Impact of Stuttering on Identity Construction. *Topics in Language Disorders*, v24(3), p200.

Davey, B. J.; and Lignugaris-Kraft, B. (2005). A Practical Approach to Functional Behavioral Assessment in a Public (State Supported) School: Successes and Limitations. *Emotional and Behavioral Difficulties*, v10(4), p255-268.

de Bildt, A.; Sytema, S.; Kraijer, D.; Sparrow, S.; and Minderaa, R. (2005). Adaptive Functioning and Behaviour Problems in Relation to Level of Education in Children and Adolescents with Intellectual Disability. *Journal of Intellectual Disability Research*, v49(9), p672-681.

De Martini-Scully, D.; Bray, M. A.; and Kehle, T. J. (2000). A Packaged Intervention To Reduce Disruptive Behaviors in General Education Students. *Psychology in the Schools*, v37(2), p149-56.

Delisle, J.; and Galbraith, J. (2005). *Kids Don't Have All the Answers: How To Meet Their Social and Emotional Needs*. Free Spirit Publishing Inc., Minneapolis, MN.

Deroma, V. M.; Lassiter, K. S.; and Davis, V. A. (2004). Adolescent Involvement in Discipline Decision Making. *Behavior Modification*, v28(3), p420-437.

DeRosier, M. E.; and Marcus, S. R. (2005). Building Friendships and Combating Bullying.

Journal of Clinical Child and Adolescent Psychology, v34(1), p140-150.

Desiderio, M. F.; and Mullennix, C. (2005). Two Behavior Management Systems, One Classroom: Can Elementary Students Adapt? *The Educational Forum*, v69(4), p383-391.

Dewatripont, M.; and Tirole, J. (2005). Modes of Communication. *Journal of Political Economy*, v113(6), p1217.

DiLalla, L. F. (2002). Behavior Genetics of Aggression in Children: Review and Future Directions. *Developmental Review*, v22(4), p593-622.

Do, S. L.; and Schallert, D. L. (2004). Emotions and Classroom Talk: Toward a Model of the Role of Affect in Students' Experiences of Classroom Discussions. *Journal of Educational Psychology*, v96(4), p619-634.

Dobbs, J.; Arnold, D.; and Doctoroff, G. (2004). Attention in the Preschool Classroom: The Relationships among Child Gender, Child Misbehavior, and Types of Teacher Attention. *Early Child Development and Care*, v174(3), p281-295.

Doveston, M.; and Keenaghan, M. (2006). Improving Classroom Dynamics to Support Students' Learning and Social Inclusion: A Collaborative Approach. *Support for Learning*, v21(1), p5-11.

Dubelle, S. T.; and Hoffman, C. M. (1987). When an Attention-Seeker Gets Under Your Skin. *Principal*, v66(4), p28-30.

Dufresne, J. (2005). Keeping Students and Schools Safe. Reclaiming Children and Youth: *The Journal of Strength-based Interventions*, v14(2), p93.

Edelman, S.; and Clin, L. R. M. (2005). Group Cognitive Behavior Therapy Program with Troubled Adolescents: A Learning Experience. *Child and Family Behavior Therapy*, v27(3), p47-59.

Edwards, C. H. (2000). The Moral Dimensions of Teaching and Classroom Discipline. *American Secondary Education*, v28(3), p20-25.

Eisenberg, N.; and et.al. (2004). The Relations of Effortful Control and Impulsivity to Children's Resiliency and Adjustment. *Child Development*, v75(1) p25-46.

Elias, M. J. (2004). The Connection between Social-Emotional Learning and Learning Disabilities: Implications for Intervention. *Learning Disability Quarterly*, v27(1), p53.

Elkind, D. (2001). Instructive Discipline Is Built on Understanding: Choosing Time In. *Child Care Information Exchange*, n141(3), p7-8.

Elkind, D. (2001). The Many Views of "Time-Out." Teaching Strategies. *Journal of Early Education and Family Review*, v8(5), p18-28.

Ellis, A. E. (1998). *The Myth of Self-esteem: How Rational Emotive Behavior Therapy*

Can Change Your Life Forever. Palgrave MacMillan, New York, NY.

Emick, J.; Welsh, M.; (2005). Multiple Regression Analysis,Cognitive Development, Memory. *Learning and Individual Differences* v15(3), p177-188.

Espelage, D. L.; Bosworth, K.; and Simon, T. R. (2000). Examining the Social Context of Bullying Behaviors in Early Adolescence. *Journal of Counseling and Development,* v78(3), p326-33.

Essa, E. L. (2000). Preschool Teachers' Use of Time-Out: Is What They Say What They Do? *Early Child Development and Care,* v165(3), p85-94.

Feldhusen, J.; and Feldhusen, H. (2004). The Room Meeting for G/T Students in an Inclusion Classroom. *Gifted Child Today,* v27(2), p54-57.

Fielding, E. N.; (1999). *Learning Differences in the Classroom.* International Reading Association, Newark, DE.

Finkbeiner, C.; and Koplin, C. (2002). *A Cooperative Approach for Facilitating Intercultural Education.* Reading Online, Oct 2002.

Floyd, M.; Coulon, C.; Yanez, A. P.; and Lasota, M. T. (2004). The Existential Effects of Traumatic Experiences: A Survey of Young Adults. *Death Studies,* v1(29), p55-63.

Foster, L. G. (1994). Discouraging Gangs in Schools: A Prescription for Prevention. *NASSP Practitioner,* v19(4), p.187-192.

Frascarolo, F.; Besse, V.; and Favez, N. (2005). Non-Verbal Behavioural Patterns in Trilogue Play Transitions and Family Alliances. *Early Child Development and Care,* v175(7) p681-696.

Fredriksen, K.; Rhodes, J.; Reddy, R.; and Way, N. (2004). Sleepless in Chicago: Tracking the Effects of Adolescent Sleep Loss During the Middle School Years. *Child Development,* v75(1), p84-95.

Gartrell, D. (2002). Replacing Time-Out: Part Two–Using Guidance To Maintain an Encouraging Classroom. *Young Children,* v57(2), p36-43.

Gendron, M.; Royer, E.; Bertrand, R.; and Potvin, P. (2004). Behavior Disorders, Social Competence and the Practice of Physical Activities among Adolescents. *Emotional and Behavioral Difficulties,* v9 n4 p249-259.

Gerber, M. M. (2005). Response to Tough Teaching: The 2% Solution. *Learning Disability Quarterly,* v28(3), p189.

Gnezda, N. M. (2004). *Teaching Difficult Students: Blue Jays in the Classroom.* Rowman and Littlefield Publishing, Lanham, MD.

Gomez, C. R.; and Baird, S.; (2005). Identifying Early Indicators for Autism in Self-

Regulation Difficulties. Focus on Autism and Other Developmental Disabilities, v20 n2 p106-116.

Gootman, M. E. (2001). *The Caring Teacher's Guide to Discipline: Helping Young Students Learn Self-Control, Responsibility, and Respect. Second Edition.* Corwin Press, Thousand Oaks, CA.

Gould, M. S.; Velting, Drew; K. M.; Lucas, C.; Thomas, J. G.; and Chung, M. (2004). Teenagers' Attitudes about Coping Strategies and Help-Seeking Behavior for Suicidality *Journal of the American Academy of Child and Adolescent Psychiatry*, v43(9), p1124.

Greenspan, S. I. (2005). Working with Children Who Have Language Difficulties. Meeting Learning Challenges. *Early Childhood Today*, v20(2), p16-17.

Gresham, F. M. (1989). Measuring the Severity of Child Maltreatment Assessment of Treatment Integrity in School Consultation and Pre-referral Intervention. *School Psychology Review*, v18(1), p37-50.

Gropper, N.; and Froschl, M. (2000). The Role of Gender in Young Children's Teasing and Bullying Behavior. *Equity and Excellence in Education*, v33(1), p48-56.

Gunter, P. L.; Coutinho, M. J.; and Cade, T. (2002). Classroom Factors Linked with Academic Gains among Students with Emotional and Behavioral Problems. *Preventing School Failure*, v46(3), p126-32.

Hail, J. M. (2000). Take a Break: A Token Economy in the Fifth Grade. *Social Education*, v64(4), p5-7.

Hamre, B. K.; and Pianta, R. C. (2005). Can Instructional and Emotional Support in the First-Grade Classroom Make a Difference for Children at Risk of School Failure? *Child Development*, v76(5), p949-967.

Harlan, J.; and Rowland, S.T. (2002). *Behavior Management Strategies for Teachers: Achieving Instructional Effectiveness, Student Success, and Student Motivation–Every Teacher and Any Student Can!* 2nd Edition. ERIC Document ED474904.

Harlin, R. P. (2000). Developing Reflection and Teaching through Peer Coaching. Focus on *Teacher Education*, v1(1), p.27.

Harms, K.; and Fritz, S..; (2001). Internalization of Character Traits by Those Who Teach Character Counts! Journal of Extension, v39 (6), p.270-278.

Harris, C. A. and et.al. (1990). To the "Kids Who Are Different". *Momentum*, v21(2), p64-67.

Harris, C. A.; and et.al. (1995). Teaching Initial Multiplication Skills to Students with Disabilities in General Education Classrooms. *Learning Disabilities Research and Practice*, v10(3), p180-95.

Harrison, Janet S.; and et.al. (1996). Teacher Instructional Language and Negative Reinforcement: A Conceptual Framework for Working with Students with Emotional and Behavioral Disorders. *Education and Treatment of Children*, v19(2), p183-96.

Havill, L. K. (2004). Levels of Involvement: The Power of Choice in a Middle School Level System. Reclaiming Children and Youth: *The Journal of Strength-based Interventions*, v13(3), p155.

Hendley, V. (2000). Collected Works Series. *AAHE Bulletin*, v52(1), p.10 Sep 1999-Jun 2000.

Hernandez, T. J.; and Seem, S. R. (2004). A Safe School Climate: A Systemic Approach and the School Counselor. *Professional School Counseling*, v7(4), p256.

Hobday-Kusch, J.; and McVittie, J. (2002). Just Clowning Around: Classroom Perspectives on Children's Humor. *Canadian Journal of Education*, v27(2-3), p195-210.

Honig, A. S. (2005). Emotional Milestones and Their Link to Learning. Infants & Toddlers. Early Childhood Today, v20, (3), p. 30-32.

Honigsfeld, A.; and Schiering, M. (2004). Diverse Approaches to the Diversity of Learning Styles in Teacher Education. *Educational Psychology*, v24(4), p487-507.

Howard, J. B.; (1999). Using a Social Studies Theme To Conceptualize a Problem. Social Studies, v90 n4 p171-76

Howes, C.; Phillipsen, L. C.; and Peisner-Feinberg, E. (2000). The Consistency of Perceived Teacher-Child Relationships between Preschool and Kindergarten. *Journal of School Psychology*, v38(2), p113-32.

Hutchinson, L. M.; and Beadle, M. E. (1992). Professors' Communication Styles: How They Influence Male and Female Seminar Participants. *Teaching and Teacher Education*, v8(4), p405-18.

Hyde, J. S.; Else-Quest, N. M.; Goldsmith, H. H.; and Biesanz, J. C. (2004). Children's Temperament and Behavior Problems Predict Their Employed Mothers' Work Functioning. *Child Development*, v75(2), p580-594.

Iervolino, A. C.; Hines, M.; Golombok, S. E.; Rust, J.; and Plomin, R. (2005). Genetic and Environmental Influences on Sex-Typed Behavior During the Preschool Years. *Child Development*, v76(4), p826-840.

Irwin, L.; and Nucci, C. (2004). Perceptions of Students' Locus of Control of Discipline among Pre-Service and In-Service Teachers in Multicultural Classrooms. *Intercultural Education*, v15(1), p59-71.

Jeanpierre, B. J. (2004). Two Urban Elementary Science Classrooms: The Interplay between Student Interactions and Classroom Management Practices. *Education*, v124(4), p664.

Jeffrey, B. (2002). Performativity and Primary Teacher Relations. *Journal of Education Policy*, v17(5), p531-46.

Johnson, F. and Edmunds, A. (2006): *From Chaos to Control: Understanding and responding to the behaviors of exceptional students*. Althouse Press, London, ON.   CA.

Johnson, F.L. (1996). *Effective Discipline for the Difficult Child*. Butler Books, Louisville, KY.

Johnson, S. M.; Birkeland, S. E.; and Peske, H. G. (2005). Life in the Fast Track: How States Seek to Balance Incentives and Quality in Alternative Teacher CertificationPrograms. Educational Policy v19(1), p63-89.

Jolivette, K.; Barton-Arwood, S.; and Scott, T. M. (2000). Functional Behavioral Assessment as a Collaborative Process among Professionals. *Education and   Treatment of Children*, v23(3), p298-313.

Kam, C-M.; Greenberg, M. T.; and Kusche, C. A. (2004). Sustained Effects of the PATHS Curriculum on the Social and Psychological Adjustment of Children in Special Education. *Journal of Emotional and Behavioral Disorders*, v12(2), p66- 78.

Kaplan, A. (2000). Teacher and Student: Designing a Democratic Relationship. *Journal of Curriculum Studies*, v32(3), p377-402.

Kearney, C. A.; and Albano, A. M. (2004). The Functional Profiles of School Refusal Behavior: Diagnostic Aspects. *Behavior Modification*, v28(1), p147-161.

Kehle, T. J.; Bray, M. A.; Theodore, L. A.; Jenson, W. R.; and Clark, E. (2000). A Multi-Component Intervention Designed To Reduce Disruptive Classroom Behavior. *Psychology in the Schools*, v37(5), p475-81.

Kim, H.-J.; Arnold, D. H.; Fisher, P. H.; and Zeljo, A. (2005). Parenting and Preschoolers' Symptoms as a Function of Child Gender and SES. *Child and Family Behavior Therapy*, v27 n2 p23-41.

Keith, S.; (1991). Whose Morals Shall We Teach? School of Education Review, v3 n1 p11-12.

Kochis, D. S.; (1995). The Effectiveness of Project DARE: Does It Work? Journal of Alcohol and Drug Education, v40 n2 p40-47.

Knobloch, L. K.; Solomon, D. H. (2002). Information Seeking Beyond Initial Interaction: Negotiating Relational Uncertainty Within Close Relationships. *Human Communication Research*, v28(2), p243-57.

Kramer-Dahl, A. (2004). Constructing Adolescents Differently: On the Value of Listening to Singapore Youngsters Talking Popular Culture Texts. *Linguistics and Education: An International Research Journal*, v15(3), p217-241.

Lane, K. L.; Pierson, M. R.; Robertson, F. E. J.; and Little, A. (2004). Teachers' Views of Pre-referral Interventions: Perceptions of and Recommendations for Implementation Support. *Education and Treatment of Children*, v27(4), p420- 439.

Larson, J. (2005). *Think First: Addressing Aggressive Behavior in Secondary Schools.* Guilford Press, New York, NY.

Lasley, T. J., II; Siedentop, D.; and Yinger, R. (2006). A Systemic Approach to Enhancing Teacher Quality: The Ohio Model. *Journal of Teacher Education*, v57(1), p13-21.

Laursen, E. K.; and Peterson, D. (2005). Chaotic Thinking, Challenging Behavior: A Reality Rub. Reclaiming Children and Youth: *The Journal of Strength-based Interventions.* v13(4), p236.

Lawrence, S. M. (2005). Contextual Matters: Teachers' Perceptions of the Success of Antiracist Classroom Practices. *Journal of Educational Research*, v98(6), p350.

Lee, Y.; Baylor, A. L.; Nelson, D. W. (2005). Supporting Problem-Solving Performance Through the Construction of Knowledge Maps. *Journal of Interactive Learning Research*, v16(2), p117-131.

Leen-Feldner, E. W.; Zvolensky, M. J.; and Feldner, M. T. (2004). Behavioral Inhibition Sensitivity and Emotional Response Suppression: A Laboratory Test Among Adolescents in a Fear-Relevant Paradigm. *Journal of Clinical Child and Adolescent Psychology*, v33(4), p783-791.

Lenze, L. F. (1996). Discipline-Specific Faculty Development. *NEA Higher Education Research Center Update*, v2(3).

Lenze, L. F. (2005). Age and Gender Effects on Coping in Children and Adolescents. *Journal of Youth and Adolescence*, v34(2), p73.

Lindberg, J. A.; and Swick, A. M. (2002). *Common-Sense Classroom Management: Surviving September and Beyond in the Elementary Classroom.* ERIC Document, ED460101.

Litrownik, A.J.; Lau, A.; English, D.J.; Briggs, E.; Newton, R.R.; Romney, S.; Dubowitz, H. (2005). Measuring the Severity of Child Maltreatment. Child Abuse and Neglect: *The International Journal*, v29(5), p553-573.

Long, J. D.; and Williams, R. L.; (2005). *Making It Till Friday: Your Guide to Effective Classroom Management. Fifth Edition.* Princeton Book Company Publishers, New York, NY.

Lopez, C.; and DuBois, D. L. (2005). Peer Victimization and Rejection: Investigation of an Integrative Model of Effects on Emotional, Behavioral, and Academic Adjustment in Early Adolescence. *Journal of Clinical Child and Adolescent Psychology*, v34(1), p25-36.

Lucas, R. W. (2003). *The Creative Training Idea Book: Inspired Tips and Techniques for Engaging and Effective Learning.* American Management Association, New York, NY.

Maag, J. W. (2001). Rewarded by Punishment: Reflections on the Disuse of Positive Reinforcement in Education. *Exceptional Children*, v67(2) p173-86.

MacKenzie, E. P.; Fite, P. J.; and Bates, J. E. (2004). Predicting Outcome in Behavioral Parent Training: Expected and Unexpected Results. *Child and Family Behavior Therapy*, v26 n2 p37-53.

Malveaux, J. (2004). Great, or Constrained, Expectations. *Black Issues in Higher Education*, v21(8), p80.

Margolis, H. (2005). Resolving Struggling Learners' Homework Difficulties: Working with Elementary School Learners and Parents. *Preventing School Failure*, v50(1), p5.

Marshall, M. (2005). Discipline without Stress[TM], Punishments, or Rewards. Clearing House: *A Journal of Educational Strategies, Issues and Ideas*, v79(1), p51.

Martin, J. E.; Mithaug, D. E.; Cox, P.; Peterson, L. Y.; Van Dycke, J. and Cash, M.E. (2003). Increasing Self-Determination: Teaching Students To Plan, Work, Evaluate, and Adjust. *Exceptional Children*, v69(4), p431-47.

Mayfield, J.; and Homack, S. (2005). Behavioral Considerations Associated with Traumatic Brain Injury. *Preventing School Failure*, v49(4), p17.

Mayselessx, O. (2004). Home Leaving to Military Service: Attachment Concerns, Transfer of Attachment Functions from Parents to Peers, and Adjustment. *Journal of Adolescent Research*, v19(5), p533-558.

McComas, J. J.; Goddard, C.; and Hoch, H. (2002). The Effects of Preferred Activities during Academic Work Breaks on Task Engagement and Negatively Reinforced Destructive Behavior. *Education and Treatment of Children*, v25(1), p103-12.

McDiarmid, M. D.; and Bagner, D. M. (2005). Parent Child Interaction Therapy for Children with Disruptive Behavior and Developmental Disabilities. *Education and Treatment of Children*, v28(2), p130-141.

McElwain, N. L.; Olson, S. L.; and Volling, B. L. (2002). Concurrent and Longitudinal Associations among Preschool Boys' Conflict Management, Disruptive Behavior, and Peer Rejection. *Early Education and Development*, v13(3), p245-63

McKinney, S. E.; Campbell-Whately, G. D.; and Kea, C. D. (2005). Managing Student Behavior in Urban Classrooms: The Role of Teacher ABC Assessments. Clearing House: *A Journal of Educational Strategies, Issues and Ideas*, v79(1), p16.

Meier, D. (2004). For Safety's Sake. Safety in Schools. *Educational Horizons*, v83(1), p55-60.

Meisinger, E. B.; Schwanenflugel, P. J.; Bradley, B. A.; Stahl, S. A. (2004). Interaction Quality During Partner Reading. *Journal of Literacy Research*, v36(2), p111-140.

Michie, F.; Glachan, M.; and Bray, D. (2001). An Evaluation of Factors Influencing the Academic Self-concept, Self-esteem and Academic Stress for Direct and Re-entry Students in Higher Education. *International Journal of Experimental Educational Psychology*, v21(4), p455-72.

Mixon, K. (2004). Three Learning Styles: Four Steps to Reach Them. *Teaching Music*, v11(4), p48.

Moorefield, L. (2005). Reflective Discipline: Providing Students a Tool for Self-Reflection Can Decrease Classroom Disruptions–And Help Identify the Problems behind Them. *Teaching Pre K-8*, v36(1), p70-71.

Mueller, A. (2005). Antidote to Learned Helplessness: Empowering Youth through Service. Reclaiming Children and Youth: *The Journal of Strength-based Interventions*, v14(1), p16.

Muris, P.; Meesters, C.; and Knoops, M. (2005). The Relation between Gender Role Orientation and Fear and Anxiety in Nonclinic-Referred Children. *Journal of Clinical Child and Adolescent Psychology*, v34(2), p326-332.

Murphy, B. (2004). Social Interaction and Language Use in Irish Infant Classrooms in the Context of the Revised Irish Primary School Curriculum. *Literacy*, v38(3), p149-155.

Nelson, J. R.; and Benner, G. J. (2005). Improving the Early Literacy Skills of Children with Behavioral Disorders and Phonological Processing Deficits at School Entry. *Reading and Writing Quarterly*, v21(1), p105-108.

Newman-Carlson, D.; and Horne, A. M. (2004). Bully Busters: A Psychoeducational Intervention for Reducing Bullying Behavior in Middle School Students. *Journal of Counseling and Development*, v82(3), p259.

Orange, C. (2000). 25 Biggest Mistakes Teachers Make and How To Avoid Them. Corwin Press, Inc., Thousand Oaks, CA.

Orth, U.; Montada, L.; and Maercker, A. (2006). Feelings of Revenge, Retaliation Motive, and Posttraumatic Stress Reactions in Crime Victims. *Journal of Interpersonal Violence*, v21(2), p229-243.

Osgood, J. (2005). Who Cares? The Classed Nature of Childcare. *Gender and Education*, v17(3), p289-303.

Oswald, K.; Safran, S.; and Johanson, G. (2005). Preventing Trouble: Making Schools Safer Places Using Positive Behavior Supports. *Education and Treatment of Children*, v28(3), p265-278.

Packer, L. E. (2005). Tic-Related School Problems: Impact on Functioning, Accommodations, and Interventions. *Behavior Modification*, v29(6), p876-899.

Panteli, N.; and Fineman, S. (2005). The Sound of Silence: The case of virtual team organizing. *Behavior and Information Technology*, v24(5), p347-352.

Parish, Thomas S.(2000). How To Improve Education: Don't get tough; just get connected. *Mid-Western Educational Researcher*, v13(1), p13-16.

Perlman, M. and Ross, H. S. (2005). If -Then Contingencies in Children's Sibling Conflicts. *Merrill Palmer Quarterly Journal of Developmental Psychology*, 51(1), p42-66.

Peskin, J.; and Olson, D. R. (2000). Young Children's Understanding of the Continuity of Biologically Determined Behavior When Appearances Change. *Child Study Journal*, v31(3), p157-76.

Pickering, J. S. (2003). Discipline: Developing Self-Control. *Montessori Life*, v15(3), p18-20.

Power, T. J.; Costigan, T. E.; Eiraldi, R. B.; and Leff, S. S. (2004). Variations in Anxiety and Depression as a Function of ADHD Subtypes Defined by DSM-IV: Do Subtype Differences Exist or Not? *Journal of Abnormal Child Psychology*, v32(1), p27.

Prusak, K. A.; and Vincent, S. D.; Pangrazi, R. P. (2005). Teacher Talk. v76(5) p21.

Putnam, R. F.; Handler, M. W.; Rey, J.; and McCarty, J. (2005). The Development of Behaviorally Based Public School Consultation Services Behavior Modification, v29(3), p521-538.

Ramos, M. C.; Guerin, D. W.; Gottfried, A. W.; Bathurst, K.; and Olvier, P. H. (2005). Family Conflict and Children's Behavior Problems: The Moderating Role of Child Temperament. Structural Equation Modeling: *A Multidisciplinary Journal*, v12(2), p278-298.

Ramos, M. C.; Guerin, D. W.; Gottfried, A. W.; Bathurst, K.; and Olvier, P. H. (2004). Teachers' Perceptions about Teaching Problem Students in Regular Classrooms. *Education and Treatment of Children*, v27(4), p394-419.

Rassuli, A.; and Manzer, J. P. (2005). Teach Us to Learn: Multivariate analysis of perception of success in team learning. *Journal of Education for Business*, v81(1), p21.

Readdick, C. A.; and Chapman, P. L. (2000). Young Children's Perceptions of Time Out. *Journal of Research in Childhood Education*, v15(1), p81-87.

Reid, R.; and Lienemann, Torri O. (2006). *Strategy Instruction for Students with Learning Disabilities. What Works for Special Needs Learners.* Guilford Press, New York, NY.

Reid, R.; Trout, A. L.; and Schartz, M. (2005). Self-Regulation Interventions for Children with Attention Deficit/Hyperactivity Disorder. *Exceptional Children*, v71(4), p361.

Reitman, D. (2004). Behavior Change and Perceptions of Change: Evaluating the Effectiveness of a Token Economy. *Child and Family Behavior Therapy*, v26(2), p17-36.

Reynolds, B.; and Schiffbauer, R. (2005). Attention in the Preschool Classroom: Delay of Gratification and Delay Discounting: A Unifying Feedback Model of Delay-Related Impulsive Behavior. *Psychological Record*, v55(3), p439.

Riedling, A. M.; (2002). Learning To Learn: A Guide to Becoming Information Literate. Neal-Schuman Publishers, Edison, NJ.

Rogers, B. (2004). *How to Manage Children's Challenging Behavior*. Paul Chapman Publishing, Division of SAGE Publications, Thousand Oaks, CA.

Rogers, C. (1961). *On Becoming a Person*. Houghton-Mifflin, New York, NY.

Rogers, W. A. (2002). *Classroom Behavior: A Practical Guide to Effective Teaching, Behavior Management and Colleague Support.* Corwin Press, Thousand Oaks, CA.

Rosenthal, R. (1987). "Pygmalion" Effects: Existence, Magnitude, and Social Importance. Educational Researcher v16(9), p37-41.

Rubin, B. C.; and Noguera, P. A. (2004). Tracking Detracking: Sorting through the Dilemmas and Possibilities of Detracking in Practice. *Equity and Excellence in Education*, v17(6), p. 162-178.

Rubin, R. (2004). Building a Comprehensive Discipline System and Strengthening School Climate. Reclaiming Children and Youth: *The Journal of Strength-based Interventions*, v13(3), p162.

Rubin, R. (2005). A Blueprint for a Strengths-Based Level System in Schools. Reclaiming Children and Youth: *The Journal of Strength-based Interventions*, v14(3), p143.

Ruenzel, D. (2001). All Children Great and Small. *Teacher Magazine*, v12(4), p24-29.

Rusnak, T.; (Ed.). An Integrated Approach to Character Education. Corwin Press, Inc., Thousand Oaks, CA.

Ryfe, D. M. (2006). Narrative and Deliberation in Small Group Forums. *Journal of Applied Communication Research*, v34(1), p72-93.

Schubert, J. L. (2004). Planting Seeds–Growing Values. *Reclaiming Children and Youth: The Journal of Strength-based Interventions*, v13(2), p114.

Schunk, D.H. (2005). Commentary on Self-Regulation in School Contexts. *Learning and Instruction*, v15(2), p173-177.

Schunk, D.H. (2005). Self-Regulated Learning: The Educational Legacy of Paul R. Pintrich. *Educational Psychologist*, v40(2), p85-94.

Scott, T. M.; and Caron, D. B. (2004). Interaction Quality During Partner Reading. *Journal of Literacy Research*, v36(2), p111-140.

Scott, T. M.; and Caron, D. B. (2005). Conceptualizing Functional Behavior Assessment as Prevention Practice within Positive Behavior Support Systems. *Preventing School Failure*, v50(1), p13.

Seay, H. A.; Fee, V. E.; Holloway, K. S.; and Giesen, J. M. (2003). A Multicomponent Treatment Package To Increase Anger Control in Teacher-Referred Boys. *Child and Family Behavior Therapy*, v25(1), p1-18.

Sheinman, A. J. (2000). 6 Behavior Tips That Really Work. Veteran Teachers Share Their Most Successful, Kid-Tested Strategies. *Instructor*, v110(1), p24.

Shulman, J. H. (2004). From Inspired Vision to Impossible Dream: The Dangers of Imbalanced Mentoring. *Journal of Teacher Education*, v55(5), p393-406.

Sigfusdottir, I. D.; Farkas, G.; and Silver, E. (2004). The Role of Depressed Mood and Anger in the Relationship between Family Conflict and Delinquent Behavior. *Journal of Youth and Adolescence* v33(6), p509.

Simons, J.; Dewitte, S.; and Lens, W. (2004). The Role of Different Types of Instrumentality in Motivation, Study Strategies, and Performance: Know Why You Learn, So You'll know What You Learn! *British Journal of Educational Psychology*, v74 n3 p343-360.

Sinkinson, A. J. (2004). Manager, Moderator, Motivator or What? Does Ensuring Consistency of Reporting Fall within the Role of the Managing Inspector in Initial Teacher Training Ofsted Inspections? *Educational Review*, v56(3), p235-246.

Skiba, R.; and Peterson, R. (2003). Teaching the Social Curriculum: School Discipline as Instruction. *Preventing School Failure*, v47(2), p66-73.

Skiba, R.; Rausch, M. K.; Ritter, S. (2004). "Discipline is Always Teaching": Effective Alternatives to Zero Tolerance in Indiana's Schools. *Education Policy Briefs*, v2(3), p. 286-299.

Smilkstein, R.; (2003). We're Born To Learn: Using the Brain's Natural Learning Process To Create Today's Curriculum. Corwin Press, Inc., Thousand Oaks, CA.

Smith, A. B. (2004). How Do Infants and Toddlers Learn the Rules? Family Discipline and Young Children. *International Journal of Early Childhood*, v36(2), p27-42.

Soodak, L. C.; and Podell, D. M. (1994). Teachers' Thinking about Difficult-to-Teach Students. *Journal of Educational Research*, v88(1), p44-51.

Spencer-Matthews, S. (2001). Enforced Cultural Change in Academe. A Practical Case Study: Implementing Management Systems in Higher Education. *Assessment and Evaluation in Higher Education*, v26(1), p51-59.

Spotts, E. L.; Neiderhiser, J. M.; Hetherington, E. M.; and Reiss, D. (2001). The Relation between Observational Measures of Social Problem Solving and Familial Antisocial Behavior: Genetic and Environmental Influences. *Journal of Research on Adolescence*, v11(4), p351-74.

Sprague, J. R.; and Walker, H. M. (2004). *Safe and Healthy Schools: Practical Prevention Strategies*. Guilford Press, New York, NY

Stecher, B. M.; and Hamilton, L. S. (2002). Putting Theory to the Test. *Rand Review*, v26(1), p16-23.

Stichter, J. P.; Conroy, M. A.; and Boyd, B. A. (2004). The Undefined Role of the Antecedent: Addressing the Measurement Quagmires in Applied Research. *Education and Treatment of Children*, v27(4), p490-508.

Stoolmiller, M. (2001). Synergistic Interaction of Child Manageability Problems and Parent-Discipline Tactics in Predicting Future Growth in Externalizing Behavior for Boys. *Developmental Psychology*, v37(6), p814-25.

Sumsion, J.; (2000). Caring and Empowerment: A Teacher Educator's Reflection on an Ethical Dilemma. Teaching in Higher Education, v5, (2), p167-79.

Sunwolf, L., L. (2004). Being Left Out: Rejecting Outsiders and Communicating Group Boundaries in Childhood and Adolescent Peer Groups. *Journal of Applied Communication Research*, v32(3), p195-223.

Sutton, R. E. (2005). Teachers' Emotions and Classroom Effectiveness: Implications from Recent Research. Clearing House: *A Journal of Educational Strategies, Issues and Ideas*, v78(5), p229.

Tan, K. H. K. (2004). Does Student Self-Assessment Empower or Discipline Students? *Assessment and Evaluation in Higher Education*, v29(6), p651-662.

Thompson, R. H.; and Iwata, B. A. (2005). A Review of Reinforcement Control Procedures. *Journal of Applied Behavior Analysis*, v38(2), p257.

Thorndike, E. L. (1932). *The Fundamentals of Learning*. New York: Teachers College Press.

Timmerman, C. E.; (2003). Media Selection during the Implementation of Planned Organizational Change: A Predictive Framework Based on Implementation Approach and Phase. Management Communication Quarterly, v68, (1), p105-102.

Topping, K.; and Ferguson, N.; (2005). Effective Literacy Teaching Behaviors. Journal of Research in Reading, v28, (2), p125-143.

Toro, J. M.; Sinnett, S.; and Soto-Faraco, S. (2005). Speech Segmentation by Statistical Learning Depends on Attention. *Cognition*, v97(2), p25-34

Toro, P. A.; and et.al. (1990). A Comparison of Children with and without Learning Disabilities on Social Problem-Solving Skill, School Behavior, and Family Background. *Journal of Learning Disabilities*, v23(2), p115-20.

Tracey, T. J. G.; and Robbins, S. B. (2005). Stability of Interests Across Ethnicity and Gender: A longitudinal examination of grades 8 through 12. *Journal of Vocational Behavior*, v67(3), p335-364.

Tsovili, T. D. (2004). The Relationship between Language Teachers' Attitudes and the State-Trait Anxiety of Adolescents with Dyslexia. *Journal of Research in Reading*, v27(1), p69-86.

Turecki, S.; (1985). *The Difficult Child*. Bantam Books, New York, NY.

Tyler, V. (2000). Why Recess? *Dimensions of Early Childhood*, v28(4), p21-23.

Urban, V. D.; (1999). Eugene's Story: A Case for Caring. Educational Leadership, v56, (6), p69-70.

Volkert, V. M.; Lerman, D. C.; and Vorndran, C.; (2005). The Effects of Reinforcement Magnitude on Functional Analysis Outcomes. Journal of Applied Behavior Analysis, v38, (2), p147.

van Grinsven, L.; and Tillema, H. (2006). Learning Opportunities to Support Student Self-Regulation: Comparing Different Instructional Formats. *Educational Research*, v48(1), p77-91.

Vitale, J. E.; Newman, J. P.; Bates, J. E.; Goodnight, J.; Dodge, K. A.; and Pettit, G. S. (2005). Deficient Behavioral Inhibition and Anomalous Selective Attention in a Community Sample of Adolescents with Psychopathic Traits and Low-Anxiety Traits. *Journal of Abnormal Child Psychology*, v33(4) p461.

Volkert, V. M.; Lerman, D. C.; and Vorndran, C. (2005). The Effects of Reinforcement Magnitude on Functional Analysis Outcomes. *Journal of Applied Behavior Analysis*, v38(2), p147.

von Tetzchner, S. (2004). Early Intervention and Prevention of Challenging Behaviour in Children with Learning Disabilities. *Perspectives in Education*, v22 n1 p85-100.

Walker-Dalhouse, D. (2005). Discipline: Responding to Socioeconomic and Racial Differences. *Childhood Education*, v82(1), p24.

Watkins, D. (2005). Maximizing Learning for Students with Special Needs. *Kappa Delta Pi Record*, v41(4), p154-158.

Watson, C. (2005). Discourses of "Indiscipline": A Foucauldian Response. *Emotional and Behavioral Difficulties*, v10(1), p55-65.

Watson, T.; Dufrene, B.; Weaver, A.; Butler, T.; and Meeks, C. (2005). Brief Antecedent Assessment and Treatment of Tics in the General Education Classroom: A Preliminary Investigation. *Behavior Modification*, v29(6), p839-857.

Weems, C. F.; and Costa, N. M. (2005). Developmental Differences in the Expression of Childhood Anxiety Symptoms and Fears. *Journal of the American Academy of Child and Adolescent Psychiatry,* v44(7), p656.

Weiler, M. D.; Bernstein, J. H.; Bellinger, D.; and Waber, D. P. (2002). Information Processing Deficits in Children with Attention-Deficit/Hyperactivity Disorder, Inattentive Type, and Children with Reading Disability. *Journal of Learning Disabilities,* v35(5), p448-61.

Weiler, M. D.; Bernstein, J. H.; Bellinger, D.; and Waber, D. P. (2005). Variability in Time Reproduction: Difference in ADHD Combined and Inattentive Subtypes. *Journal of the American Academy of Child and Adolescent Psychiatry,* v44(2), p169.

Weisser, S. O. (2005). "Believing in Yourself" as Classroom Culture. Academe, v91(1), p27-31.

Wilde, O.; (1959). *Wit and Wisdom.* Dover Publishing, Mineola, NY.

Wilkinson, L. A. (2003). Using Behavioral Consultation To Reduce Challenging Behavior in the Classroom. *Preventing School Failure,* v47(3), p100-105.

Willert, J.; and Willert, R. (2001). An Ignored Antidote to School Violence: Classrooms That Reinforce Positive Social Habits. *American Secondary Education,* v29(1), p27-33.

Wendorf, C. A.; and Alexander, S.; (2005). The Influence of Individual- and Class-Level Fairness-Related Perceptions on Student Satisfaction. Contemporary Educational Psychology, v30, (2), p190-206.

Winter, T.; and Haines-Burnham, J. (2005). "Just Because" Interventions: Engaging Hard-to-Reach Students . Reclaiming Children and Youth: *The Journal of Strength-based Interventions,* v14(1), p37.

Witzel, B. S.; and Mercer, C. D. (2003). Using Rewards To Teach Students with Disabilities: Implications for Motivation. *Remedial and Special Education,* v24(2), p88-96.

Wood, J. G.; and Benton, S. L. (2005). Attributional Responses to Students with Attention-Deficit-Hyperactivity Disorder Who Fail. *Teacher Education and Special Education,* v28(3), p153-162.

Xin, J. F.; and Forrest, L. (2002). Managing the Behavior of Children with ADD in Inclusive Classrooms: A Collaborative Approach. *Reclaiming Children and Youth,* v10(4), p240-45.